THE WORLD WATER SPEED RECORD

THE FAST AND THE FORGOTTEN

THE WORLD WATER SPEED RECORD
THE FAST AND THE FORGOTTEN

ROY CALLEY

AMBERLEY

First published 2014
Paperback edition published 2016

Amberley Publishing
The Hill, Stroud
Gloucestershire, GL5 4EP

www.amberley-books.com

British Library Cataloguing in Publication Data.
A catalogue record for this book is available from the British Library.

ISBN 978 1 4456 5534 5 (paperback)
ISBN 978 1 4456 3798 3 (ebook)

Typesetting and Origination by Amberley Publishing.
Printed in the UK.

CONTENTS

	Foreword	7
	Introduction	9
1	The Steam-Powered Battle	11
2	The Harmsworth Trophy	18
3	The Hydroplane	25
4	Gar Wood	31
5	Is it a Boat or is it a Plane?	37
6	Boats and Planes Again	38
7	1928: Ratification and Drama	40
8	Henry Segrave	44
9	Segrave's Grand Prix Dreams	49
10	Segrave Breaks the Land Speed Record	55
11	Wood Against Don	65
12	The Campbell Dynasty	73
13	Campbell the Hero and Then to Zero	81
14	Campbell Dominates	84
15	From Land to Water	89
16	The Race for 200 mph and Another Campbell	94
17	Slo-Mo-Shun	100
18	Sayres, Cobb and Verga: A Tragic Time	107
19	Donald Campbell Dominates	115

20	Campbell and Butlin: All About the Money	122
21	Land and Water in the Same Year, But Only Just!	129
22	1967: The Defining Year	138
23	The Aftermath	149
24	America Grabs the Record Back	153
25	Australia Enter the Race	159
26	Australia's Lost Spirit	168
27	'Three will Die Before the Record's Broken'	174
28	The Aftermath	181
	Statistics	185
	Acknowledgements	188

FOREWORD

I'm leading a team that's striving to bring the world water speed record back to Britain, and so I can't claim to be an impartial contributor to this new book from Roy Calley. Our boat, *Quicksilver*, is well under construction. Let's hope we can bring something fresh to the story of the record. My firm belief is that we can.

I will say straight away that I disagree with Roy's assertion that the world water speed record lacks the glamour of its land speed counterpart. I happen to think that the truth is the exact opposite – that the world water speed record is more alluring by far, and that it holds an enduring place right at the very heart of the public consciousness. It's a classy record. Classier than the land speed record. And it's a more difficult record to get, and therefore all the more valuable if you can get it.

So where did it go wrong? For Roy is right when he says that water speed's ultimate prize is seemingly contested by a succession of 'unknowns'.

Well, I think the problem lies in the fact that such a giant figure as Donald Campbell dominated the water speed arena for so long. Donald is a tough act to follow. And the way that he left us was so spectacular. As spectacular as it was tragic. It cast a shadow over everything else that has gone since.

Campbell's life and death added immeasurably to the record's mystique, yet in doing so left a dark and cavernous space in which we see little or nothing and hear only echoes.

What will alter the status quo? Only another British record success! Because only Britain, with its national history steeped in nautical achievement, can serve up the antidote. A British boat and driver, a new design inspired by the past. A new record attempt for a public hungry for that special magic the world water speed record summons up.

It is not for want of interest that the record has languished in the doldrums. It was for want of a bold new challenge, and the unleashing of the potential there has always been for Britain to take up once again its rightful place and rule the waves.

Britons have broken the world water speed record more times than any other nationality. It is high time we brought the record 'home'.

Nigel Macknight
2014

INTRODUCTION

Unlike its land counterpart, the world water speed record is an unheralded endeavour, lacking the glamour and recognition that is so associated with the fastest wheel-driven vehicle, yet many have attempted it and few have succeeded. Whereas the names that have driven the land speed record to its never-ending pinnacle have become international personalities and celebrities, the water version has by and large been contested by unknowns or, in some cases, by the very people who have succeeded in the more recognised format.

Few people would have heard of Gar Wood, Stanley Sayres or Ken Warby, but the names of Henry Segrave and Kaye Don and the inevitable Malcolm and Donald Campbell resonate immediately. All at some stage held the world water speed record, yet the well-known and instantly recognisable among them had firstly broken the land speed record before making any attempt on water. In fact, if a straw poll were conducted among the less interested, then surely only that of Donald Campbell would register, as his crash of January 1967 in *Bluebird* has effectively defined the water speed record.

An explanation as to why the water speed record seemingly fails to capture the imagination of the public is a varied thing. A car is now the expected desire of most people living in the western world, a necessity that enables them to travel with comfort and ease, whereas a boat is still seen as a luxury item, normally only available to the more prosperous. A wheel-driven vehicle attempting speeds that are unimaginable is therefore a source of excitement. It explains fully why motor racing of all forms is far more popular than powerboat racing.

The speed differential is also responsible for a certain amount of apathy towards the WSR. Whereas the current land version record stands in excess of 700 mph, with an attempt at 1,000 mph due, the water speed record currently stands at 317 mph. This doesn't sound anywhere near as impressive, but anyone who has travelled in a boat at a three-figure speed can testify to the danger involved. A 100 mph journey on land can feel swift and almost comfortable, and in the twenty-first century, not necessarily dangerous, but a similar journey on water can feel like double the speed, stunningly uncomfortable and will involve more than a certain amount of danger.

The danger is as great, if not greater, on water. A fatality rate that would be shocking in any other form of sport is the true testament to that. On land, a smooth course can be attained – on water anything but. Many have tried to become the official fastest person on water, but only a handful have succeeded. In fact, since the ratification of the record in 1928, only nine men have laid claim to the world water speed record. During the same period, six lost their lives in their attempts.

This book is the story of the *fast* – the ones who raced across the unforgiving water to inch the record higher – and the *forgotten* – the ones who were also fast, but ultimately paid the price of failure with their lives.

1

THE STEAM-POWERED BATTLE

There will always be a 'fastest' when it comes to any type of driven machinery. Whether it is the fastest steam-powered car, the fastest locomotive or the fastest propelled aeroplane, the progression of speed is inevitable due to human nature. So it is with water vessels. Once man devised a way of replacing the sweat and strength of numerous men pushing wooden oars through the water as a means of forward trajectory, the race began to make boats and ships faster and more efficient.

The earliest record of a boat that didn't need the endeavours of man to make it move was in the late eighteenth century, when the Marquis Claude Jouffroy d'Abbans and his partner, the Conte de Follenay, designed a steam boat, powered by a single-cylinder James Watt engine, which they called *Pyroscaphe*. This engine actually powered paddles, working like the webbed feet of a duck, and in front of thousands of spectators, the boat moved of its own accord along the River Saône. There is no record of the speed attained, but the sheer awe and wonder this must have provoked can only be imagined. Steam ships soon became the norm, but speeds were little better than those made by traditional sail ships, or indeed man-powered vessels.

Speeds were measured in miles per hour, as the early designers were essentially land people and had no other way of defining their progress. The nautical term 'knot' was first used in the seventeenth century from the practice of counting the number of knots tied in a length of rope measured against a sandglass as the boat moved. The measurement wasn't exact, and most people recognise the land equivalent, so that is how speeds were recorded in later years.

In 1873, the Government of India commissioned a steamship they wanted to be capable of reaching speeds of around 20 mph to ferry people up and down the Orissa Canals in Bengal. At that time there were two boatyards in London capable of building such a vessel, and eventually the tender went to the yard owned by John Thorneycroft in Chiswick. They supplied an 87-foot-long teak and steel boat that had a beam of 12 feet and called it the *Sir Arthur Cotton* after the well-known irrigation expert, who was based in India. The following spring, on 14 April, the boat was taken out on the Thames near Chiswick, piloted by Lt-Col. Felix Thackery Haig of the Royal Engineers. After two runs with and against the tide, an average speed of 24.61 mph was recorded, leading *The Times* newspaper to herald her as the 'fastest steamer in the world'. More tests followed, proving her reliability, and she was then shipped to India where she gave sterling service at a previously unknown speed. This first trial can reasonably be assumed as the first unofficial world water speed record, starting a process that was to intrigue and interest right up to the present day.

From the very beginning, the accolade of having the fastest boat was a straight battle between Great Britain and the USA. After a decade of pre-eminence, Britain was usurped by America with the navy torpedo steamer *Stiletto*. This had been designed by the naval architect Nathanael Greene Herreshoff, or 'Captain Nat' as he became known. Herreshoff later became famous for designing a number of America's Cup defenders with a huge amount of success, but *Stiletto* was the first boat to bring his talents to prominence. In 1885, she had an 8-hour test run where she reached the speed of 26.6 mph, prompting the *New York Times* to declare that the boat was 'a perfect water knife'. So impressed were Congress that eighteen months later they purchased the boat for a navy commission the following July. This boat was primarily a torpedo war boat, helped enormously by its speed, and it certainly sealed what was already a very favourable reputation for the Captain.

Herreshoff went on to fame and fortune, designing boats with his brother John Brown, who sadly went blind at the age of fourteen. Between them they built up a huge business in the Bristol, Rhode Island area, employing around 400 people, and so earning Herreshoff another nickname – 'The Wizard of Bristol'. As well as designing vessels for America's Cup defenders (as opposed to challengers, as America was completely dominant), they designed luxury yachts for the likes of William Randolph Hearst and Cornelius Vanderbilt III, plus racers too. Sadly, his career was hit by tragedy in 1888, when a boiler exploded on his 875 hp steamboat *Say When* and a member of the crew was fatally injured. The accident saw him lose his steam engineer's license, but unperturbed, Herreshoff continued to build his business until his death in 1938.

The unofficial record changed hands on a number of occasions over the next ten years. Few were really interested in setting a fastest speed for posterity, with more interest in the technological advances of the time. John Thorneycroft's 147-foot boat *Ariete* reached 30 mph on the Thames. Eight years later, another of his torpedo boats, *Boxer*, recorded the incredible speed of 33.75 mph.

In between these two successes, a 13-tonne yacht powered by a 600 hp quadruple expansion steam engine managed to become the fastest boat at 31.6 mph. It was originally called *Still Alarm*, but was later renamed *Feiseen*. Her defining feature was that she was actually built to become the fastest boat on water. She'd been commissioned by William Cogswell and designed by William Gardner and Charles Mosher, and was built in complete secrecy. The builder, Benjamin Franklin Wood, was so confident once she had been completed that he said publicly at her launch, 'I am willing to rest my reputation as a shipbuilder on her. She is built of mahogany throughout, but with 30,000 wooden rivets in her frame, I think that she is any day as strong for seafaring purposes as if she were made entirely of steel. She will be polished like a piano and will not only be the swiftest but the most beautiful and symmetrical craft afloat.'

She was everything that was required, and on 25 August 1893, she set that speed, making her the fastest boat at the time. Soon afterwards, she was sold to the Brazilian Navy, who extended her hull and added an armoured deckhouse and deck-mounted guns.

The next significant advancement of speed on water can be attributed to a 100-foot steel vessel called *Turbinia* in 1897. It had been designed by the Hon. Charles Algernon Parsons, the Anglo-Irish son of the 3rd Earl of Rosse, the famous astronomer William Parsons, and had been the fruit of a long labour to perfect the invention that he became known for, the steam turbine.

Parsons had grown up with a naval and engineering background. Born in Dublin, but raised in London, he'd always had a fascination for invention and the mechanical. That interest manifested itself early when, in 1869, he and his older brother Richard had constructed a steam-powered car that resulted in the first recorded fatal traffic accident; his cousin Mary Ward fell from the vehicle and died from a broken neck. Despite this, he continued his mechanical advancement by attending Cambridge University, spending five years studying maths and also spending a long time rowing in races and designing model boats. There then followed numerous appointments at engineering firms, where he started to look at the possibility of devising the steam turbine.

In 1884, with the help of a model consisting of cotton reels, cardboard strips and sealing wax, and shared with his two young children, Rachel and Algernon, he'd effectively built from scratch an engine that would run up to 18,000 rpm – an astonishing feat of engineering for its time. By now he was part of Clarke, Chapman, Parsons & Co., based in Gateshead, but a falling out with his partners meant a less than amicable split and, after a lengthy and failed court case, he was forced to form a new company in Heaton, minus many of his original patents for the steam turbine. That company became the Marine Steam Turbine Co., with the sole aim of producing a demonstration steam turbine vessel. To give some idea of his inventiveness and adaptability, he again created models to prove to his partners the worth of his dream. A 2-foot hull was towed up and down a freshwater pond on the end of a fishing line to show the manoeuvrability of the design, and then later a 6-foot model was produced and 'powered' by a rubber band to measure the resistance of the hull through water. This master of improvisation also built a cardboard box on the hull with a light fan inside to see the workings at various speeds.

In 1895, the craft was ready. *Turbinia* was built on a slipway in the River Tyne and had cost an enormous £16,000 to produce, mostly self-financed as he had effectively worked free of charge on the whole project. For the next few months, it was trialled time and again with a crew of his two children and his wife, but tests were disappointing. For the boat to be considered a success, a speed of 30 mph was expected, but at no stage did this become a vague possibility. The vessel could only reach 20 mph, which was effectively slower than traditionally steam-powered boats, so Parsons had to look closely at what was going wrong with his invention.

It seemed that the reason for the lack of forward thrust was due to a fault termed 'cavitation'. This means that the high speed of the rear propeller forms a cavity in the water and causes it to spin round without pushing the boat forward. To overcome this, the agile and brilliant mind of Parsons devised three propshafts to be driven by three turbines at various intervals, and after numerous tests of a model in a tank of water with photographic evidence to prove their worth, they were fitted to *Turbinia*, which hit the dizzying speed of 33 mph in just 20 seconds! This was later described by him as a ship that would convince passengers aboard 'that the vessel was Charles Parson's winning North Sea greyhound'.

To make the ship profitable, Parsons had approached the Admiralty with an unbiased and official report. Unfortunately, they were totally unimpressed and refused to commission the boat, despite numerous tests alongside the Northumberland Dock with members of the Admiralty in attendance. Not one to be bowed by such a snub, Parsons then used his renown to effectively advertise his project in front of an appreciative crowd.

On Sunday 27 June 1897, there as a huge naval review as part of Queen Victoria's Diamond Jubilee at Spithead, with 170 ships spreading over 27 miles. All of them were to be reviewed by the royal yacht *Victoria and Albert* in what was, at that stage, the largest gathering of marine vessels ever. Parsons saw his chance and, bedecking the funnel in bright red and yellow, he took *Turbinia* alongside and immediately reached a speed of 32 mph. As he had prearranged, he was then asked by His Royal Highness Prince Henry of Prussia to put her through her paces, which he duly obliged.

The fast run wasn't without its problems, as other small craft, totally unaware of *Turbinia*'s speed, attempted to outrace her and, in some instances, actually cut across her bow, but with the help of two heavily worked stokers down below feeding her coal at an unprecedented rate, she reached the astonishing speed of 39 mph. To say this was impressive is something of an understatement and, later that evening, Parsons was invited as guest on board the German warship *Koenig Wihelm* to explain the advantages of his vessel to Prince Henry. It was clear that *Turbinia*'s had made the fleets of the great powers obsolete, with the publication *The American Shipbuilder* commenting that the ship was a huge success and 'not to be sneezed at'.

Eventually, the Admiralty saw sense and commissioned a turbine-driven destroyer from the Parsons Marine Steam Turbine Co., which was delivered in 1900. It was called *Viper* and was capable of speeds of 42 mph. That was followed by another, *Cobra*, and although both ships were eventually lost at sea, they convinced the Admiralty that all future Royal Naval vessels should be turbine-powered. *Turbinia* became an exhibition piece and was at the Paris show for some time before being hit by another ship, the *Crosby*, in 1907, virtually cutting her in two. Once repaired, she actually sailed alongside the RMS *Mauretania* when she was launched on the Tyne, but mechanical problems forced her to dock after just a few miles. Soon she began to deteriorate and the company decided to take her out of the water in 1926. She was loaned to the London Science Museum, where she was exhibited for some time, although in a rather sorry state. To then complete what had been an unusual life on the waves, the ship was 'blessed' by descendants of the native Navajo American tribe who had located to the North East of England. The reason behind the 'blessing' was to ensure a safe return to the land of its birth, and the ceremony was attended by notable dignitaries, including Nicholas Parsons, the son of Charles. After many years, when the boat was cut in two with the aft section, complete with engines and propellers, exhibited at South Kensington Museum in London, it was eventually taken to the Municipal Museum of Science and Industry, Newcastle, in 1961 with both sections now intact. In 1983, it went through a complete reconstruction and now stands in the Discovery Museum in Newcastle where, in 2000, a £10 million refurbishment took place, with the boat the focal point of the exhibition.

Charles Parsons went on to many other successes in his life, inventing, among many other things, the Auxetophone, which was the first compressed air gramophone. He was knighted in 1911 and made a member of the Order of Merit in 1927. His Parsons Company became part of Siemens in Newcastle and, in 1931, at the age of seventy-six, Charles Parsons died on a cruise ship following a collapse. He had a memorial service at Westminster Abbey later that year, and it's fair to say that without his engineering genius, the forward passage of nautical technology would have been a lot slower.

At the turn of the century, a wealthy New York entrepreneur, Charles R. Flint, was attempting to sell a torpedo boat to the US Navy with the Spanish-American conflict uppermost in his mind. Unfortunately for him, the short war was soon over and the two 3,500 hp steam engines he'd acquired were of little use, so instead he decided to build a boat to become the fastest on water. With that in mind, he commissioned Charles Mosher (of *Fieseen* fame) to design her. In 1902, a 132-foot yacht was ready to break new barriers.

Arrow was so called because of her narrow 12.5-foot beam and 3.6-foot draught, meaning she could scythe through the water. She was made of mahogany and aluminium and powered by two engines, giving her a combined total of 7,000 hp, plus she was quite luxurious. It was said that twenty-five people could comfortably sit aboard while sailing the seas, with a cruising range of 3,000 miles on her 30 tonnes of coal. It was the perfect boat to take the unofficial title of world water speed record, or more accurately for the time, fastest vessel on water.

What took place afterwards is of some dispute. In early 1903, the boat raced on the Hudson River (which had 'no perceptible tide') at a speed claimed as 45.06 mph. This would have been a remarkable advancement, but no serious records were kept from that day and many experts of the time had suggested that the boat didn't go anywhere near as fast, simply because she didn't attempt it again. Shortly after the run, one of her boilers was removed and the boat never again reached that speed. For an entrepreneur like Charles Flint, it's quite astonishing that no official record was kept on an attempt upon which he had set his heart and spent a lot of money. It's also suggested that various US steam ships were able to go faster – sadly this is one record that is never likely to be ratified. Whatever the real story, the fact is that the speed of 45 mph attributed to *Arrow* stood for many years, and it took nearly a decade for any petrol-engined craft to match that speed.

2

THE HARMSWORTH TROPHY

At the turn of the twentieth century, the motor boat was beginning to gain a certain amount of favour among the competitive. It lagged badly behind the motor car in terms of performance and popularity, with the famous Gordon Bennett Cup now in existence. This was a long-distance car race introduced by the American newspaper proprietor James Gordon Bennett with the express intention of beating the supremacy of France on the roads, who, up to that point, had been dominant in the promotion and success of road racing. One of the first to beat the French was a racing cyclist by the name of Selwyn Francis Edge, who also had a car salesroom in Regent Street, London. He won the event in 1902 and, the following year, he was granted home advantage to defend his title. Racing was forbidden on English roads, so Cork in Southern Ireland was chosen, which was still part of the United Kingdom in those days. As well as entering three Napier cars, powered by an 80 hp engine, he also used the same power plant for a boat to compete in the Alfred Harmsworth International Challenge Cup at the same time.

The Harmsworth Trophy, as it later became known, was the idea of the proprietor of the *Daily Mail* newspaper, Alfred Harmsworth. He'd enjoyed the heady thrill of travelling in a car and had described the sensation of going fast as 'like being massaged in a high wind', and in 1900 had sponsored the 1,000-mile trial around the country, in which eighty-three cars participated. Soon his attention turned towards the water equivalent and, in 1902, he commissioned a silver trophy to be awarded to the winner of a head-to-head contest between two boats from separate countries. The rules were pretty straightforward – the boats were to be no more than 40 feet in length, the build plus the engines had to originate from the competing country, no more than three boats could compete from each country and each had to be crewed by three people of naturalised subjects. No limits were put on the construction, but the boats had to be mechanically powered.

The craft that Edge entered was about as radical as it could have been for the age. Instead of the traditional shape, he designed a flat bottom so that the hull could skim the water as opposed to cutting through it, as tradition had always demanded. It took some time for anyone to really take this seriously, but eventually a company in Camden Lock built the curious-looking device and painted it in British racing green for the race.

The challengers came from Germany with a boat called *Mercedes*, but this was destroyed a week before the race, and the substitute French boat was immediately disqualified for not being entirely built on French shores. Two British boats also aimed to beat the odd-looking curiosity called *Napier*. They never came close. In the first race, Edge's boat won by over 3 minutes over the 12-mile course, watched by thousands of spectators in Queenstown, despite giving challenger *Durandel* a head start. That was followed by a winner-takes-all race against *Scolopendra*, a boat built by the highly successful Thorneycroft shipyard. This boat actually hadn't raced before the final, as there was no one to race against, but the organisers, mindful of the attraction to the impatient spectators, decided to give *Scolopendra* a time trial, which it passed by reaching a speed of around 13 mph.

The final was just as one-sided, with *Napier* completing the course at a speed of just under 30 mph, and nearly 1½ miles ahead of *Scolopendra*. This speed was regarded as being quite impressive, as earlier in the year the *Mercedes* vessel had been clocked at 22.36 mph off the French coastal resort of Nice, and had been described in the German press as 'the fastest launch on Earth'. This victory meant that she was now the swiftest petrol launch afloat.

Napier, the first recipient of the Harmsworth Trophy, continued to race with success. She was eventually sold to a French industrialist for the astonishing amount of £1,000 and renamed *N'a pas Pieds*, literally translated as 'Footloose'.

At the same time, a boat from America, *Argo*, was rumoured to have beaten *Napier*'s speed by 6 mph. This remains a rumour, as sadly no records exist, but witnesses at the time suggested she hit around 30 mph and was good for 10 miles an hour more. The boat, 63 feet long and powered by two 150 hp engines, staggered so as not to extend the width, could only travel in a straight line as it needed to virtually stop to turn around, but the New York built craft travelled along East Penobscot Bay at a speed fast enough to make the few spectators watch in wonder. Even at this early stage, and unbeknown to the participants, the battle for the fastest boat on water was taking on a distinctly Anglo-American feel.

With this in mind, the sporting authorities of Monaco, ever mindful of their burgeoning reputation for glamour and excitement on the harbour of Monte Carlo, decided to organise an exhibition and a race meeting on the bay for powered-boats. The idea was to showcase the fastest French boats and maybe break a speed record or two at the same time. It was tremendously popular and many of the motor car companies of the time, looking to test their new, powerful engines in any type of craft, entered the competition. The likes of Panhard, Peugeot, Delahaye, FIAT, Mercedes and Napier all in some way or other participated by either having a boat designed around their engines, or simply acquiring an existing vessel and re-powering it with their mechanicals.

One such boat, which went on to great success, was the French-built *Trefle-a-Quatre-Feuilles*, which entered the Prince of Monaco Cup with an engine supplied by Henri Brasier, used for George Richard to power his car in that year's Gordon Bennett car race, and won convincingly at a speed of 25.1 mph. It therefore picked up around £700 in prize money, a huge amount for the time. This speed was of course still some way off the steam-powered 'record' set a few years previously, but it was clear that petrol engines were now the way forward as far as speed and comfort were concerned. As an aside, the Prince, whose name was given to the trophy, was apparently so impressed with *Trefle* that he actually asked if he could steer her himself on a run around the harbour. No records exist for the speed attained with royalty at the helm.

The French boat continued to have success at the Monaco meeting, beating even Selwyn Edge convincingly, although he did make amends by winning a regatta in Germany a month later. At the same time, *Trefle-a-Quatre-Feuilles* proved herself to be the fastest boat afloat by recording a speed of 26.65 mph on the River Seine just outside Paris over a course measuring a staggering 108 kilometres. Whatever the British and Americans could do on water, the French were determined to match or better, and with some style. *Trefle* was an attractive 30-foot boat that was powered by an 84 hp engine and was clearly the standard-bearer for the rest to beat.

In 1904, along with seven other entrants, she challenged Selwyn Edge for the second Harmsworth Trophy in English waters, overseen by King Edward VII on his royal yacht. Sadly, the whole event was a disaster, with four of the boats failing to turn up and the remainder playing out a mock competition with interminable heats and run-offs that bored the thousands of spectators senseless. It became so tedious that two of Edge's boats, *Napier II* and *Napier Minor*, ran off against each other, with the former hitting an obstacle after winning and nearly sinking. That meant she couldn't defend her title in the final against *Trefle*, which had also had numerous race-offs to reach that position, and so *Napier Minor* was put forward in her place.

The British boat won, but the French crew challenged and protested that it was the wrong vessel they had been racing and so won the trophy on a technicality, much to the annoyance of the King and the British spectators. At the same time, one of the boats that had been beaten in the earlier heats, the American *Challenger*, went out on the same waters and recorded a fastest average speed of 29.3 mph over the measured mile. It was hardly surprising that most onlookers were confused by the shambles that had played out in front of their critical eyes.

Edge was undeterred and determined to regain the unofficial record for the fastest boat on water. Three weeks after the trophy races, he took *Napier II* out on to the Greenwich waters, with Harry J. Swindley of the Automobile Club of Great Britain (the forerunner of the RAC) as a timekeeper, and recorded a mean average speed over two runs of 29.9 mph, to just pip *Challenger*. After that, he sold the boat to John Scott Montagu of Beaulieu and Lionel de Rothschild; although she continued racing, she never recreated the success or speed of previous times.

An even sadder end came to *Trefle-a-Quatre-Feuilles* – she caught fire while preparing for the second Monaco meeting and sank to the bottom of the harbour. Although she was eventually salvaged, she never sailed again. The Prince of Monaco Cup was actually won by another French boat, *Dubonnet*, built for the owner of the famous drinks firm Emile. It was a 50-foot craft powered by two massive 200 hp Delahaye engines and reached an incredible speed of 32.46 mph, then raised to 33.80 mph two weeks later at Juvisy, where *Trefle* had been successful. Unfortunately, the boat was too big to be considered for the Harmsworth Trophy (now renamed the British International Trophy after the Automobile Club had taken control of proceedings), but French honour was supplied by *Mab* for the races on the Bay of Arcachon off Bordeaux. This was a last-minute entry by the Automobile Club of France after every one of the entrants from France and America failed to turn up, leaving only the newly owned *Napier II* to race.

The event was even more disappointing than the previous year for the thousands of spectators. With four boats racing each other, the British craft easily won each heat and the final made amends for the 'technicality' loss of 1904. The winning speed of 24.30 mph was underwhelming for Montagu and Rothschild, though, who had both been at the helm.

However, the record was broken again in 1905, when a curious Anglo-French 12-metre boat called *Legru-Hotchkiss* went out on to the River Seine in winter and reached 34.17 mph. The vessel was designed in London and built in Paris by English craftsmen, and was powered by two engines developing a combined total of 170 hp. This was unofficial, but so impressed were the authorities that they were keen on 'inviting' the owners to compete in the next Harmworth/BIT in 1906, seemingly forgetting their strict rules on nationalities. As it was, the boat wasn't entered, and the trophy limped on the following year with the *Yarrow-Napier,* a boat built for the two rich owners, winning by half an hour over the steam-engined *Rose-en-Soleil.* That could hardly be described as a spectacle for anyone watching from the shores.

Despite *Legru-Hotchkiss* being the fastest boat, it was *Challenger* that had created all the headlines and caught the public imagination. H. L. Bowden, a racing driver who had just driven his Mercedes at 109.75 mph along Daytona Beach in an attempt at breaking the land speed record, announced that he would transfer the engine from the car, plus the addition of a second engine, and install it in the *Challenger* in an attempt to increase the speed of the American boat and make it the fastest vessel on water. A year later, in February 1906, at a motor boat carnival held at Fort Worth, Bowden took the boat out on to the water with the two engines installed and could only manage a mean speed of 28 mph, proving the difficulty and difference between land and water; *Challenger* could not go any faster.

Around the same time, a young engineer by the name of Clinton Crane was making a name for himself as a boat designer, and specifically a racing boat designer. He'd graduated at Harvard University and had found himself in New York after a year at Glasgow University. Teaming up with a couple of naval architects, he built the business of Tam, Lemoine & Crane into a successful boatbuilding enterprise by the turn of the twentieth century. Among the boats that heralded the business were *Vingt-et-Un,* a 30-footer that had huge success and achieved a top speed of 22 mph in trials and various races, followed by the second version, which increased the speed to 25.67 mph, but still some way off the fastest of the time.

Crane's big success came when he and his partners were approached by a certain Sam Thomas from Kentucky, who wanted to win the Harmsworth Trophy for America and needed a fast boat to do it in. This boat was called *Dixie* in deference to Thomas' place of birth, but almost immediately hit problems. The 40-foot boat struggled to reach the 30 mph mark until ballast was added to her stern to help her lift out of the water, and then she missed the Trophy event altogether as it was clear the boat wasn't ready. Not to be dismayed, however, Thomas commissioned a second boat, inevitably called *Dixie II*, from Crane and by the summer of 1907 it was ready.

The boat was 40 feet in length, made from pure mahogany and weighed around 1,000 lbs. It was powered by a 2,200 lb V8 engine, designed and supplied by Crane's brother Henry, and on a private trial on the Hudson River, she reached the previously unattainable speed of 37 mph. It was encouraging to say the least.

Although the Harmsworth Trophy, or the British International Trophy as it was known at the time, was not an official world water speed record event, the fact was that most of the races were won at a best speed or certainly nearly as close, and so the 1907 event saw two of the fastest boats in the world go head-to-head for the honour of national pride and the claim to be the fastest boat on water. *Dixie II* was challenged by the British boat *Wolseley-Siddeley*, owned by the richest man in Britain, the 2nd Duke of Westminster, Hugh Richard Arthur Grosvenor.

Grosvenor, or the Viscount Belgrave, was a hero of the Boer War. As well as regular appearances in the House of Lords, plus taking care of his vast wealth, which included some of the richest property in London and estates in Cheshire and Scotland, he was a keen sportsman too. At the age of twenty-four, he'd ridden in the Grand National, but had fallen when his horse Dumfree had thrown him. The horse was shot after breaking its neck, and the Duke was quite badly injured. Undeterred, and with the exuberance of youth and the carefree attitude of the rich, he continued his sporting pursuits, with car races at Brooklands and the occasional motor boat challenge too.

He came across the *Wolseley-Siddeley* after it had successfully won races in Monaco and Nice at speeds approaching 35 mph. Built by the Wolseley Tool & Motor Car Co., the boat was a 40-foot hull and powered by two 200 hp engines that would normally sit in a Wolseley car, plus had many mechanicals from a 4-cylinder car that had been designed by John Siddeley (hence the name). After its successes, the Duke bought the boat and its pilot, Noel 'Robby' Robbins, and proceeded to enter it against *Dixie II* at the next Harmsworth Trophy. It wasn't successful, and *Dixie II* won comfortably. To prove the worth of the *Dixie II*, the Crane brothers then took the craft to Hemsptead Harbour, racing it over the same course, and recorded a fastest speed of 35.75 mph over four runs (timed by New York Yacht Club officials), making it 'officially' the fastest boat on water. Later that year, on another specific run, they increased *Dixie II*'s speed to 36.6 mph, leaving no doubt as to the claim to a new world record.

The Duke of Westminster was not the type to give up easily, and in 1909 he had a successor to *Wolseley-Siddeley,* inevitably called *Wolseley-Siddeley II*. This was a boat of revolutionary design starting with a sharp V shape and rounding to a U shape at the rear. It was 49 feet long, and made of mahogany planks that were 50 feet in length and moulded together in such a way that the whole boat looked as if it were built from one long piece of shining timber. Also, the cockpit had been moved ahead of the two 400 hp Wolseley engines, meaning the helmsman and engineer wouldn't be suffocated by the fumes from the motors – a radical invention.

The boat was all-conquering, winning the Coupe des Nations in Monaco at a speed of around 40 mph on its first outing. This speed was clearly the fastest, but records were not officially submitted during races, with times being recorded as stand-alone 'speed attempts'. However, in April 1910, the boat, now renamed *Ursula* after the Duke's daughter, tackled a 25-kilometre course off Monaco harbour and officially recorded a top speed of 43.6 mph, so gaining the title of the 'fastest vessel in the world'.

3

THE HYDROPLANE

Up until this point, all speedboats had ploughed through the water in traditional fashion, using brute force from the power of their engines to displace the solid water. Now the idea of hydroplaning – skimming across the water – was becoming more and more popular. This had first been suggested in 1872, when a Reverend Ramus from Rye in Sussex had experimented with models to that purpose and was so enamoured by his 'invention' that he even offered the idea to the Admiralty free of charge. They in turn had rejected it as at that time no steamship was light enough or indeed powerful enough to plane across the water. The idea was shelved, much to the sadness of the Reverend, who seemed to be a forerunner in one of the most significant nautical inventions of all time.

Others tried to perfect the idea, notably John Thorneycroft, and he indeed had a certain amount of success with a hydroplaned boat called *Miranda III,* which had reached 31 mph on the River Thames in 1909. An American by the name of William Fauber, who mostly built bicycles and accessories, attempted to hone the 'skimming' idea and took out numerous patents in Europe after his explanations and promotions fell on deaf American ears, but it was the Crane brothers who had the first and most significant success with a hydroplane boat.

The Harmsworth Trophy of 1911 saw another challenge from Britain, and so *Dixie IV* was built. She was 40 feet long, as stated by the rules of the competition, built of mahogany and powered by two 270 hp engines and a hull that would lift out of the water at speed. It was said that the vessel was worth around $10,000 and was possibly the most expensive boat ever built at that time.

It was to be driven by Vice-Commodore Fred Burnham, although his cockpit position was unusual to say the least. In an age well before aerodynamics had been seriously thought of, he sat well above the boat in a bucket seat so that he could see above the spray that would inevitably wash over the craft. It didn't protect him from the fumes from the exhausts, though, so a combination of muffler and goggles made for a curious sight. It worked though, and in trial runs, the boat reached nearly 46 mph.

The trophy was won convincingly again in front of over 10,000 spectators on Huntingdon Bay, this time against the Duke of Cornwall's white-painted *Pioneer,* driven by 'Robby' Robbins. Despite the Viscount betting £3,000 on his boat being victorious, his vessel never came close to *Dixie IV.* To prove the worth and superiority of the American boat, three days after successfully defending the trophy (which, by the way, had now dropped the British International Trophy title for pretty obvious reasons), Fred Burnham arranged to take her out on the same bay in an attempt at becoming the fastest boat on water.

On 9 September 1911, *Dixie IV* successfully navigated the measured mile, officiated by timekeepers from the New York Yacht Club with a complex set of flags and timepieces to gain as an exact speed as possible, and with her bows out of the water, she recorded a mean speed, from no fewer than eighteen timekeeper's readings, of 45.21 mph – a new world record. It also gave her owner a prize of $1,000 and a trophy for the speed trial. That should have been the crowning glory for one of the most radical designs in boatbuilding, but sadly the accomplishment was blighted by tragedy some six days later.

While leading the Great Lakes Championship on the Niagara River at around 40 mph, the steering failed as she turned a stake boat for the return run downstream. Seeing that the boat had effectively become out of control, Burnham, who again was driving, shouted to his engineers to abandon while he attempted to slow her down, as it was clear the boat was heading towards the shore where most of the spectators were watching. Two jumped and two stayed on board, thankfully all four were uninjured, but the boat careered onto the bank and headlong into the crowd, killing a thirteen-year-old schoolboy, seriously injuring his mother and causing an amputation of the leg to another fifteen-year-old boy.

It was a tragedy of the highest order and in the inquest that followed Burnham was criticised by the judge for 'criminal negligence in not signalling to his engineers to stop the boat', and of 'cowardice in deserting his post at the steering wheel when the boat was within 300 feet of the shore and might have brought it under control'. Harsh judgements, which, given appeal, were changed to 'accidental death', effectively ended Clinton Crane's involvement in boat racing. A quote from a 1952 publication called *Yachting Memories* explains his feelings fully:

> When I remember the way Mr Burnham drove *Dixie IV* around the crowded harbour at Huntingdon, where many yachts were at anchor, I shudder to think what might have happened if she had taken a sudden sheer at that time. I am sure she could have gone right straight through any one of the yachts. That ended *Dixie*'s racing career and ended my work in the design of hydroplanes, as I saw no way of making them safe and useful.

The Crane brothers didn't return to boatbuilding or racing professionally again, although Clinton did race for a hobby from 1922 until his death in 1958. As chairman of the St Joseph Lead Company, he had led it from a company in serious debt to a business with a Wall Street evaluation of $100 million. His brother Henry actually designed his own custom-built car before becoming General Motors, consulting engineer, designing the engine that would be used in future Pontiacs. He died in 1956.

What of Fred Burnham? Well, despite his racing successes in both *Dixie III* and *Dixie IV,* he will always be associated with the terrible tragedy on Niagara River. Meanwhile, a month earlier, the Duke of Westminster had suffered a serious accident when his now aged *Pioneer* boat flipped at around 40 mph. It was also effectively the last time he was involved in boat racing at that level.

The next small increase in the fastest boat on water went to a Canadian boat, racing for Britain in the Harmsworth Trophy and, after eight years, finally surpassing the steam record held by *Arrow.* Montreal-born Mike Edgar had lived in England for five years, worked as a successful and wealthy stockbroker, and had a passion for motor boats, among other things, such as acting and tennis. *Maple Leaf IV* (bizarrely the fifth boat to hold the title of the Canadian emblem as there were two *III* versions) was a winner of the trophy in September of 1912, but one month earlier in trials had posted a speed of 46.51 mph over a 33-mile course. This 40-foot hydroplane boat with two 400 hp engines had been driven by Thomas Sopwith, a twenty-four-year-old aviator who had recently gained his pilot's licence at Brooklands. He'd also been a quite adept long-distance ballooning expert, so steering a petrol-engined boat at a previously unheard of speed was of no real concern to him. Sadly for the crew of *Maple Leaf IV,* their 'record' lasted for all of six weeks before being smashed by another American Harmsworth challenger (and loser too), *Tech Jr.* This hydro, driven by Coleman DuPont, covered a nautical mile in 1 minute and 12 seconds, meaning she had reached the quite astonishing speed of 58.26 mph, completely destroying any other boat at that stage. At one stage during the brief run, it was suggested that the barrier-breaking 'mile a minute' had been reached, something that an automobile had first achieved in 1899 with the French *La Jamais Contente* setting the incredible speed. Almost immediately, *Maple Leaf IV* was readied by Edgar for another attempt at proving his boat was the fastest, but the First World War intervened and the dreams of the boat were not realised. Just to rub salt into the raw wound, weeks before the conflict began, Frenchman Victor Despujol's new hydroplane *Santos-Despujols* went to Monaco harbour and attained 59.96 over the nautical mile – again a new world record.

The 'mile a minute' was finally achieved in America in 1915 by a fifty-four-year-old boatbuilder called Christopher Columbus Smith living in Algonac, Michigan. He'd been building boats since 1881 and had local success with his enterprise, building his first powered boat in 1906, which had reached the speed of 9 mph. A couple of years later, he supplied a pleasure craft for a well-known wealthy gambler called John 'Baldy' Ryan, and so impressed was he with the boat that he arranged for movie mogul J. Stuart Blackton of Vitagraph Pictures, who also enjoyed racing boats, to commission a vessel off Smith for an attempt at the Harmsworth Trophy. Not only that, but Blackton also commissioned smaller boats to take part in the Mississippi Valley Powerboat Regatta, and *Baby Reliance I, II* and *III* all swept to victories in their respective classes. Unfortunately, the number two version failed against *Maple Leaf IV* in the trophy race, but Smith's reputation had now been established.

Ryan went bankrupt shortly after, unsurprisingly so bearing in mind his gambling habits, and so a source of valuable income was lost to Smith. However, like all true entrepreneurs, he saw this as a challenge as opposed to a setback and immediately started a sponsorship scheme from the citizens of Detroit to build a boat that would be capable of breaking the longed for 60 mph – some stories suggest that Smith had dreamt the idea one night and had seen in his visions spectators dropping dollar bills into a bucket! The Miss Detroit Powerboat Association was a success and funded the boat *Miss Detroit I*, but unfortunately any extra funds from J. Blackton were unlikely, as his picture company had been supplying mostly to a German market that was now at war.

Miss Detroit I was fast, but not fast enough, and fell short of the MAMBOAT title (mile a minute). The syndicate lost interest and couldn't afford to continue, so Smith started all over again and built

Miss Minneapolis for three eager sportsmen from the area. He piloted it himself, and in an effort to sell it to any prospective owner, took it down a measured half-mile on Put-in-Bay in Ohio at the Interlake Yachting Association and over four runs averaged 66.66 mph. It was an astonishing speed, never seen before on water, and some sixteen years since a car had reached the same velocity. It's also worth noting that at that stage in 1915 the world land speed record, which was officially ratified, stood at 124.10 mph. Nonetheless, it was impressive enough and that afternoon, 6 September, the *New York Times* headlined 'POWERBOAT QUEEN' and followed with 'Wins one mile title and sets new record in burst of dazzling speed' in its leader. Christopher Smith's reputation was made and his chance meeting with Gar Wood at that time was to have a serious impact on powerboat racing and the attainment of speed on water. Before that, a surprising figure was to make an impact on the 'fastest vessel on water'.

Alexander Graham Bell is of course known for his many inventions, notably the telephone, but what is not widely known is that he was jointly responsible for the 'record' being broken with a boat he helped to design. The hydroplane was a 'new' idea in boat design that had first been trialled in the mid-nineteenth century. Thomas Moy was looking to add a couple of wings to his flying machine in an attempt to lift it into the air, so he used a boat as a trial, and with the help of two hydrofoils, he managed to get the craft to rise off the water briefly at a sustained speed. There is no record as to whether he eventually managed to get his machine into the skies, though. Whereas hydroplanes 'skim' along the water supported by planing forces as opposed to simple buoyancy, hydrofoils (i.e. struts that support the hull) lift the boat out of the water to effectively glide. This was a radical departure at the time, despite other designers experimenting with the idea.

One person who spent a lot of time looking at the possible success of hydrofoils was Professor Enrico Forlanini. He was based in Milan and in 1906, he'd built a cigar-shaped hull that had four-laddered foils at the front. When he took it out on Lake Garda, it reached a speed of 45 mph in almost supreme comfort. These foils were made up of three steps each, to give strength to the struts. The hull was effectively lifted out of the water and supported on the foils, meaning that a fast boat no longer needed to scythe a route through the density of water beneath. This was quickly taken up by other boat designers, and an article written by American William Meacham alerted Bell to the idea, who in turn described the design as 'the most significant invention in years' – heady stuff from one of the most revered and successful inventors of all time.

Bell met up with Forlanini, with his colleague and boatsman Canadian Casey Baldwin, in France in 1910 during a world tour, after experimenting himself with a home-built hull on the lake of Beinn Bhreagh, next to his house in Nova Scotia. The three spent some time together and Forlanini gave the two regular rides across Lake Maggiore at speeds of around 45 mph. It left a huge impression on Bell.

When they returned to Canada, they set to design a hydrofoil boat that would be fast and appealing to the Canadian and US Navy, as at that time the First World War was now involving the United States. Bell, a Scotsman by birth, had become a citizen of Canada and with that country's initial neutrality, had first approached the US Navy. Sadly, the boats, named *Hydrodome I, II* and *III*, failed to impress – the first actually breaking in half at a speed of 50 mph – especially as their speed was hardly faster than any 'conventional' craft. Bell became depressed at the lack of success, and described the rejection from the US Navy of his craft as 'a bomb landing in their camp and shattering all his plans'. However, his sister Mabel came to the rescue and put up the money for more development. Eventually a 60-foot cigar-shaped vessel riding on two sets of hydrofoil ladders, one forward and one rear, powered by two 400 hp Liberty engines, was built. The engines had been loaned by the US Navy, who at first had been less than enamoured with the idea. Once they had been installed, some ten years after Forlanini's trials, *Hydrodome IV* took to the waters.

Casey Baldwin piloted the boat and on 9 September 1919, on Beinn Bhreagh, the boat reached a mean speed of 70.86 mph, smashing the previous record by 4 mph. *Hydrodome IV* was now the 'fastest vessel on water', but although both the British Admiralty and the US Navy witnessed the run, neither considered making an order for the boat now that the First World War was at an end. The craft lay on the shores of Nova Scotia and was hardly used again. With Alexander Graham Bell died just three years later, and it was an invention that was effectively lost among some of the great man's finest achievements. He will, though, forever be associated in nautical circles with designing a successful 'water speed record' boat.

4

GAR WOOD

There are few people outside of boating circles who have heard of Garfield Arthur Wood. However, in the first half of the twentieth century, he was not only one of the most successful, influential and recognisable businessmen in America, but in a twelve-year period, he held the world water speed record no fewer than six times, and was also officially the first man to take a boat to 100 mph on water.

'Gar' Wood was born on 4 December 1880 to Elizabeth and Walter Wood, the third of an astonishing twelve children. He was named after the successful Republican Presidential 'ticket' of James Garfield and Chester Arthur, and ultimately became more famous than both of them. The family originally lived in Iowa, but in 1890 they moved to Minnesota, where Walter became the captain of a ferryboat. Walter was a father who demanded respect, and in that regard Gar was unfailing. The ten-year-old would spend many days travelling on the ferry with his father, and one particular instance effectively created the man that Gar would become. He was busy helping his father when a rival ferry operator started to overtake them in a vastly superior boat, but Walter refused to cede and, in Gar's own words, did everything he could to ensure they finished the journey first. The following is a story that he loved in later years to recount on a regular basis.

The first boat race I ever took part in was on Lake Osakis. My father operated a ferry on that lake, and we had some great old times with it. Our ferry was named the *Manitoba* and its only rival was the *Merry Mann,* owned and run by old Wes Mann. Wes couldn't give up the idea that his ferry boat, which was a wood burner like ours, was the faster of the two, and that someday he would catch Dad unawares and prove it.

> On one memorable trip across the lake, Wes caught us short of wood! His old boat was pushing us hard because we couldn't feed ours enough fuel.
>
> 'Why don't you row that old tub in?' he jeered at us as he edged alongside. 'I'm passin' you standing still!'
>
> 'Blast his hide!' roared Dad. 'Hey you lads, give us a hand with this furniture! Bust her up and shove her into the firebox! We'll beat the old pirate if we have to tear up the deck!'
>
> So we fed the fire with the chairs and tables, and though old Wes pushed his boat for all she was worth, we beat him fair and square! I was only a kid then, but I still feel the thrill of winning that race. Right then I resolved that someday I was going to build race boats of my own.

It was clearly a defining moment in young Gar's life, and when his father was transferred to Duluth to captain a large freighter for the Great Lakes, the family moved again and Gar actually started to work in an engineering department attached to the company, using his vast technical knowledge gained at such an early age to build small boats and launches for local fishermen. He even looked at the design of a carburation unit and attempted to improve on it – all of this while still at school.

In fact, school bored him as his talent and enthusiasm for engineering far outweighed that of his exasperated teachers, and soon he was leaving to advance his career. By the time he was twenty, he had already sold lightning rods to farmers, taught automotive engineering to schools, bought himself a garage and became an official Ford car dealer. That wasn't as successful, as he only sold ten cars in a year (not helped by a tardy distribution process), but to show what a resourceful man he had become he immediately attempted to sue the distributor, who was so impressed that he gave him a highly paid job with his firm.

Soon afterwards, and after his marriage to Murlen Fellows, a student at Minnesota University, he opened his own machine shop called G. A. Wood Company, which specialised in boatbuilding and repairs. He was commissioned to build a vessel called *Leading Lady* for a Mr Cleveland and the two of them took the boat to the Mississippi Valley, where they won virtually every race they entered at the then astonishing 10-mile speed of 31 mph. His ability and talent was soon making people take notice in that small boating circle.

Surprisingly, his breakthrough to fame and definitely fortune had nothing to do with boats, but actually concerned a hydraulic lift that he invented for lifting the beds of trucks. It came by chance when one day he and his wife witnessed a couple of sweating and cursing labourers who were hand-cranking a winch to lift a heavy bed filled with coal. He knew there was an easier way, and the two of them decided to invest their small savings into the building of a prototype.

It was all pretty simple, as he took the old cylinder from the *Manitoba* (used to reverse the engine) and, adapting it successfully to the truck, persuaded the owner to try it. The mechanism seemed pretty basic and simple, but Gar Wood's charm and authority persuaded the owner after initial scepticism. It could only work with a heavy load, and as nothing was at hand, he then suggested that some of the truck owner's friends, who were actually returning from a dinner party and dressed appropriately, should stand on the bed while Gar winched it with his mechanical device. The guests agreed – full of humour and ridiculing comments, but were deposited quite quickly onto the dusty floor once the bed had been winched upwards – Gar had sold his product! The owner ordered enough winches for every one of his trucks and soon a successful and extremely profitable business was formed.

The winch was patented and orders far outscored the products. Wood soon decided to expand and move to a larger factory with the help of a $5,000 investment from a local car dealer – something Wood regretted for many years, especially as the buy-back cost him around £750,000 twenty years later. Interest and eventual orders from the US and British Army for use in the First World War, where the winches were used on lorries that were used to rebuild bombed and battered roads, made him into a millionaire. After just four years of owning and running his own business, Gar Wood was now rich enough to indulge in the one abiding passion he'd had ever since that day on his father's ferry. From that moment in 1916, his successful businesses were there to provide for his family, and that meant his parents and eight brothers and three sisters, and also to finance his motor boat racing. For the next seventeen years, Gar Wood all but dominated the waters with his specifically designed boats and in that time wrote his name in the water record books. None of it would have been possible without the invention of the hydraulic winch.

In 1916, Chris Smith was owed a considerable amount of money from the association that had sponsored him and the *Miss Detroit* boat. To try to resolve the problem, the members of the group had a luncheon in downtown Detroit to discuss the debt and hopefully put the boat up for auction to sell and then in turn pass on the proceeds to Smith. The boat had been successful, but was now battered and bruised, with a hull that needed completely replacing, but they were still confident that someone would make a high enough bid to pay off the debt. Lee Barrett was the head of Detroit's Bureau of Conventions and Tourism and he conducted the auction. His words told the story of what happened next.

It happens that the one man in the world who was interested in a used race boat was in the room when I spoke. He stood up – a slim, dark-haired man in his mid-30s whom I had never seen before.

'How much do you want for that boat?' he called out from the back of the dining room. Silence swept the room. The man did not look like he could buy the boat. I leaned over the chairman and asked, 'Shall I tell him the price?'

'Sure,' said Judge Callender, 'take a chance,' I straightened up and told the stranger $1,800. The dark man stood up again said, 'I've got $1,000 with me and I'll sign a six months note for the balance.'

I leaned over to the judge and whispered, 'Is his note good?' The judge smiled and said, 'His word is good for a million,' and *Miss Detroit* was sold to Gar Wood.

Wood had bought his first proper racing boat and he immediately drove to Alganoc on the St Clair River to see his new purchase. After locating the business of C. C. Smith Boat and Engine Company, he soon spotted *Miss Detroit* and saw the sad state she was in. As he examined her, he was joined by Chris Smith and his oldest son, Jay. They talked about the boat, and the knowledge that Gar Wood had bought her earlier that day was the best piece of news the Smiths could have received. It meant that the debt they were owed could now be paid off in full. It was also the start of an astonishing business relationship, which, within a few hours of their first meeting, saw Gar Wood become the majority owner of C. C. Smith Boat & Engine Company and employing the Smiths as his sole racing boatbuilders. In one day, Wood had bought his first race boat and then bought a company that would build further models for him. For the next six years, the Smiths built boats and Wood raced them to victories and speed records.

In 1917, the combination of Chris Smith's building expertise, helped by his son Jay, who also crewed the boats, and Gar Wood at the wheel, saw the *Miss Detroit* and *Miss Detroit II* sweep the board in just about every race they entered. They were completely and totally dominant against any kind of opposition, including winning the prestigious Gold Cup. The following year they were even more unstoppable, especially when Gar Wood suggested they use a Glenn Curtiss aircraft engine to power *Miss Detroit III*. This powerful engine would turn the propellers of the boat at 2,000 revolutions per minute and make it the fastest vessel in any race condition.

This advancement of the mechanics of boat racing was advantageous to Wood and the Smiths, who were glorying in their success, but the American Powerboat Association took an extremely dim view of proceedings and decided to change the rules wholesale so as not to negate competition. They were concerned that Wood's dominance would be counter-productive and scare off any potential opposition. They decided, among other things, to completely outlaw aircraft engines in boats, plus disallowed any type of hydroplane boat, preferring to retain the safer displacement hulls. It was an act aimed purely and totally at Gar Wood and his partners. After five consecutive Gold Cup triumphs, Wood decided enough was enough and turned his attention elsewhere – to the International Harmsworth Trophy being held in England. It was at this race in 1920 that the first of the *Miss America* hydroplanes was used, and over the next twelve years, nine more would be built and raced, taking seven world water speed records. Before that, though, a major split in the working relationship of Chris Smith and Gar Wood took place.

The Smiths were now financially secure, mainly based on the successful input of Wood, and after the shock of the rule changes implemented by the APBA had registered, Chris Smith in particular lost interest in powerboat racing. He wanted to build family leisure boats at the higher end of the market and, with that in mind, ended his business association with Gar Wood. It wasn't exactly amicable, but later Wood decided to invest in the new, larger factory that the Smiths had built in Alganoc, and as he was still passionate about his powerboating, gave the Smith family commissions for the building of powerful engines for his boats. One of those, the first *Miss America*, was raced on the St Clair River and recorded a speed of 77.85 mph – a new world water speed record, and a boat that was officially the fastest vessel on water. This speed had smashed the previous record by nearly 7 mph, set by *Hydrodome IV* the previous year. It was a 26-foot racer powered by two Liberty engines and made from sleek Philippine mahogany. It was now ready for its big challenge – the International Harmsworth Trophy in England.

The trophy was won back in some style on the English Channel, beating three British defenders after boats from France and Spain both failed to turn up. *Miss America* was completely dominant, winning its heat against timid opposition and the final in an even more complete way. Soon afterwards, Gar Wood took the boat to victory in the 30-mile classic called the APBA Gold Cup, and at that point there seemed little left for Wood to achieve, but as well as being a successful businessman, he was also a showman and a self-publicist. This came to the fore at the beginning of 1921.

At the stroke of midnight on 25 April, Wood took his boat, *Gar II Jr*, a 50-foot cabin cruiser powered by two Liberty engines, out of Indian Creek Harbour. He'd announced to the population of America that he would race the famous express train *The Havana Special* from

Miami to New York and was confident he could beat it. The stunt caught the imagination of the public and thousands lined the shore to see the boat travel along a parallel line to the railway tracks where the *Special w*ould run. In fairness to the rail company, they didn't see it as a race and continued to travel the route at a normal speed, making the necessary stops along the way. That didn't matter to Wood, and after 47 hours and 23 minutes, plus the use of 700 gallons of aviation spirit, *Gar II Jr* pulled in at the Columbia Yacht Club at the end of West 86th Street some 21 minutes before *The Havana Special* arrived at Grand Central station. It was an amazing achievement, made even more remarkable by the fact that heavy fog had at one stage forced him to go at least 25 miles off course, yet still he covered the 1,260-mile trip at an astonishing speed. His name was in the newspapers and on the radio and, not for the first time, Gar Wood had captured the hearts of the American people.

Not content with his feat, or maybe not satisfied with the level of media coverage he'd been given, he decided almost immediately to set another 'record' by travelling from New York along the coastline and up the Hudson River to Detroit, a journey of a further 2,200 miles. He started the very next day and arrived 84 hours later, with a media entourage in full flow.

There is no doubt that Wood was the top boat racer of the time, but his insatiable need for publicity seemed to have taken him to endeavours and attempts that now seem almost futile, for three months after his success against an express train, he was doing the same against an aeroplane with *Miss America*. The distance was just 16 miles on the St Clair River from Algonac to Marine City, and with at an average speed of around 70 mph, Wood and his vessel triumphed again, this time by just 2 minutes. The publicity was priceless. It helped to sell his boats – a surprisingly small part of his business empire – which in turn paid for his passion. Gar Wood was the biggest name in powerboat racing at that time.

IS IT A BOAT OR IS IT A PLANE?

A new type of boat arrived on the scene in the early 1920s. After the success of the hydroplane and the hydrofoil, along came the hydroglider. In 1922, Marcel Besson designed a 32-foot wingless seaplane, powered by a 350 hp aero engine that drove a huge 7-foot propeller. The basic idea was that the high speeds would effectively lift the craft out of the water with air passing under a central tunnel, while a water rudder would stabilise the boat at slow speeds. It didn't look like a boat and it didn't look like a plane either. A year later, in pretty horrendous conditions on the River Seine at Meulan, just north-west of Paris, an aeroplane pilot called Pierre Canivert drove the craft six times over the water through a measured kilometre. The tests were officially and carefully timed, and a brief top speed of 88 mph was recorded. This wasn't long enough to be ratified as the 'fastest vessel on water', but the concept had been proved.

The so-called 'record' was reported in Europe, but totally ignored in America, not least by Gar Wood, who was strongly against this new and radical boat-plane design. Two years later, however, another American, Jules Fischer, a well-known aeroplane pilot, took a new hydroglider, designed by Frenchman Maurice Farman and powered by a 450 hp engine, to a new 'record' of 87.392 mph on the Seine between Sartrouville and Maisons-Laffitte near Paris. The date 10 November 1924 was the only time a hydroglider held the title as the 'fastest vessel', as this mismatch of aeroplane technology bolted onto a boat was deemed to be stretching the unwritten rules too far.

BOATS AND PLANES AGAIN

In 1925, Gar Wood was at it again. Looking for the oxygen of publicity once more, he and his brother, George, decided to race another express train, *Twentieth Century Ltd*, over 150 miles from Albany to New York. *Baby Gar IV*, yet another powerboat built for the pleasure of Wood, was to sail the Hudson River, while the express would travel its normal route. To their equal consternation and delight, the train was packed to capacity with new passengers wanting to be part of a little piece of history. Again, the railway company made a point of saying that they were in no need of a race and didn't recognise it as such, but the Wood brothers disregarded that, and with all the media publicity they could attract, they prepared for the attempt. The stunt was extensively advertised, not least with the major New York newspapers, with Wood saying, 'A mile-by-mile descriptive report will be broadcast on low power from an airplane and rebroadcast on high power...' The race was on. Numerous aeroplanes followed the route, sending the aforementioned broadcasts, and thousands of spectators lined the route once more.

Baby Gar IV, a 33-foot pleasure 'runabout', actually crossed the 'finishing line' some 41 minutes ahead of the train's final destination, but what was not immediately disclosed was that the original boat, *Baby Gar V*, had broken down midway through and the Wood brothers had switched vessels. Not against any rule, of course, as this was a self-indulgent stunt made by and for Gar Wood. They had also used 110 gallons of petrol with the empty barrels being tossed unceremoniously overboard into the Hudson River to keep the weight down. None of that mattered though, as an average speed of 46.5 mph was enough to win the 'race'. It was yet more publicity for Gar Wood and his boats. Still, none of this had anything to do with breaking a water speed record, something that slowly but surely was beginning to capture the attention of the racing media around the world.

The personality of Gar Wood seemed simplistic at first glance. He was an entrepreneur and family man who provided for his parents and sisters and brothers, didn't drink and smoked occasionally. He studiously went to bed at 10.30 p.m. and rose at 5.30 a.m. for a day's work, and outside of racing boats, only seemed to have piano playing as a hobby. He was devoted to his wife, and despite his dangerous hobby, was a fatalist who made sure that every possible safeguard was put in place before he travelled on water at speed. In fact, he always wore a life jacket. His family were God-fearing people, and his mother was probably the most influential person in his life. As he described,

> She'd tell us that she didn't want us to lie, or to cheat, or to smoke and drink and be shiftless. They're nine of us boys alive today (1922) and not one is a smoking or a drinking man. More than that, not one of us is ashamed of anything the others have done, and the credit belongs to Mother.

This personality was the driving force behind his subsequent speed attempts. He'd held the title of the 'fastest vessel on water' once and wanted it back, but firstly he had to stand by and watch as another took it – his brother, George.

7

1928: RATIFICATION AND DRAMA

The year 1928 saw the governing body of powerboat racing, the Union Internationale Motonautique (UIM), finally ratify the rules and regulations for the official 'water speed record'. The Monaco-based committee were mindful of how the sport was being perceived around the world, and with the land speed record at that time standing at 206.956 mph, set by Malcolm Campbell's *Blue Bird*, it was clear to them that any attempt at breaking the 'fastest vessel on water' tag now had to be governed in a professional way.

The rules and regulations were effectively based on those that registered the land speed record, in that two runs were required over either a 1-mile or 1-kilometre course in both directions and had to be completed within a 60 minute limit. The average speed of the two runs would determine the outright speed and a record could only be broken if it was at least 1 per cent faster than the previous one. It also meant that none of the previous 'records' were recognised officially, and so up to that point in 1928, the world water speed record did not exist.

Rather surprisingly (and, one can only assume, annoyingly) for him, Gar Wood was not the first man to set a water speed record. It was his brother George on 4 September 1928, when he took the newly renovated *Miss America II* along the Detroit River to a mean speed of 92.838 mph, beating the hydroglider of Jules Fischer of four years previously by some 5 mph. The achievement was hardly publicised as inevitably Gar Wood had made all the headlines just a month earlier for entirely different reasons.

Gar and his racing mechanic, Orlin Johnson, had, on 12 August, taken out a new boat, *Miss America VI*, on to the St Clair River and had successfully reached around 100 mph. This was by far and away the fastest that any boat had ever travelled on water, and was perfect preparation for the Harmsworth Trophy once again. The speed wasn't officially recorded, but enough eye witnesses and the speedometer paid testimony to the rate. Unfortunately, at that speed the boat simply broke up after, it was later reported, one of the hull planks cracked and disintegrated. Johnson was thrown against an exhaust pipe and badly burned, and in the violence of the actions, both were tossed overboard. Jay Smith, who had been following in a support boat, raced to the scene and rescued Orlin Johnson, whose throat had been slashed near the jugular vein and was bleeding heavily, while Wood resurfaced clutching a gasoline tank. Both were taken to hospital immediately and stayed there for quite some time. Undeterred, Gar commissioned a stronger boat to be built for another crack at the Harmsworth Trophy and eventually the water speed record, but it's fair to say that he was severely shaken by the incident and seriously questioned any more participation in speed events.

As an aside to this tale of near tragedy, Gar Wood was the forerunner of a small superstition that seemed to take hold of powerboat racers down the years. His wife Murlen had, some time earlier, given Gar two small toy bears to be attached to the steering wheel for good luck. He won the first race where they were present and, from that moment, Wood wouldn't go on to the water without them. He called them Bruin and Teddy (although there is no explanation as to why), and on the one occasion when he'd actually forgotten to place the bears in the boat, due to a rushed start to the race, he'd lost. That convinced him that they were both lucky mascots. On the day of the huge accident, divers were sent to the bottom of the St Clair River to retrieve the broken engine, plus the steering wheel with the two bears still attached. Wood was convinced they had saved his and Johnson's lives. They were found and were then made two miniature life jackets and stayed with him for the rest of his racing career. In later years, another famous speed racer, Donald Campbell, was similarly attached to his lucky mascot, Mr Whoppit.

One year later, Gar Wood finally took the world water speed record for the first time (although of course he had already piloted his craft to the 'fastest vessel on water' title twice) by taking the stronger and more powerful *Miss America VII* down the Indian Creek at his estate in Florida to an official 93.123 mph. He did this on 23 March 1929, meaning his brother George held the record for just over six months. It's worth noting too that there was never any true sibling rivalry between the two, as these events might suggest. All of the Wood children seemed to be successful in their own right, and George was a co-owner, with another brother Edward, of the Locktite Patch Company in Detroit, one of the largest tyre repair companies in the world. Of the other brothers, Winfield was president of the Everlock Patch Company in Minneapolis, Logan managed the Gar Wood Industries, Lewis was the chief engineer there, Clinton managed production, Philip was in charge of the Canadian branch and Harvey was responsible for overseas operations. They were essentially one big happy family, with only Gar and George having the racing spirit within to enjoy powerboat racing.

At this point, the Wood brothers had dominated racing around the world and Gar's reputation, especially in the United States of America, was huge. He was so powerful and influential in a business sense that he could consult any politician and also give counsel to the President. In terms of his racing success, he was almost untouchable, with water speed records to his name and (far more importantly at that time) no fewer than five Harmsworth Trophy wins to his name (with two more to come). There were challengers, though, with two coming from Great Britain. One male and one female. One successful and one failed.

The 'failure', if that term can be used to describe such a person, was Betty Carstairs, one of the richest women in the world after inheriting her grandfather's fortune. He was Jabez Abel Bostwick, the founder of the Standard Oil Company. Betty was born in England in 1900, but her American mother took her back to the States within six months, and there Betty was brought up and schooled in Hartford. When she was sixteen, she left and made her way back to England to help with the war effort. Within a year, she was on the battlefields of France, driving an ambulance to care for the wounded, eventually signing for the American Ambulance Service once that country had entered the war.

As soon as peace had been declared, she returned to England where she built a new life and started to take an interest in powerboats as a way of occupying her time and a continuing adrenaline boost. She met up with the boat designer Sam Saunders on the Isle of Wight and commissioned a boat that would compete for international trophies, and despite only being 5 feet in height and slightly built, she was determined to pilot the craft herself. For the next few years she raced *Newg*, as the 17-foot boat was called (Gwen backwards as a tribute to her very close friend, the actress Gwen Farrar), in all kinds of competitions with a huge amount of success, plus she set a record on Lake Windermere for all 1½ boats at 54.97 mph over a 30-mile course. Her many successes of 1926/27 included victories in the *Daily Telegraph* Cup, the Betsie Cup, the Lucina Cup and the prestigious Duke of York Trophy against French, German and American opposition. Her boats, painted black with a wide white stripe, were powered by a Sunbeam engine, designed and built by Sam Saunders and entirely financed by herself. By this time, Betty felt she was ready and prepared to challenge the all-conquering Wood brothers, especially Gar, for the Harmsworth Trophy, which had been out of British hands for so long that the original British International Trophy title had been well and truly forgotten.

Being a feisty and forward woman, Betty Carstairs didn't do anything half-heartedly, and for the challenge for the trophy she'd commissioned four boats! Three of them were expected to reach a speed of 100 mph, powered by the Napier-Lion engine that had so successfully driven Malcolm Campbell's *Blue Bird* to the land speed record of 206 mph, and had also forced the Supermarine seaplane, piloted by Flight Lieutenant Webster, to 340 mph. The fourth boat was designed to cross the Atlantic Ocean from Cowes on the Isle of Wight to New York at an average speed of 55 mph and take in the region of 90 hours. These were brave and optimistic goals, but within a mile of taking the *Jack Stripes* – a 78-foot cruiser shaped like a bullet that could cut through the unpredictable ocean waters – on to the English Channel, she became so unstable as to be totally dangerous and the attempt was immediately abandoned.

The other three boats, named *Estelle I, II* and *III,* fared little better as none of them could reach a speed above 60 mph. With this crushing blow, she telegramd Gar Wood to withdraw her challenge:

> I have now had an opportunity of thoroughly testing the British challengers for the Harmsworth Trophy. After most careful consideration and review of the seaworthiness and safety of the hulls I have reluctantly come to the conclusion they will not uphold the prestige of Great Britain in this important international event. Please therefore accept withdrawal of my entry.

It seemed a lost cause, but after hearing of his terrible accident on the St Clair River, she changed her mind and travelled to America with her challengers. It was a disaster. In the very first heat, *Estelle II* hit the swell of a passing speedboat and capsized, flipping into the air and throwing her and mechanic Joe Harris into the water. Her lucky mascot, a 12-inch doll called Lord Tod Wadley, was also despatched into the river, and while Gar and George Wood raced among themselves for the trophy, Betty and Joe were taken to hospital with broken ribs. Betty decided there and then that she would build a bigger boat to challenge again, and would also build a boat that could break the 100 mph mark and take the water speed record. She would return in future years.

8

HENRY SEGRAVE

If Betty Carstairs was regarded as a failure in her attempt at finding the fastest speed on water, another from the British Isles, Henry O'Neal de Hane Segrave, would be regarded as a complete success and become as well known for his water speed record as he was for his motor racing and land speed records. It's quite ironic that the second most successful record-breaker on water, Gar Wood, should be all but anonymous in this day and age, and his exploits almost forgotten as a moment in unrecorded history, yet the name of Henry Segrave resonates far stronger and wider among the knowledgeable and interested, mainly due to the fact that when he arrived for a water speed record attempt, he had already taken the land version three times and had reached over 230 mph. Segrave, or de Hane as he was more commonly known at the time, was an iconic figure in the world of motor racing and a man whose name in later years would epitomise the image of the daring, devil-may-care racing driver who flirted with danger and defied death at every opportunity. The fact that he had joined motor sport after becoming a war hero just added extra lustre to the name and reputation that he had already acquired. It is also quite ironic that it was Gar Wood who had first introduced Segrave to the world of powerboat racing and in turn became Wood's most accomplished challenger. He won the water speed record for Great Britain in 1930 in the most tragic of circumstances. There have surprisingly been few books written on this ultimate speed merchant, or indeed few moving images of his racing career both on and off land and water, but the name of Henry Segrave is as recognisable today as that of Malcolm and Donald Campbell and Kaye Don. The fact that he died in his attempt at 100 mph on water gives him a legendary status that only Donald Campbell has matched or surpassed since. His story to that point is one of thirty-three years of a life well lived and full to the extreme.

Henry Segrave was born on 22 December 1896 in Baltimore, USA, to Charles and Mary. His father had been brought up in County Wicklow, Ireland, but as soon as he was old enough, Charles left the quiet and sedate life of the Kiltymon estate and set sail for America. There he joined the British Consulate Service alongside his uncle William, but his natural Irish charm and vigour for a far more frenetic life led him to making a fortune in real estate. At the age of twenty-six, he married American Mary Lucy, the daughter of a US Naval Officer, and three years later, Henry was born.

Sadly, Mary died just two years later after a long illness, and with the grief tearing him apart, Charles decided to cut all ties with America and return to Wicklow in Ireland with Henry, his mother-in-law and a nurse. In fact, the day they set sail was Independence Day 1899, a time when Irish immigrants would traditionally arrive on the shores of New York looking for a new life in the 'New World'. Charles and his family were unusual in going the other way. The move was a success, though, and in 1901, Charles married for a second time, this time to a Liverpool girl called Jessica. They produced a brother for Henry three years later, and the family settled down to a life of peace and quiet in rural Ireland. Of course, no speed freak could start without the inevitable guiding hand of his parents – no matter how clichéd that role is later described, but with Henry it was genuine.

His father Charles was an official at motor race meetings held by the Automobile Club of Great Britain and Ireland (the forerunner of the RAC), and in time started to compete in long distance races himself. He drove a twin-cylinder Argyll, and Henry would attend and watch in awe and wonder as his father dismantled the car and rebuilt it in their home garage. In fact, he actually drove it for the first time when he was just nine years old. This came about when the car was undergoing a repaint in a local garage, and the proprietor took him out around the country lanes and let Henry take to the wheel. Little could he have known that it would lead the youngster to eventually become the first man to hold the world land speed and water speed records simultaneously.

Henry's interest in cars and indeed boats blossomed from that point onwards. The boats were due to his father also purchasing a fast vessel to race around the Shannon Lake with Henry on board, but in fact he was interested in just about any type of mechanical device, including a huge toy train set that he developed and increased down the years.

Eventually, though, schooling got in the way and terms at Bilton Preparatory School and later Eton College made the boy into a man. It was while he was at Eton that his father bought him a motorcycle at the age of fifteen. This monster of a machine that was belt-driven with hard and inflexible tyres was a difficult beast to tame, but Henry actually rode it over 200 miles along rough Irish roads on only his second day of ownership. Soon races with other students took place around the college, which, according to legend, Segrave invariably won, and it was with this machine that he joined the Army in Tipperary (where the family had now moved to) as the First World War approached. Henry was seventeen and, at over 6 feet tall and with his privileged upbringing, was destined for an officer's role in the armed forces, possibly with the Irish Guards.

War was declared in 1914, when Segrave and his cousin Barry Close were working as despatch riders in North Wales for the regular Army, and as soon as they heard the news the two of them rode over 300 miles down to Aldershot to 'join up' for the war effort, which at the time was of enormous excitement for youngsters, unheeding any possible alarm about the prospect of a conflict that ended up being the most bloody and terrifying in human history.

Sadly for the two, they were rejected for being too young, but Henry was advised to go straight to Sandhurst to take an officer's cadet course. This he did and passed, receiving his commission. By January 1915, Henry Segrave found himself on the battlefields of Northern France as a 2nd Lieutenant. A month later, he was posted to the 2nd Battalion of the Warwicks and became directly involved in the horrendous battle at Neuve-Chapelle. At the age of just eighteen, he was in command of a battalion that was fighting almost hand-to-hand combat, and at one stage he'd captured a trench with the help of just fourteen men after starting with sixty. He was calm under pressure and was respected by his platoon, which speaks volumes for the measure of his maturity, although it's fair to say that war very quickly turns a boy into a man. One of the enduring songs of the time, which had its title and place changed for the British version, was 'It's a Long Way to Tipperary', which must have only brought about homesickness in the young lad.

Soon after, he was involved in the battle of Ypres, which saw over 9,000 British soldiers die as they attempted to advance. Segrave was injured himself, when, on 16 May, he was hit by a bullet from a German revolver from just 4 yards. Thankfully, the bullet went straight through his shoulder finding his gun useless and clogged up with sticky Belgian mud, Segrave threw his ammunition belt at the enemy. The German soldier was so surprised at this action that he fell while discharging his revolver, and so the bullet passed through Henry's left shoulder and out near the shoulder blade. A lucky escape to say the least!

He was sent back to Belle Isle in Southern Ireland to recuperate at his father's estate. As a reward for his quick recovery, Charles bought him his first car – a two-seater Singer that he was able to thrash around the lanes at around 50 mph. The speed bug had caught hold of him again.

That drive for speed manifested itself after his recovery when he reported to the Royal Flying Corps school in Wiltshire in an attempt to rid himself of any more time in the trenches and join the flying aces who were buzzing the skies with their precarious and fragile biplanes. He passed his flying tests after a total of just 2 hours and 32 minutes of solo flying time, and was soon transferred to Castle Bromwich, where he was to test the new types of aircraft in readiness for them being sent to action at the front. This was not quite the dream job that a potential speed maestro may have longed for – the aeroplanes were far from reliable and, with many being shot down, new ones were being readied without any major technological advancement or mechanical production. To give an idea of how perilous this type of work was, this is what Henry Segrave said in a letter to his father after crash-landing one of these deathly machines:

> Excuse this scrawl but my hands are so shaky. Curse these rotten machines the Arrol-Johnston people are turning out ... At 5,000 feet, over Kineton near Banbury, first a control wire broke and then immediately afterwards, two rocker arms broke clean in half and so the engine stopped. The machine nose-dived at once and I just righted her in time and landed without breaking a single thing!

His persistence eventually paid off, and by 1916 he was back at the battle zone of Ypres again, but this time looking down on the maze of trenches and the horrendous conditions. He saw action in the sky as much as he'd seen it on the ground, and numerous engagements with enemy planes followed, with him shooting down German Aviatiks, but also being shot down himself. On the last occasion, after he had been promoted to Flight Commander (at the age of nineteen), he was flying one of the faster and more reliable FE8 single-seater scout planes when he was caught by anti-aircraft fire and crashed near Abeele. The plane hit the earth and somersaulted, with Segrave hitting his head badly in the process and also breaking his ankle. It was the last action he would see in the war, and his ankle was so badly injured that there were strong suggestions from many in the Air Force that it should be amputated. Thankfully, in later years a London surgeon rebuilt it with silver plates, but he always walked with a limp from then on. It's also quite interesting that if the military surgeons had had their way, then the subsequent land and water speed record attempts may never have taken place.

9

SEGRAVE'S GRAND PRIX DREAMS

In October 1917, Henry Segrave married the musical actress Doris Stocker after meeting her the previous year. He also saw out the war in an administrative capacity for the Royal Flying Corps after his injury (a year before they amalgamated with the Royal Naval Air Service to become the Royal Air Force), and in 1918 went to America to help assist military training for aviation, taking his new wife with him. They settled in Washington, but on a wedding anniversary trip to New York, he met a man by chance who would point him down a path he had never considered taking.

Bill Bruce-Brown was the brother of the famous American racing driver David, who had won numerous honours in the sport, but was killed in 1912. Inevitably, the conversation revolved around this fledgling sport and it immediately hooked Segrave. He was told that there was a meeting coming up on Long Island, and he was more than keen to attend. It was a typical American race meeting of its time, run over a 2-mile board speedway where the cars would circulate at speeds of around 100 mph in a somewhat dangerous fashion. The hero of the day in the sport (after the war, racing drivers really were regarded as heroes) was Ralph de Palma, and Segrave watched him win every race with ease and decided there and then that this was going to be his future. That determination was confirmed just a few days later when he tried the track himself on an 'open' day and, at 82 mph in his private car, lapped a 60 hp Apperson. He was even given a plaque by the owner of the track to commemorate his achievement. It proved to him that he could drive a car at speed and the exhilaration far outweighed any misgivings his young wife may have had – once he'd decided that this was his future, she supported him fully, as was expected in those days.

When peace was officially declared, Henry and his wife returned to England and moved into a flat in London. There he started a motor sales business, selling second-hand cars at reasonable profits. He also sought out the acquaintance of a Captain Alistair Miller, who had in his possession two 4½-litre Opel Grand Prix cars (the name Grand Prix coming from the one and only race that had the title in its name, run in France, the birthplace of motor racing) and soon came to an agreement to race one of the vehicles. Like now, motor racing then cost quite a lot of money, but Segrave had made plenty from his business, and so made his debut in early spring 1920 at the famous Brooklands circuit (although it was the only circuit in Great Britain at that time). He was able to lap the huge banking at around 90 mph, and on 20 May 1920, he entered his first official race in the Opel.

Brooklands was in those days a place where people went to be seen, and the rich and the famous would take their expensive cars and habits to the members' paddock and watch the cars speed around them, making the occasional bet in the process. The race circuit was run along the lines of horse racing, and so each day there could be numerous races with separate handicaps, depending on the size of the car and the ability of the driver. Segrave found himself in race No. 9 and competing against the likes of Captain Malcolm Campbell and Kenelm Lee Guinness, a competent race driver and the founder of the KLG spark plug company. He performed quite well in his Opel, and after one particularly nervous moment when he lost a wheel at the top of the banking at over 100 mph, giving Doris a near heart attack, he crawled back to the paddock with applause from the spectators ringing in his ears. It was a promising start, and just an hour later he won race No. 11 against the likes of Tim Birkin at an average speed of 88.5 mph. A victory in only his second race proved that he had the ability and the raw courage to race against the best and come out on top. In fact, his performance in the first race in particular was quickly noticed by some of the national newspapers who were there reporting on the race day. *The Times* said of his driving after losing a wheel, 'Major Segrave ... supplied the big thrill of the afternoon ... by a fine piece of driving. He kept his car absolutely in hand and saved what for a moment looked like being a terrible accident.'

Another who was impressed was a certain Louis Coatalen, manager of the Sunbeam Motor Company racing division and a former racer himself. The two had already met before and Segrave had enquired about a seat in the team even before he'd raced a car in anger – he hadn't received a particularly encouraging response, so this incident had certainly helped his cause. A few months later, Coatalen was there at Brooklands to watch

Segrave win a short handicap race of just 5¾ miles, again against some of the eminent names in the sport at the time, including Tony Vandervell, who would go and create his own Formula One team in later years, and Malcolm Campbell again. Segrave was making a name for himself at a very early stage of his motor racing career and the motoring press were beginning to take note.

The dream of any racing driver in the 1920s was to compete in the Grand Prix. That was a race held in France annually and would usually last for around 6 hours on dusty and unyielding roads and tracks, but the top car manufacturers of the time saw it as an ideal opportunity to advertise their products, especially if they won! One such company was Sunbeam, who at that time were one of the leading motor manufacturers and had a successful racing division. The year 1920 had been a good first year for Henry Segrave in his quest to become a racing driver. He'd raced mostly at Brooklands, although he had taken the Opel to speed events at other venues, and had managed three victories in handicap races. This, he believed (rather unreasonably), was enough to be given a drive at the Grand Prix by Coatalen in the Sunbeam. The fact that his now close friend Bill Guinness had been selected for one of the three available seats just encouraged him more. With that in mind, he drove to the company's Wolverhampton offices and spent some time pleading and begging with Louis Coatalen to be given the third seat. It must have had an effect of some sort – maybe he wore down the Frenchman or maybe the suave and sophisticated Breton saw something in the English gentleman – because two days later it was announced that Henry Segrave would drive the third Sunbeam car at the Le Mans Grand Prix in 1921. His father was overcome with happiness and Henry looked to the future with a new glint in his eye.

If there was anything that could maybe take the gloss off this shining moment, it would have been the fact that this new endeavour was to cost him quite a lot of money. Sunbeam didn't pay their drivers in those days; in fact, they didn't even give them expenses for living or entertainment. They would pay the travel costs, but drivers of the 1920s were expected to make a living from start money and prize money, should they be good enough to win. Sadly, the Le Mans Grand Prix offered neither. In fact, all they supplied was a medal for each entrant, but for Segrave that didn't matter. He knew that if he performed well in the Grand Prix the following year, he would be considered for a permanent seat, and then he could earn some serious money. Henry Segrave the racing driver had arrived.

The Grand Prix of that year was held on the 10¾-mile sandy and tree-edged Circuit de la Sarthe at Le Mans, and was to be competed over 325 miles. Segrave took it so seriously that when there was a suggestion that the Sunbeam Company were about to withdraw from the event due to their cars being hopelessly unprepared, he personally confronted Coatalen and forced him to change his mind. He also spent some time helping the mechanics to get his car ready for the event too. Segrave didn't drink, but his intake of cigarettes increased as the stress of the weeks leading up to the race took its toll.

The 1921 French Grand Prix took place on a Monday, as the organisers had set the Sunday date aside for the motorcycle race. Their reasoning was that the car fraternity didn't need to worry too much about taking time off work as they were obviously financially sound. As it was, thirteen cars set off in pairs at 30-second intervals (in an altogether incomprehensible format guaranteed to confuse and alienate the thousands of fans who were watching) along un-tarred roads that almost immediately cut up the basic tyres of the day. Add to that the stones being hurled into the air from the wired spinning wheels, and it shows how very dangerous motor racing was nearly 100 years ago.

After only a few laps, and after Segrave was forced to do some emergency repairs to the ignition timing at the side of the road, a boulder flung up from the leading Duesenburg car, driven by Jimmy Murphy, as it was lapping the Sunbeam, hit Segrave's passenger mechanic Jules Moriceau full in the face and knocked him unconscious. Such was the speed and the wind and the noise that Segrave drove on totally unaware for another 5 miles before the Frenchman woke up, wiped off the blood from his face and continued his duties. That included changing the tyres no fewer than fourteen times during the race!

Segrave and his mechanic finished ninth and last, but they had finished and that was an achievement in itself. In his biography, *The Lure of Speed*, he was quoted as saying that finishing the race 'meant more than anything else in the world to [him] at that time'.

The 'success' of his first Grand Prix led to his becoming an official driver for the Sunbeam team, and lesser races saw him triumphant in the remainder of 1921 and for the full season of 1922, but it was the French Grand Prix of 1923 where Henry Segrave made his mark as a racing driver, and achieved the defining moment in a career that eventually led to the world land and world water speed records.

The circuit of Tours was the venue for the race on 2 July 1923, and again Segrave would be racing for Sunbeam. It was his first race of the year and he took it as seriously as ever (the previous year he'd been running in second place before the car retired due to mechanical trouble, something of a relief to him as petrol had spilt into the cockpit during a pitstop and he was in excruciating pain as his skin began to burn). He practiced on the triangular circuit over and over again in an attempt to get to know its every bump and hollow, but despite this, he still lapped some 34 seconds slower than the favourites for the event, the Italian FIAT cars.

The race day was stiflingly hot and the new 'rolling start' saw all seventeen cars set off at the same time on the 14-mile circuit. For the first four laps, Segrave ran in sixth position, struggling with a clutch that was refusing to engage. It meant he was lapping nearly 1 minute slower than his competitors, but midway round the seventh lap, a huge bang emanated from the engine and the clutch was free. It was later discovered that a restricting plate had sheared off and now the clutch could be used fully. This meant the Sunbeam could now lap at a regular pace, and as the three FIATS were one by one retiring due to supercharging problems, the Sunbeams capitalised. His progress was only halted during a pitstop when he was handed an oil funnel with the cap still in place, which refused to be opened, forcing him to smash it vigorously to get the liquid into the engine. Segrave made his way up to second place, and this was in no small part due to the other two Sunbeams having mechanical problems. One of them, driven by Albert Divo, was forced to stop in the pits every lap to refuel due to the filler cap being jammed solid and petrol having to be siphoned into a reserve tank, but Segrave was driving superbly anyway.

He was closing on the leader at around 30 seconds a lap when the leading Italian car ran out of petrol 1½ miles away from the pits. The mechanic sprinted to pick up a churn of fuel from the garage, arriving gasping and panting. He was then forced to carry the heavy load back the 1½ miles as organisers had firstly refused a substitute mechanic to take over and then stopped him from commandeering a bicycle. One can only imagine his consternation when once arriving at the stricken car and pouring the fuel into the empty tank, the driver, Feretti Salamano, set off and immediately stopped again with a blown engine!

With two laps to go, and the final FIAT retired, Segrave had the lead in the most important race of his career. He covered the last 28 miles without any misfortune, although his crowning glory wasn't quite the moment that dreams are made of, as the ACF (Automobile Club de France) organisers actually forgot he was leading and didn't wave the chequered flag as he passed the winning line. No matter as Henry Segrave had become the first Briton to win the French Grand Prix (remember this was regarded as *the* Grand Prix of the season) at an average speed of 75.3 mph, taking the 496-mile race in 6 hours 35 minutes and 19 seconds. He actually completed a 'warm-down' lap too, which took some time. Also, despite it being 1923 and Ireland was now independent of Great Britain, Segrave still represented the Union Flag in his racing.

After tasting the champagne, which he didn't like, he was then feted for the rest of the evening and news services from all over Britain caught the story and announced it via the radio and the early morning editions of the newspapers. The next day, he drove the car to the Channel crossing at Le Havre and hundreds of people waved him by. Once back in Britain, he took the car to the Sunbeam Hanover Square showrooms, where it stayed on exhibition for the thousands of fans who wanted a glimpse of the mighty machine. He then went on a public speaking tour and was honoured by the newly formed RAC at Pall Mall, such was his achievement. Henry Segrave was known throughout the country and was rightly regarded as the best racing driver from the British shores. In fact, the legend of the time was that any unwary driver caught for speeding would inevitably be greeted by the accusing policeman with the words, 'Who do you think you are, Henry Segrave?' His stock was high and although he never matched the success of the 1923 French Grand Prix, he did continue to win races around the country and on the Continent. He was a natural speed freak and his quest for more would soon lead him to the most dangerous of exercises.

10

SEGRAVE BREAKS THE LAND SPEED RECORD

In the 1920s, motor racing and speed records effectively went hand in hand. It was reasoned that if a driver could race a car quickly, then he would also have the capability of attacking whatever speed record may be on offer. Henry Segrave was a recognised and successful racing driver by 1926, and had already attempted numerous class records in his capacity of Sunbeam employee. For the Sunbeam Company, their presence on the Grand Prix scene now waning, the publicity surrounding a successful attempt at the land speed record was prestigious and profitable, and since the end of the war, the record had been raised officially five times, three in a Sunbeam car. By the time Segrave was commissioned to try to raise it again, it stood to Capt. Malcolm Campbell, driving a Sunbeam but calling it *Blue Bird,* at 150.76 mph.

Southport Sands offered the best place for the 4-litre Sunbeam Tiger that had been put together from old racing car parts and enhanced by a supercharged V12 engine. So in March 1926 Segrave was despatched to the Lancashire coast to attempt to wrestle the record off a man who was already beginning to make a name for himself in the discipline. A huge crowd turned up for the event and the car, now painted bright red, was an instant hit as it had a streamlined look that others lacked. It also had a smaller engine than others, relying on its design as opposed to sheer brute force. As is the way with record attempts, none of it went smoothly. The fine sand entered the engine casing on so many occasions that the aluminium cracked constantly and after three weeks, the chief mechanic and designer Capt. J. S. Irving was ready to return to the Wolverhampton base to affect mechanical improvements. Segrave was reluctant and persuaded him to upgrade one of the superchargers so that it would be capable of at least lasting the 3 minutes required for a true record attempt. He was also concerned at the expense of the official timekeepers from the RAC, who had been waiting patiently on the beach to be employed.

On 16 March, the car was towed to the starting position to save any wear and tear on an already fragile engine, hot water was poured into the radiator to save any running time to heat it, and the machine was push-started. It seemed to work as Segrave, on only three-quarters power, sped down the first run at a pretty impressive speed. Mindful of the stress the engine was under, he turned immediately and proceeded with the second run. The return was even faster, but as he neared the end of the standing kilometre, the car hit a gully in the sands and leapt into the air, landing some 50 feet later. Obviously, the engine over-revved and immediately failed again, but it didn't matter as once the car came to a halt, Segrave was told that his average speed over the two runs was 152.33 mph, beating Campbell by 1.57 mph. Henry Segrave held the world land speed record, the nineteenth man at that time to attain such a feat. He was heralded by the press and his standing in the world, not just in the world of motor racing, was as high as ever.

It didn't last long. Six weeks later, Welshman Parry Thomas took his 27-litre *Babs* to 169.30 mph on Pendine Sands, and then increased it by 2 mph the next day. This was then increased to 174 mph by Campbell in the *Blue Bird* the following year. Thomas then lost his life in horrifying fashion on 1 March 1927, when his newly streamlined *Babs* took off on Pendine Sands, rolled and nearly decapitated the burly Welshman. Undeterred by this, Segrave now had 200 mph in his sights and had approached his employer Coatalen again about the possibility. What came out of the discussion was a 4-ton monster called the *1,000hp Sunbeam*. It had two V12 engines that produced a capacity of nearly 45,000 cc and was designed to be the first car to break 200 mph on land. Coatalen had now decided that sheer brute force was needed as opposed to streamlining and elegance. It was everything that Henry had asked for, but he was told in no uncertain terms that the only commitment the company would make would be to build the car, while the rest of the expenditure and arrangements were entirely down to him. With that in mind, Segrave approached a number of companies who agreed to back the endeavour, becoming in a way an early form of sponsorship.

It was deemed that 9 miles was needed to run the huge car, and there were no sufficient places in Great Britain to accommodate the attempt, so Segrave took on the expense of sailing the boat and the numerous mechanics across the ocean to Daytona in America. The

Beregaria was the liner they used and the crossing must have been uncomfortable to say the least for him. Despite his later breaking the water speed record, Segrave was a terrible sailor and often suffered seasickness. The journey was also an emotional one as while on there he was cabled with the news of Thomas' terrible tragedy, something that affected him badly as he had been involved in record-breaking attempts with Thomas at Brooklands some years before. He was ready though and he looked forward to the challenge, if not overawed by it all. He wrote at the time,

> I think I stood and stared at the monster rather as a child would have done. Racing cars I had seen and driven by the dozen, but this was something more gigantic than any yet dreamed of. It fascinated me. The thought that I was to drive it, control it, unleash all its potentialities, was, one must admit, a little unnerving. I can honestly say when I have stood in front of a car and doubted human ability to control it.

They arrived in Daytona in March 1927 and were greeted by the Americans as heroes. From the berth in New York to the journey down to Florida, Segrave and his team were feted wherever they went, followed by news reporters and well-wishers. His natural charm had endeared him to many and he'd even managed to persuade the AAA (American Automobile Association) to join with its European counterpart so that any record could be recognised worldwide, something the Americans had previously refused to do.

Once at Daytona he became the star attraction, with thousands of spectators taking up positions on the beach to watch this monster car roar up and down the yellow sand. In fact, there were so many that police had trouble controlling them and their constant movement affected the timing equipment, so much so that an early run was timed at anything between 160 mph and 280 mph. It took some time before the officials were able to protect the delicate apparatus.

There were inevitable teething problems with the red monster, much to the amusement of some of the American newspapers, who secretly seemed to want the Briton to fail, but on 29 March 1927, Henry Segrave became the first man to break the 200 mph barrier on land.

Over 30,000 people had turned up for the pre-announced record run, many of them sleeping in their cars overnight to ensure a good position the next morning, and at 9.30 a.m., with the sun shining, the 1,000 hp Sunbeam roared into life. The first run along the beach was dramatic to say the least as, after flashing through the measured-mile, the car swerved due to the wind and Segrave had no alternative but to head towards the sea to slow it down as the brakes were ineffective and had proved troublesome throughout the time in Florida. On its way, it sliced three 4-foot marker poles like a razor and then hit the water at 55 mph before slowly turning round to face a second run. Segrave remained calm and motored slowly to the 'pit' area. Four tyres were changed and the red machine set off again.

'A rushing blur enshrouded in a cloud of sand' was the way it was described in many newspapers the next day, and the sight of a car travelling at such a speed kept the spectators stunned and awestruck as it raced past. Within seconds of it coming to a halt, it had been confirmed that the average speed was timed at 203.792 mph, smashing the previous record by the highest margin recorded in land speed record history. For the second time, Segrave held the record and also became the first ever to pilot a car on land at over 200 mph.

Inevitably, his achievement was broadcast around the world and his fame extended beyond anything previously imagined. The *London Evening News* actually conducted a telephone interview with him within 25 minutes of getting out of the car and 1 hour later had the story on its front page that day. Quite remarkable, bearing in mind the age and year it took place. His wife, Doris, was busy conducting interviews back in her London home after receiving a telegram from Henry saying simply, 'World's record. Over 200. All is well. De Hane.'

The Americans took to him as if he was their own, and a couple of days later he met Gar Wood, who at that time was attempting to take the newly ratified world water speed record. The two of them became good friends, and Wood took Segrave out on the water in a couple of his high-speedboats, and also showed him *Miss America V.* Segrave was impressed and in turn Wood bought the run-around Sunbeam car that Henry had been driving. That friendship was of course to result in Segrave eventually swapping land for water.

A couple of weeks later, he returned to London and was banqueted at the RAC, interviewed by the BBC, given a public ceremony in Wolverhampton and numerous other engagements. Even Malcolm Campbell had been pressed to offer his congratulations, although that only served to push him into another attempt himself. After all of the attention, Henry Segrave announced publicly his intention to retire with immediate effect from all forms of motor racing. 'I've had a good innings ... and I would rather go out at the top than go on, getting slower and slower.' This was expected, but what wasn't expected was his next announcement:

As a substitute ... I shall take up motor boat racing. I am hoping to do for the British motor boat what I have been fortunate enough to do for the British car. We are years behind America in hull design, and the United States have held the Harmsworth Trophy for six years. I am going to see if I can get it back to this country.

The change from land to water was already underway.

From Land to Water to Tragedy

Segrave still had a few motor racing events to compete in as part of his contract, but it's fair to say he didn't really attack them with any enthusiasm. Water was the new attraction, and he made his sea racing debut at the Hythe Regatta in May 1927, where he actually won an outboard dinghy race at the rather sedate speed of 17.9 knots. By the end of the year, he had taken up a position with the Portland Cement Company, which certainly paid him well. This was an unusual employ for a man who was officially the fastest driver on land, and maybe that was the problem for him. He had broken the land speed record, was indulging his new hobby on the water and was actually enjoying some success – he won the Hythe Regatta again in August 1928 at a speed of 60 mph with his recently purchased 200 hp hydroplane (effectively equivalent to twice the speed on land) – but the day-to-day running of being a director for a cement firm was hardly going to keep him occupied. Something had to give, and inevitably it did.

On 19 February 1928, Capt. Malcolm Campbell, driving another *Blue Bird* on Daytona Beach, took the land speed record to 206.95 mph and so wrestled it from Segrave. Whereas previously he'd said he would be 'content' to leave it be should his record be broken, there was no way he would relinquish his record without a fight, and so on 19 April, the *Wolverhampton Express and Star* announced exclusively that a new car was being built for Henry Segrave with a 900 hp Napier engine, designed to be capable of a speed exceeding 230 mph. Four days later, American Ray Keech, driving a horrifying looking beast called *Triplex*, increased the record to 207.55 mph, and so gave Segrave the ideal excuse to travel to the States to win the record back for Britain.

The *Golden Arrow* car was heavily backed financially and looked every bit the record-breaker she was expected to be. There was the single Napier-Lion 12-cylinder engine, which had been developed for aircraft racing, and the whole body, painted in glorious gold, was made of aluminium with encased wheels and the cockpit low down for streamlining purposes. The record bid was promoted in the daily newspapers, where Segrave gave each individual interview ahead of departure in order to avoid being misquoted. He then released another bombshell, announcing some five months later that he would also attempt the world water speed record soon after his land attempt and was not only trying to take George Wood's record of 92.8 mph, but was going to take his new boat, *Miss England* to Florida too, in an attempt at a head-to-head with Gar Wood. It was a remarkable challenge.

Miss England was a single-step hydroplane boat with a Napier engine similar to the one being used in the *Golden Arrow* and had been built by the British Powerboat Company at Hythe. It was expected she would be capable of reaching 100 mph on water, a remarkable speed for the time. The two speed machines set sail for America on the 30 January 1929, with Segrave saying to the gathered press at the dockside of *Miss England*, 'It's this boat that puts the breeze up me. Kill me before I'm through with her I expect.' He didn't appear to harbour any such concerns for *Golden Arrow* though.

There were the usual teething problems for *Golden Arrow* to contend with over the first fortnight or so of testing, and when the Daytona Beach didn't satisfy the car's desire, Segrave just took *Miss England* out on the water for trial runs. All of this was of much interest to the American public, who had warmed to the Major the last time he was there. On the day of the record run, 11 March, a crowd of anything between 100,000 and 120,000 turned up packed on the shore ready to see yet another record broken. They weren't to be disappointed. The measured mile was illuminated by huge red arc lights atop 50-foot trestles, so that there was no danger of Segrave not being able to see where he was heading, bearing in mind the wind-forces at those speeds were difficult to navigate with just a helmet and a set of goggles.

The first run was only distinguished by a leap of 30 feet after hitting a bump, but he flashed through the timing equipment in 15.55 seconds. First gear had been changed at 80 mph, second to top at 160 mph. It was smooth and serene. The second run, starting just 6 minutes later, was slightly slower at 15.57 seconds, but once he'd rolled to a halt the speed was calculated, and a mean average of 231.446 mph meant for the third time in his life, Henry Segrave was the holder of the land speed record, and this time he'd broken the record (held by America) by 24 mph.

If the record run seemed almost easy, then the next day was to remind everyone how dangerous and unforgiving speed can be when tempted and teased in the wrong way. The *Triplex* came out to retrieve the record, not driven by Ray Keech, but mechanic Lee Bible.

He attempted to wrestle control of the fearsome 81-litre beast on the bumpy Daytona Sands, and after reaching around 180 mph on his first run, lost control and careered into a photographer before rolling and swerving down the beach. Bible was thrown out and all four wheels were detached as the chassis bounced and rolled frighteningly. When help arrived at the stricken scene, Bible and the photographer, Charles Traub, were dead. Ironically, the tripod that held the camera quickly vacated by Traub still stood. It was this horrific accident that convinced Segrave not to take the *Golden Arrow* out again.

Instead, he concentrated on the water attempt, helped by the fact that Gar Wood took the water speed record on 23 March 1929 on Indian Creek at 93.12 mph, and a race he'd had with Wood for the International Championship at the Biscayne Regatta, Miami, on *Miss England*. In one heat, Segrave beat Wood, driving *Miss America V,* at 55.22 mph (although Wood retired due to steering problems) and then lost the second by some considerable margin while averaging 42.75 mph to Wood's 61.27 mph. However, Segrave had won the trophy on points and he returned to England shortly afterwards, convinced that his boat was good enough to take the water speed record.

Just to prove his popularity with the British public, and indeed around the world, as he and his wife were sailing home, he received a telegram informing him that he was to be knighted by King George V for his achievements in the realms of speed on behalf of Great Britain. Once home, he was given the usual public acclaim, including a special train laid on for him and Doris, and then a cavalcade along the roads to the Houses of Parliament, with crowds six deep on the pavements cheering him on. He was feted for weeks afterwards with the usual round of celebrity appearances and public speaking, all of it a distraction from the next big challenge in his life. The water speed record.

Miss England was a fast boat. In races over the next year she proved that, beating Gar Wood on many an occasion and at one stage actually clocking 93.5 mph (faster than the current record), but Segrave wanted a boat that would take the record by a huge margin, the way *Golden Arrow* did. So a new boat, *Miss England II*, was built and was ready to not only break the water speed record, but to take back the Harmsworth Trophy for Britain. It was a twin-engined, single-propeller craft that would spin the blades at an astonishing 13,000 rpm. The boat was a 38-foot single-step hull made out of steel and mahogany, painted black and white and polished with graphite. It looked like a record-breaker and the team travelled to Lake Windermere full of confidence.

The decision to attempt the record on a British lake was deliberate as Segrave wanted the attempt to be as British as possible, and the

Windermere authorities could not have been more helpful. They lay out a measured mile course on the west of the lake and this potential 115 mph boat, laden with Segrave and his two mechanics dressed in immaculate white overalls, took to the water. It was a hot day, on 5 June 1930, when the boat was officially launched after numerous weeks of tireless work to get her ready in time. Unfortunately, the first run was frustrating as the hundreds of pleasure craft there to witness the event had created a swell on the lake, and so *Miss England II* could only cruise gently, eventually overheating her engines and had to be towed back to shore. Further runs were a lot more successful, though, with the boat being timed at speeds approaching 107 mph, but time and again the weak propellers broke, meaning more repairs and lengthy delays. The crowds that had flocked to see Segrave on that June day had receded, and so the lake was calmer and untroubled. With this in mind, and with the knowledge that the timekeepers were due at the Isle of Man TT motorcycle meeting at the weekend, Henry Segrave announced he would try for the record on the Friday before – 13 June.

Friday the 13th has an unlucky omen about it, yet that wasn't a consideration back in 1930, and thousands of spectators packed the shores of Windermere to see history being made. The press had virtually given Segrave the record even before he'd attempted it, such was their confidence in the man who already held the land version.

At 1.15 p.m., *Miss England II* was towed into position, but what followed was tragic. These are the words of one of his two riding mechanics, Michael Wilcocks, as reproduced in the wonderful biography of Segrave written by Cyril Posthumus:

> On the way, Sir Henry made an alteration in the programme. Instead of returning to the boathouse after a run in each direction to fit the other propeller, he decided to do two runs at only just over record speed. 'You and I, Halliwell, will take the times of the first run, and if not good enough for the average I will increase slightly on the return. Then, if everything is OK, I'll run her up again all out, and see how much over 120 she'll do. I hope to Heaven she'll behave herself.'
>
> I said, 'She'll be alright sir, Friday the 13th is my lucky day.'
>
> Sir Henry smiled and said, 'That's something anyway.'
>
> *Miss London* cast us off. I started the motors and away we went, just a nice ruffled surface on the water. Past the first milepost, then the second, Sir Henry and Vic Halliwell comparing watches. We swung around for the return run, revs a little higher this time, completed the mile and slackened the speed … Sir Henry tapped me on the shoulder … pointed to stopwatch and jerked both thumbs up. I yelled, 'Broken?' meaning the record. He nodded and smiled, signalled for OK and pointed to the course. I returned OK. The boat swung round and we set off on a

second northward run. She was running beautifully, infinitely faster than on any of the trial runs. She felt as though she was just touching the water. One has a similar feeling in a plane just as the wings are taking the full weight of the machine.

I glanced at Sir Henry. He was smiling and evidently delighted, the water temperatures of the engines were rising and getting very close to the maximum allowed, and the water control was full open. I glanced ahead to see how much further we had to go as I would soon have to ask for less revs…

Then there was a slight thud from forward, a slight list and swerve to port. We straightened, then to starboard, and straightened again, the bows were rising up … she oughtn't to do this … going over … water coming up to meet … bang!

Everything went yellow. I couldn't see very well when I at long last scrambled to the surface. There was Vic Halliwell, quivering gently and sinking a few yards away – no movement of limbs, leaving just a swirl of water. A figure went past me, jerking along backwards – no movement of arms – he also disappeared and I was alone, *Miss England II* a dark, blurred mass, and two air cushions a few yards away.

I longed to catch hold of something but I could make no progress, couldn't use my eyes and was gasping for breath. I slithered across one of the hatches and went under again. I could see better, but no sign of the others – everything grey and utterly desolate, and I felt horribly scared.

Two boats appeared, and from their spray were travelling fast. I set my eyes on the nearest, tried to get my wind, and put out just enough energy to keep up. I knew they would have to be quick. I tried to point and tell them where the others were, but couldn't hear my voice. Then I understood them to say that they had got both of them, but I know one at least had gone down…

They put me to bed, with so many assurances that the record was broken, that the others were alright save for broken arms, that I realised I had panicked and had imagined I had seen things. I was feeling happy again, the cold going from my bones, when one in attendance blurted out, 'Your chief passed away twenty minutes ago.'

There are some feelings in life which no words can ever describe, mine cannot. I had failed to help the finest Chief man ever had in his hour of need, and let my teammate go down. I was the meanest thing in the world.

The Doc saved me, I think – bless him. I told him I knew the truth and what I felt about it, and described everything in detail. He said, 'When we find Vic Halliwell, from what you have told me, we shall find he broke his neck in hitting the water. Sir Henry was brought up from under the surface, but with his internal injuries he was beyond human aid. Don't worry laddie – you have a blow on your side which prevented you using your legs, and you couldn't see properly because blood was coming from your eyes. Your duty is to keep your mind clear on what actually happened up to the time of smash. Your Chief would wish you to do this for the sake of everyone. There will of course be an inquest, and you must remember the facts for it.'

Sir Henry's first words were, 'How are the lads? Did we break the record?' I have kicked myself over and over again, I have puzzled scores of times – I knew she was going over, why didn't Sir Henry get clear of the wheel in time, for his brain would know long before mine? His reactions were like lightning. Lady Segrave, brave lady, told me she knew Sir Henry wouldn't wish to live on with one of his companions dead.

I didn't begin to see daylight until long afterwards. When talking to Commodore Gar Wood, he told me that Sir Henry once declared the one thing that worried him about racing boats was the necessity to have someone else in the boat ... had Sir Henry been solo, and had only himself to think of, he could easily have got clear. It was all progressive until the port side of the step burst away with hydraulic pressure and folded back in area ten times as great as the rudder, therefore putting the boat beyond human control. All this in five seconds ... one of my legs was torn from below the knee to the ankle, and the shoe pulled off. I found Sir Henry's air cushion right under the foredeck (after she was pulled out of the water). Unfortunately Vic Halliwell was very tall and slightly built, and being on the port side was shot fairly high into the air. He was unmarked, with the exception of a bruise on the top of his head.

It seems that *Miss England II* had hit a submerged log on a fast run that was unnecessary as the record had been broken at 98.76 mph. Segrave was rescued from the water with both arms and two ribs broken, plus a crushed thigh and serious head injuries. Somehow he remained conscious as he was taken to a house on the west bank and still had time to speak to his wife. He died 2½ hours later.

Henry Segrave held the world land and water speed records at the same time, but sadly lost his life in pursuit of the latter. He was thirty-three years of age. The world mourned, his demise front page news in every Western country. His funeral was a quiet affair at the wishes of Lady Segrave, but later in the year a memorial service was held for him in Westminster, attended by hundreds. His ashes were then scattered over the playing fields of Eton College, where he'd enjoyed some of his happiest times. Segrave became the first 'name' casualty of the quest for the water speed record, but as Sir Henry Norman wrote to Lady Segrave in tribute, 'What a man he was. I suppose he was foredoomed. To him life was nothing – it was just incidental to the great objects he had in view...'

11

WOOD AGAINST DON

Betty Carstairs had witnessed the tragedy on Lake Windermere, and despite the horror of that day, she proceeded to attempt the water speed record herself. Nine days after Segrave's death, she sailed for Canada and with her went her two latest boats, *Estelle IV* and *V*. The Muskoka Lakes in Ontario was where the attempt took place and by the end of June, she'd managed successive runs of 70, 80 and 90 mph in the *IV* boat. Then on 13 August 1930, in *Estelle V*, Betty Carstairs made an official attempt at the world water speed record, but could only reach 94.5 mph in a one-way flat out sprint. It wasn't enough and she gracefully retired, knowing that there was no more to be gained from the vessel. The run was witnessed by Gar Wood, who challenged her to a race in Detroit a fortnight later at the 14th International Motorboat Regatta. She accepted and *Estelle IV* took on *Miss America IX* driven by Gar, *Miss America VIII* driven by George, and *Miss America IV* piloted by Phil Wood. Betty also brought *Estelle V* for Bert Hawker to race but, as was always the case when taking on the Wood brothers, glorious failure followed and Betty Carstairs announced to the press that she would no longer attempt any more records or indeed any more races. Despite being a millionairess at the age of thirty, she simply could not afford to continue. It was now left to Gar Wood to regain his water speed record and try for the first 100 mph speed on water.

It came on 20 March 1931, when Wood took *Miss America IX* out onto his private runway at Indian Creek and set a new three-way average of 102.155 mph, beating Segrave's record by nearly 4 mph. This was the fourth time Gar Wood had held the record, the second time 'officially'. The 100 mph barrier on water was broken some twenty-seven years after it had been attained on land, when Louis Rigolly raced on

Ostend beach at 103 mph. At the time that Gar Wood broke the special barrier, the land speed record stood at 246 mph, proving how difficult it was to move quickly on the waves.

Gar Wood was now all-dominant in powerboat racing, with successive Harmsworth Trophy victories and the holder of the water speed record, but of course that kind of success inevitably leads to a challenger, and that challenge came in the shape of an Irish-born racing driver, very much in the mould of Henry Segrave, who seemed to follow his career path for path.

Kaye Earnest Donsky (or Kaye Don as he was later known) was born in Dublin on 1 April 1891 and educated at Wolverhampton Grammar School. His father died when he was seventeen, meaning it was left to him to support his mother and sister, and for the next few years he worked as a clerk at a tyre dealer. He joined the Army in 1915 with the world at war, but was discharged some nine months later on medical grounds, and then, like Segrave, learnt to fly and saw action on the Western Front. In March 1919, he was transferred to Ireland for motorcycle liaison work. Following the armistice, he then became a racing driver at Brooklands, where he competed in a 4-cylinder car and actually broke the record for the hour at 90 mph. The record-breaking bug had already started to interest him.

Don combined his time as a sales manager at the tyre company he'd served for with racing Sunbeam cars around Brooklands circuit, setting an outer circuit record of 131.76 mph in a Sunbeam, and then increasing it to 134.24 mph in August 1929. Also that year he started to show interest in powerboats. In April, he'd attempted a national speed record for unlimited outboard motorboats in a 10-foot hull powered by a supercharged Dunelt engine. He failed as the boat only reached 22.5 mph.

Two months later, he looked to set a record of a double-crossing between Dover and Calais in less than hour in a boat called *Kaye Don Special,* a 30-foot standard model that was powered by a 200 hp Kermath engine. It was a glorious failure when at 4.30 a.m. on 23 July, caught in strong winds and stormy seas, the boat hit a huge wave and had to be rescued with a spluttering engine and smashed windscreen. Three days later, he tried again and succeeded. The boat crossed the English Channel and back in 1 hour and 23 minutes, beating the two-year record by 24 minutes. Later that year, he set a new kilometre record for cars at the Brooklands circuit at 140.95 mph again in a Sunbeam (he'd called individual cars *Cub, Tiger* and *Tigress* down the years) and decided that the time was ripe for a full attempt at the land speed record, which was held by Henry Segrave in the *Golden Arrow.* The attempt turned out to be one of the most shambolic and disappointing in the history of the LSR and lowered Don's standing in the motoring world.

Louis Coatalen designed the *Silver Bullet,* an astonishing-looking car that weighed 4 tons, created 4,000 hp from two 12-cylinder supercharged engines and had fearsome looking bodywork with rear fairings and wheel covers, sprayed of course in silver with the name of Sunbeam emblazoned on its side. Daytona Beach was again chosen for the record attempt, but almost immediately the whole project hit problems. The two engines, which had hardly been tested in Wolverhampton, decided to exhibit all of their teething problems publicly as the car lurched on a very bumpy beach. March was hardly the ideal time for a smooth surface on the east coast of America, and the uneven course gave serious handling problems too.

Team morale fell markedly and friction between Don and Coatalen hardly helped. This transmitted itself to the record attempts, with the highest speed attained being only 186.046 mph, some 45 mph short of the current record held by Segrave. The American press, rather tired of the British coming over to their territory and routinely setting records, made much of the 'failure'. Some suggested that Don was afraid of the car, others that the whole attempt was amateurish, bearing in mind that little of the mechanicals appeared to work correctly, and when the decision was made to abandon and return to Britain, one American newspaper described it as '...their bulldog tails between their legs'. The *Silver Bullet* was modified when it returned to Wolverhampton, but never ran again. It was a complete failure.

Meanwhile, *Miss England II* had been salvaged, restored and repaired by the consortium led by Lord Wakefield, the man who had financed the original bid with Henry Segrave. He was convinced the boat could travel faster and was looking for a suitable pilot when the name of Kaye Don was suggested. After numerous tests on water in lesser craft for the inexperienced boat racer, the decision to attack the water speed record again officially was taken in December 1930, with the idea of an attempt in spring the following year at the British Empire Exhibition in Buenos Aires, Argentina.

The new *Miss England II* was repaired in Derby and strengthened by a stainless steel hull addition, plus tough new propellers. Michael Willcocks bravely agreed to get back onto the boat that had nearly killed him, and he and Segrave did some freshwater testing in Northern Ireland before shipping the vessel to South America for the official attempt. Willcocks was instrumental in helping Don acclimatise himself to the powerful boat, but once the attempt took place, he gracefully and understandably stepped aside to observe from the shore.

The British Empire Exhibition had every manufacturer from the country advertising their wares to a new public clientele. The reason for an attempt on the water speed record during the exhibition was to prove to the world that Great Britain could again rule the waves, with the emphasis now on technological advancement as opposed to the old military reasons. The team chose the Paraná River in the heart of the South American rainforest, with the boathouse a rather inconvenient 4-hour ride away from the 'measured' course. Surprisingly, despite its remote location, large crowds turned up to see this impressive boat that was about to go faster than any before it, save for the Windermere attempt, of course. Predictably, though, there were delays – and long ones, too. The river was hardly conducive to record attempts, with the waters clogged with broken logs and trees, meaning the Argentine Navy had to help with the dredging and clearing. There were also the usual mechanical problems that accompany any speed attempt, with the exhaust manifolds proving particularly troublesome. It needed local engineering companies to come to the aid of the team, while the timekeepers sweltered in the high temperatures.

Finally an attempt was made. On 2 April (and not the 15th as is regularly reported), Don took *Miss England II* on to the river, warming up with a few 90 mph runs before an official attempt. Unlike the shambles that was Daytona, this went about as smoothly as possible, and Don recorded a mean average of 103.49 mph, to take the world water speed record off Gar Wood by just over 1 mph. It was a celebratory moment for the speed ace, but news of it took some time to reach Great Britain due to the unusual remoteness of the location. In fact, no record attempt has been conducted since in such an unlikely place.

Mission accomplished for Don, that night he boarded the *Andalucia Star* bound for England, leaving *Miss England II* behind to take centre stage at the British Empire Exhibition. Within four months, the boat and Don were at it again and increasing the speed even further.

The boat was shipped to Lake Garda in Italy, where she and Don were to compete for the d'Annunzio Cup, in honour of the man who financed the lavish event, the political arch-rival of Benito Mussolini. He was a war hero from the First World War and, in 1920, had defied the United Nations by attempting to take the East Coast of the Adriatic for Italy from Austrian hands, helped by a small army. He was rich and powerful and had a love for all things speedy. For this, he invited the world record holder to race his craft on the lake against an Italian opponent, the 1000 hp *Torino*.

Unfortunately, *Miss England II* was beset by mechanical problems and failed to finish the course, but as *Torino* also retired midway through the race, there was no winner and no trophy awarded. It was something of an anti-climax, but the hospitality from the Commandante was lavish enough to make it of no concern.

A month later, on 9 July (again, not the 31st, as is reported), Don took the boat on to the lake again and recorded another record – a mean average of 110.23 mph, increasing his own speed by 7 mph. This was celebrated in the most impressive of fashions, with d'Annunzio arranging for fireworks and parties within the gardens of the Vittoriale. Whereas the previous success was played out in front of bemused locals and news took time to be delivered, this one was greeted as if it was an Italian feat and was immediately broadcast around the world, and presumably also to Gar Wood. Within the space of three months, Kaye Don – pilloried for his 'failure' with the *Silver Bullet* in Daytona on land – had broken the world water speed record twice and seemingly with consummate ease. All it needed now was for Gar Wood to challenge again and, as was expected, that challenge came very quickly, not just as a record attempt, but a direct head-to-head for the coveted Harmsworth Trophy.

The trophy was run that September and proved to be a destructive and combative clash. *Miss England II* had a new crew, including a dwarf named Tommy Fisher, who could crawl between the engines and the hull of the boat, while *Miss America IX* was supercharged again in an attempt to retain the trophy that had been held by the States for a decade. Nearly half a million spectators crowded the Detroit River to witness a grudge match that saw all vestiges of sportsmanship disappear in a fog of desire and ambition.

The first heat was won by Don in the British boat at a new heat record of 89 mph, but the second was to prove to be the light that ignited the volcano. The fuel tank of the American boat had split after the opening race, and Gar Wood had naturally requested an extension of preparation time of 45 minutes to fix the problem. This seemed entirely reasonable, as in the past he had generously shown leeway to other competitors who had experienced problems, but not so Kaye Don. He refused the request, and in Wood's anger, there was an incident at the start of the second heat that almost caused a serious accident. *Miss America IX* crossed the start line ten seconds early, making *Miss England II* follow quickly. Both boats were immediately disqualified for starting the race early, but the British boat hit the heavy wash as she trailed the American vessel and overturned, throwing Don and his crew overboard. They were rescued unhurt, but *Miss England II* sunk to the bottom of the river, eventually being salvaged with a wrecked hull. The heat was deemed a 'no contest', and two days later *Miss America VIII*, piloted by George Wood, cruised the course and so retained the trophy for the United States once more. The controversy caused a major break in relations between the two men, and Gar Wood's reputation in the British press was destroyed, albeit unfairly.

The following February, on the 5th, Wood took the same boat on his traditional Indian Creek river and regained the water speed record with a mean average of 111.712 mph, just 1.5 mph faster than Don's record. It was Wood's fifth water speed record, and his third 'officially'.

Mindful of America wresting control of the record once more, and in keeping with the America-Britain battle for supremacy, a new *Miss England* was commissioned by Lord Wakefield. This was built by Thorneycrofts and powered by a Rolls-Royce engine that produced 2,350 hp and had recently been used to take the air Schneider Trophy at a speed of 340 mph. The boat was a departure from the previous one, with a more solid bulkhead as opposed to the streamlined version of *II*. It also dispensed with the normal requirement of two riding mechanics, and made do with just one.

The first trials were on Lake Garda again, but they proved to be a disappointment as only 106 mph could be reached. The boat was taken back to the workshops, with Don expressing his frustration to a newspaper reporter: 'I wish the boatbuilders would think less of my life and more about speed, which is what I want in a boat. After all, risk is my stock in trade.'

The problem with the vessel had been the heaviness of the nose, so the front step had to be planed to make it more aerodynamic. This took some time, but once ready, the team then transported the boat to Loch Lomond in Scotland, chosen due to the fact it had a 24-mile freshwater runway and was nearly as good as Lake Windermere. The latter had been discarded following the tragedy to Henry Segrave, leaving an almost earthly gloom to hover over the place.

Sadly, Scotland didn't exactly make the team welcome with expected rains and thunderstorms, and at one stage the boat fell loose of its mooring as it was being lowered into the water and had to be rescued by Royal Navy divers and specialists from a Glasgow shipyard. Then the early runs saw the boat porpoise badly at speeds in excess of 80 mph, meaning yet more work to the hull and more delays. The team were getting anxious and public interest was waning, but finally, on 18 July 1932, Don recaptured the record with a run averaging 117.43 mph, and then an hour or so later, he increased that to 119.81 mph, actually reaching 2 miles a minute at one stage, the first to ever to reach that speed on water (some twenty-six years after the same barrier had been broken on land). It was a remarkable achievement, and effectively brought an end to Don's exploits on water, bar another futile attempt at winning the Harmsworth Trophy at Lake St Clair. In the two heats in which he competed against Gar Wood, *Miss England III* nearly flooded and then broke a piston, giving the American a straightforward victory once more.

That was the end of Kaye Don as a powerboat racer as Lord Wakefield pulled out his financial backing 'for personal reasons', and the record-breaker returned to his businesses and the occasional motor race at Brooklands. As an aside, he also spent three months in prison in 1934 after being found guilty of causing the death of a mechanic, Francis Taylor, as the two of them were preparing an MG Magnette on the Isle of Man. They had taken the car out at night without lights and hit a hackney carriage on a public road. The MG lost a wheel and crashed. Six hours later, Taylor succumbed to his injuries in hospital and Don was arrested. He was found guilty by a jury and sentenced to four months imprisonment, despite appealing the original verdict. After just under three months, he was released on 10 December on medical grounds. Don then went into the motorcycle business and built up the company Ambassador Motorcycles, which thrived until it was taken over by BMW in 1962. Kaye Don died in 1981, his water speed reputation far outliving his 'failure' at the land speed record attempt. As he said in later years about his life, 'One or two experiences that I have had have been somewhat thrilling.'

Sadly, sentiment plays little part in record-breaking, and Don's achievement lasted just over two months. On the very same morning that *Miss England III* was taking the record twice, Gar Wood was testing his new boat, *Miss America X*. This vast juggernaut, made of mahogany and powered by four Packard engines, had cost in the region of $250,000 to design, build and run, a huge amount for the day and a big drain on his company's resources, but Wood lived for powerboat racing and breaking records. Frankly, money was no object. The test was successful and he took the boat out on the Alganoc course at around 100 mph. Later, he was told of Kaye Don's success in taking the water speed record off him and remarked, 'I think we will wait until after the Harmsworth race is over before making a straightaway run.'

Inevitably, the trophy was won again, actually against Don in virtually his last competitive boat race. A crowd of 400,000 had lined the shore to see *Miss America X* and *Miss England III* go head-to-head, but the usual mechanical problems beset the British challenger and the trophy remained firmly in American hands. To add insult to injury, Gar Wood then regained the world water speed record on 20 September 1932 when he took his new vessel along the St Clair River in wet and drizzly conditions and set a new high of 124.86 mph, some 5 mph faster than Don. His mechanic, Orlin Johnson, said of the run, 'The telegraph poles lining the canal became like a fine-toothed comb.' For the sixth time in his life, Gar Wood was the fastest man on water. His reputation was as high as ever and his relentless quest for speed on water went a long way to pushing the progress of mechanical reliability and safety with his boats. Gar Wood was a legend in the nautical world he inhabited, with an industry that he founded strong enough to sustain his personal achievements. It seemed at that time his name would always be synonymous with record-breaking on water, but as in all walks of life, there is always a new and younger challenger who takes everything that has gone before and pushes it to a further limit. That challenger (or, to be more precise, challengers) came in the name of Campbell. As well as their successful exploits on land, father and son would effectively dominate water speed record-breaking for a thirty-year period, with only one real challenger to interrupt their duopoly. The Campbells were coming!

12

THE CAMPBELL DYNASTY

Gar Wood actually attempted to better his own record in 1935, mainly to see if he could reach 130 mph, but also because there were simply no other challengers around. He'd won the Harmsworth Trophy in 1933 against the British driver Hubert Scott-Paine, who had pushed him all the way, and then a year later had effectively been given a 'walkover' when successive challengers failed to emerge. So with little competition, he took an improved *Miss America X* to Indian Creek once more with the intention of lifting the record to a level that wouldn't be touched for quite some time. Unfortunately, this didn't go according to plan. Despite having new superchargers that increased horsepower to 7,500, the boat couldn't match the previous speed. It was the last time that Wood was to be involved in record-breaking. He retired from racing with the advent of the Second World War and concentrated on helping the American effort and then continued to run his successful business. In later years, he acquired Fisher Island, off the Florida coast, and spent his days with his family on the retreat. A millionaire, he could afford to live his life as he chose and still have the influence to effect change in business and politics. He died in Miami in 1971 at the age of ninety after a life of success in competition and business. He will always be associated in nautical circles with the world water speed record.

So along came the name Campbell, one that is now almost a byword for speed records. It started with Malcolm, continued with Donald and ended with Gina. Malcolm Campbell was born in 1885 to William and Ada in Chislehurst. The family originally came from Scotland, and in fact their ancestors were clansmen who fought for and alongside Mary, Queen of Scots, so their rich heritage meant that it would be unlikely that a Campbell would not be involved in the public eye with an extraordinary life. William Campbell had inherited a diamond business and when he died in 1920, he left an estate that would translate to around £11 million today. Malcolm grew up in a privileged environment, but he was also taught to be self-sufficient, with a strict upbringing from a disciplinarian father.

Malcolm went to preparatory school in Guildford, where he took up boxing as a way of protecting himself from the bullying that was endemic at such establishments. That was followed by a spell at Uppingham School, where his natural talent for misbehaving and adventure came to the fore. One of the stories recounted from his early days was ignoring strict orders from the headmaster of the school not to walk through the railway tunnel at Glaston on the Kettering to Manton line. This was too tempting to overlook so he and a friend entered the tunnel in the dark and managed to reach the halfway point before being forced to rush to safety when an express train came speeding through. What made the act even more dangerous was that they couldn't tell which track the train was on until it came around the curve. The headmaster was suitably unimpressed and one of the many thrashings was handed out to him and his accomplice.

Once school had finished, his father, never the most paternal or affectionate, sent Malcolm to Germany to learn business. He teamed up with a young German he called 'Fritz' and the two of them looked for as many ways as possible to stem the boredom of business studies. It was the time of the Boer War and Great Britain wasn't exactly at its most popular around the world, so Malcolm's habit of raising a Union Flag wherever he went wasn't always appreciated, but he had been brought up to love 'King and Country' so his patriotism was inbred and a part of his character that prevailed as the years passed.

More tomfoolery followed, with stories of poaching and hunting and a moment when a bullet just passed by his head when the two played war games with rifles. It left him shaken but didn't deter his quest for fun and frolics. Shortly afterwards, he was sent to France to live with a clergyman and his family, again to understand French business methods. It was all a precursor to taking over the family diamond business, but at no time did Malcolm seem to grasp the technicalities of business or indeed embrace the life that was being planned for him. His relationship with his father was fractious to say the least, and after joining a city broker, Tizer & Co, he moved out of the family home, although for his twenty-first birthday, William bought his son a partnership in the firm of Pitman & Dean, making him a Lloyd's underwriter. It was this that helped Malcolm make his own fortune.

In 1906, a newspaper writer had reported on a car rally in Dieppe but had added a mythical story concerning the behaviour of an English spectator to make the story more appealing. Unfortunately for him, he chose a name for the Englishman that coincided with someone who was at the rally and was entirely innocent. That man then brought a legal action against the journalist and the newspaper and won damages equivalent to over £100,000 in today's money. Malcolm Campbell, after being tipped off by an uncle, decided to start a new insurance business to combat such instances in the future and, after attempting to sell the idea to many companies, he found success with Oldham, Southwood & Co., and was just in time to cash in on many copycat legal actions. His fortune was assured.

Of course, for the speed king Campbell was to become, there needs to be a starting point to his obsession with the fast and the quick. That point was earlier at the age of seventeen, when he paid the equivalent of today's £1,000 for a Rex motorcycle, a machine he rode frighteningly quickly and crashed many times. By 1906, he was racing and won a gold medal three years in a row in the London to Land's End trial, but his passion was also matched by a wandering mind, and within two years he'd switched his allegiances to flying. Newspapers at the time were offering huge amounts of money for feats of aviation following the Wright Brothers' successful first flight in North Carolina, so Campbell just knew he had to give it a try, despite having absolutely no knowledge of the fledgling aeroplane industry. He was determined to build his own plane one day and helped to finance it by betting on Louis Blerot being the first man to fly across the English Channel. Campbell won £750 when the Frenchman succeeded (approximately £43,000 in today's values) and so prepared to construct the 'Campbell Flyer'.

As a way of understanding the aviation industry, he caught a steamer to France for a meeting in Reims, but it ran aground and Campbell then was forced to hitch a ride across the difficult French countryside, arriving just in time to attach himself to President Loubet, who was inspecting the planes. He was already proving his resourcefulness.

The plane, however, was a disaster. He'd employed a carpenter to help build it and, powered by a two-cylinder motorcycle engine, it produced around 6 hp, but it never looked likely to be successful. The maiden flight near Orpington saw it lift a few feet and then crash back to the ground, almost completely wrecking the machine. At the same time, unbeknown to him, Campbell was being burgled and lost a fair amount of money. It had proved to be a sobering experience.

During 1910, he worked tirelessly on the plane, but each time he launched it would fly just a few feet and again land unceremoniously with extensive damage. He attempted to auction it off to raise funds for a new model, but somehow managed to bid against himself and so ended up paying for the plane that he already owned. A week later, he tried again and sold it for a much smaller fee that just about covered the commission he owed from the previous auction. His foray into the aviation world was expensive and ultimately very brief.

Within a year, he'd found a new passion – motor racing. He'd already dabbled in a few races at Brooklands, but it became very serious when he purchased a 10-litre Darracq that he called *Flapper*. In fact, the first three of his cars were to be named this, but following one defining night in Campbell's life, a new name was born and one that always resonates when anyone, knowledgeable or not, talks of speed records. *Blue Bird* was created.

One night in 1912, he went to see an opera at the Haymarket Theatre in London. It was a popular variation on a theme of happiness and contentment, written by Maurice Maeterlinck and performed in front of packed audiences. The opera was called *The Blue Bird*, and as he had enjoyed it immensely, Campbell decided to rename his car *Blue Bird*. Even though it was after midnight when he drove home, he then went to a local shop, got the proprietor out of bed and purchased every pot of pale-blue paint he had. That was followed by an all-night session of repainting the whole car blue – when he arrived at the start line at Brooklands the next morning, the car was still in the process of drying. Like the story surrounding the colour of the Mercedes 'Silver Arrows' (where the general consensus is that the night before a race the paint was sandpapered off to save weight and so leaving the bare silver metal, a story that has never really been verified), this act eventually took on far greater significance as the years passed than could ever have been imagined at the time. It's also worth noting for historical accuracy that Malcolm Campbell's cars and boats were named *Blue Bird*, whereas when Donald continued the tradition, he called them *Bluebird*.

The car won its first two races, proving that blue was going to be a lucky colour, but in an August Bank Holiday meeting, Campbell burst a tyre at 100 mph on the steep banking and very nearly hit the many spectators watching from the enclosure. One of those was a lady called Dorothy Whitall, who had gone with her father. She had reason to remember the incident, for in years to come she ended up marrying the man who nearly crashed into her! As she said after watching Malcolm wrestle with the car to avoid hitting anyone, he was '...worthy to be installed in the gallery of heroes, and there in my young mind I placed him'.

In 1913, Malcolm Campbell married a wealthy socialite called Marjorie Trott. She was rich enough to help to finance Campbell's racing career, which she appeared to do with enthusiasm, but in 1914 all forms of entertainment were shelved as the First World War broke out. Campbell enlisted as a motorcycle despatch rider before fighting in Mons after his commission as a 2nd Lieutenant came through. He then joined the Royal Flying Corps, meaning he was taught to fly properly, but he was eventually turned down as a fighter pilot as the instructors didn't believe he could make the grade and thought him to be a little too clumsy. Instead, he was given the tedious duties of flying old and new planes back and forth over the English Channel to France. This wasn't without its dangers, as a crash-landing in fog left him badly injured and seriously shaken. Once recovered, though, he became a flying instructor and published a book at his own expense on flying tips for new recruits. This service led to his being given an MBE for aviation duties during the war.

Sadly, his marriage didn't last as Marjorie soon became tired of Campbell's selfishness and financing every one of his projects. She was a strong woman and wasn't the type to stand by her man's every mood and tantrum. Malcolm had started to show a part of his character that became more pronounced as the years passed. He was egoistical, self-centred and at times almost incapable of dealing with people. He courted publicity constantly and had an overinflated opinion of himself, yet these characteristics were essential in the future bloody-minded pursuit of speed records. The two divorced in 1915 and, five years later, Malcolm married the aforementioned Dorothy. In 1921, his son, Donald, was born, with a daughter, Jean, two years later.

After the end of the war, Malcolm, who was now reasonably well off due to his membership of Lloyd's, could indulge his passion for motor racing. Unfortunately, his business acumen didn't improve as he persuaded a few of his friends to invest in a car trading company that saw deposits taken for scarce new models, only for the cars never to make an appearance. He also turned down the opportunity of marketing cars made by William Morris, saying they weren't sufficiently well finished. Morris cars, of course, became a huge success story of the British motor industry during the twentieth century. It was clear that business was not his forte, and so he concentrated on racing cars instead of attempting to sell them, yet he kept his company going before it went bankrupt in 1927, owing around £1 million in today's value to his backers. A combination of long absences while record-breaking and some pretty unhealthy dealings with customers eventually killed the business.

Campbell had success on the race tracks, but when he saw a Sunbeam car raced by Kenelm Lee Guinness and built by Louis Coatalen, a new passion took hold. He had to break the world land speed record. Firstly, he hired the car off an unwilling Coatalen and immediately took it to Redcar, where he raced it in one direction at around 134 mph, matching the existing record. It wasn't officially recognised as only one run had taken place, but it proved to Campbell that the car was capable and he had the bravery to handle such a beast of a machine. The following year, he finally bought the car for an inflated price off Coatalen and took it to Denmark, where he managed to break the record at a mean average of 137.72 mph. Unfortunately, the timing apparatus wasn't accepted by the governing body of speed records, the AIACR (Association Internationale des Automobile Clubs Reconnus), and so the record wasn't recognised. Undeterred, he returned a year later (now with the correct timing equipment) and attempted the record once more. In the interim it had been raised to 146 mph, but Campbell was convinced he could reach the landmark 150 mph. This he did, but tragedy followed when on the first run the car skidded and sheered a tyre, which then careered into the spectators who were standing behind a single rope barrier. The tyre hit a boy, who later succumbed to his injuries. Campbell was exonerated of any blame, but the tragedy must have surely played on his mind when taking the painted blue Sunbeam to Pendine Sands in Wales.

On 25 September 1924, Campbell broke the first of his nine world land speed records when the huge monster of a car ploughed along the wet sands at 146.16 mph, breaking the record by 0.15 mph. Nearly a year later, he became the first man to break 150 mph on land, only to see it beaten by Henry Segrave eight months later in Southport. Campbell was a national celebrity and his stock was as high as ever. He'd broken the 2½ miles a minute barrier, so now he wanted the 3 miles a minute record, and another *Blue Bird* was built with the express intention of travelling at 180 mph.

Helping Campbell at this time was a man who, alongside Malcolm and Donald, is a name that resonates around the world when people talk of speed record-breaking. Leopoldo 'Leo' Alphonso Villa was born in 1899 in London, and for most of his life was closely linked to both *Blue Bird* (or *Bluebird* as it later became known) and the Campbell family.

After school, Villa had a succession of jobs, including one rather unsuccessful stint as a page boy in the Strand (unsuccessful in that he was sacked after falling out with a fellow porter and then threw a bottle of ink all over him), but his true calling was mechanical engineering. At the age of sixteen, he was working as a racing mechanic to the Italian driver

Giulio Foresti (surely one of the best racing driver names ever), and for the next five years they raced around Europe with conservative success. Motor racing in those days was terrifyingly dangerous, and at the French Grand Prix in Strasbourg, Villa was seriously hurt when he suffered extensive burns following a generator explosion. He then convalesced for a while before meeting up with Captain Malcolm Campbell at Brooklands. Villa had driven a car to the circuit for Campbell to test and they immediately forged a bond that persuaded Campbell to employ Villa as his chief mechanic. As the years passed, he became a firm friend of Campbell and, after Malcolm's death, with his son Donald too, and was instrumental in building the cars and boats that succeeded in record-breaking.

In 1926, with the enormous input of Villa and some of the best engineers in the country, Campbell built a new *Blue Bird*, with a Napier-powered 24-litre engine. It was suggested that Campbell had spent in the region of £10,000 building the car, a huge amount for the time. It was seen as a straight battle between himself and Parry Thomas, in *Babs*, to see who could break the 3 miles a minute barrier, and on 4 February 1927, Campbell took the blue monster down the Pendine Sands at a mean average speed of 174.883 mph, his third land speed record. After the run, Campbell was quoted as saying, 'I never want to experience anything like that again.' This was hardly surprising as the beach was wet, with the sand bumpy and clingy and the flying winds had torn his goggles off midway through the run, meaning that in effect he had been blinded by the spray and the breeze. If anyone attempted to take a modern-day racing car along a wet and bumpy sandy beach at a speed of 170 mph today, they would rightly be described as being crazy, yet Campbell and his ilk stared danger in the face with machines that were totally inadequate and, for the most part, came out successful at the other side. Sadly, one month later, Parry Thomas was killed on the same beach while driving the *Babs* car in an attempt to raise the record. The crash was horrifying and Thomas was virtually decapitated in the accident. It was the first fatality in land speed record-breaking in nearly thirty years. It wasn't to be the last.

As an aside, in 1926, Campbell actually organised and travelled on an expedition to the Cocos Islands to find buried treasure that he had convinced himself existed. Despite all of the work needed to ready *Blue Bird* for a record attempt, he simply dropped everything, boarded the *Adventuress* and sailed to the south of Costa Rica. A few months later, he returned empty-handed after an adventure that he described as 'futile'. It perfectly described the man who had never really grown from a boy.

With the public outcry over the death of Thomas, it was down to Henry Segrave to raise the record to an astonishing 203 mph, but he had to take his Sunbeam to Daytona Beach in Florida to do it. This was as much to do with the length of the beach as opposed to any outcry another record attempt in the United Kingdom might deliver, but there was not be another land speed record attempt on the shores of the British Isles again.

Campbell prepared another attempt at the record, but he and Villa were almost killed well before any thoughts of such a thing could take place. They'd been racing at Brooklands in one of the smaller engined *Blue Bird* cars when the bonnet flew off at high speed. The huge piece of metal hit Campbell full on the head and knocked him unconsciousness, leaving Villa to calmly take hold of the steering wheel from the passenger seat and bring the machine to a safe stop. Capt. Malcolm, never one to underplay a drama, especially if it involved himself, later said, 'By all the laws that we know, my mechanic and I should have been killed that day. It is my belief that no man dies before his time, and I've never been able to explain these things.' They were articulate and heroic words spoken by someone who seemed to face death regularly, but they were also spoken by someone who at times gloried in the melodramatic. Years later when asked, Villa gave a rather different view of the proceedings and even suggested it had happened at a totally different time.

It was irrelevant, though, as in February 1928, Campbell went to Daytona and took a new and improved *Blue Bird* to a new record speed of 206.956 mph, just 3 mph faster than Segrave. It was a brave and glorious attempt as the car had hit a bump badly on the first run and nearly ran out of control, but after months of redesigning and financing the original car, a small margin of increase was scant reward. As ever, Campbell played to the crowds:

> I am no physical weakling and it required all my power to keep her on an even course. The wheel had to be gripped. When I hit that bad patch, my muscles were being torn from me and I had to wrestle with *Blue Bird* … when she skidded and presented a broadside to the wind, well, I was fate's plaything, and fate decided to let me get back … If I ever imagined that my end had come, I believed it in the moments that followed…

Campbell held the land speed record yet again.

13

CAMPBELL THE HERO AND THEN TO ZERO

Malcolm Campbell was now known around the world due to his record-breaking antics. It's difficult to imagine now why breaking speed records became such an attraction in his age, but this was a time in between world wars and a time when Great Britain still strived to be the best at everything. Even something as simple as going faster than the last man was important; it was vital that it was a Briton (or Britisher as the parlance of the time dictated) that did it. In the United States, Campbell was revered as if one of their own, helped enormously by the characteristic British sense of fair play and clipped tones. Two of the more prominent newspaper headlines read, 'Britain beats speed record' and 'England's speed wizard'. Enlighteningly, there was another that shouted: 'Capt. Campbell's triumph – American's fail!' The battle for supremacy for land speed records was a straight one between the Mother Country and its newer and more brash junior, and the Americans were itching for an opportunity to get it back. At a reception in London, the United States Ambassador, Alanson B. Houghton, made a speech that was a direct challenge aimed at his people back in America: 'When a man goes to the United States to win a speed contest, he has to go quickly. Captain Campbell has beaten the Americans fairly and definitely on their own soil, but it is no secret that Americans intend to bring the trophy back!'

Campbell was constantly in the newspapers and used for a variety of reasons. At a time when the country was struggling with debt and the popularity of the Chancellor of the Exchequer, Winston Churchill, was at a low, many cartoons depicted Campbell in an imaginary car attempting to break free of the shackles of 'Debtona' – a play on words, helped somewhat by the clipped accent of Malcolm, which made Daytona sound like the word used. Sadly, this notoriety was given a major knock when, within two months, Ray Keech bettered his speed on the same beach and became an instant hero in America. That was then followed by Henry Segrave taking the record back for Great Britain by an astonishing margin, but Campbell had already faced the biggest failure of his life and one that took him from hero to zero in a very short space of time.

He'd decided to make another attempt at the record, and this time it was going to be on Empire soil (there was nowhere suitable in the United Kingdom and, for reasons not fully explained, he didn't particularly want to return to Florida). Seemingly scanning the globe in a light aircraft in an attempt to find a suitable territory, he and his travelling companion, Squadron Leader D. S. Don, actually managed to crash land in Spanish North Africa and were held hostage by the Riff tribesmen. According to Campbell, they made their escape the next morning by climbing over their captors while they were asleep, but not before they'd been held in a hut and forced to eat 'rancid butter' and 'harsh, sour bread', plus drink 'water that was almost black'. The tale went that the two of them ran, walked and swam some 70 miles before being rescued by Spanish officials. It was a great story.

Eventually, after more searching, Verneuk Pan in South Africa was discovered. This was a huge expanse of salt and mud from a dried-up lake, and although some 100 miles from the nearest railway line, it had the geography and the geology essential to allow a car to travel at speeds of 250 mph. Campbell and his team set up camp with a new and improved *Blue Bird* and proceeded to empty his bank account into the glaring white mud. The whole adventure turned out to be an unmitigated disaster. The temperatures were unbearable and any work during the day was almost unimaginable. The top layer of the arid lake bed had to be scraped to make a smooth and flat surface and then relaid with mud, but this was beyond the team, so the local authorities came to help. This took weeks, and the few journalists who had come to cover the event were bored out of their minds in the hell hole that they had inhabited. This boredom manifested itself in less than complimentary reports back in Britain, and sponsors started to question their involvement in the whole process. The car didn't turn a wheel as the arid temperatures became baking during the day so that even leaving the shade of the makeshift tents and huts was akin to putting your head in a heated oven. At night, the temperatures fell to an alarming degree, which left everyone shivering. The question of why Daytona, with its hospitality and amenities, had been eschewed for the middle of a dry lake miles from anywhere was asked on a regular basis.

To make matters worse, it started raining. This wasn't the kind of rain found in the counties of England, this was torrential, battering rain that flooded the lake within minutes. The car and the homestead were completely stranded. In an attempt to find another suitable location, Campbell took his aircraft and surveyed the surrounding area, but then crash landed, suffering cuts to his mouth and cheek, and lost a few teeth. To compound his misery, the plane that was sent to rescue him also crashed and caused yet more injuries. If that wasn't enough, his wife Dorothy became unwell and returned to England accompanied by fellow racing driver Brian Lewis. The two then embarked on an affair once they returned to their home shores. To add to Campbell's almost insurmountable misery, his eyesight started to cause him problems and the thought of travelling along an expanse of salt at 250 mph seemed a little crazy to say the least.

Campbell gave up on Vereuk Pan after spending thousands of pounds, generating negative publicity and employing a local populace who excelled in their apathy. The car came nowhere near a land speed record and he returned to Britain in a less heralded fashion than the last occasion.

At this time, there was a question asked by the British press as to why Campbell wanted to continue. The land speed record was in British hands, but sadly Henry Segrave had now been killed on Lake Windermere. Another Briton, Parry Thomas, was also dead, Frank Lockhart was dead, and even Ray Keech had been killed in a car accident. There was simply no one now to challenge, but Campbell wanted the record back and nothing would stop him. His business interests (those that weren't losing money on a regular basis) hardly kept him busy, and there was a part of him that wanted back the glory from the now deceased and much fantasised Segrave.

Whatever it was that drove him on, it drove him to a successful run that in four-and-a-half years took the record five times and increased the speed record to over 300 mph.

14

CAMPBELL DOMINATES

Malcolm Campbell gave *Blue Bird* to Reid Railton, who engineered a faster and slicker looking car. He also decided to return to Daytona Beach, where the Florida authorities welcomed him with open arms. This was more to do with the tourist attraction than any affectionate feelings. They were also a little more reluctant to finance the attempt like last time, meaning that Campbell was effectively using his and his sponsors' money to pay for the large team to be shipped over to the east coast of America. It was worth it, though, as he took the blue streamlined car to a new record of 246.09 mph on 5 February 1931, tantalisingly close to the 250 mph barrier he wanted to break. It wasn't without its mishaps, of course – nothing Malcolm Campbell did was ever smooth – as on one run his brakes faded and he just missed some of the thousands of spectators who had gathered, forcing the machine to slow by using second gear, and on the final record run itself, a motorcycle policeman had inadvertently crossed his path in the gathering mist, only to be knocked off his bike by the draught caused by a giant machine travelling at 240 mph. These things were what made the attempt romantic, and Campbell was again the fastest man on land.

For the umpteenth time in his life, and a relieving moment for him too, he was feted wherever he went. The American press again headlined his exploits and again questioned when a challenger from their country would be ready to take on the British. The answer to that question would be 'many years hence'. Campbell travelled back to England with words of praise from the American President and a companion in Charlie Chaplin, who just happened to be on the same ship back across the Atlantic.

Of course, no story on Malcolm Campbell can be complete without the usual strange happenings and fantastical stories. On board the *Mauretania*, a passenger fell overboard on the leg from Cherbourg to Southampton and the story followed that Campbell raced to the deck and threw a lifebelt into the sea for the poor individual. The man was rescued, but then as the ship was cruising up the River Solent, accompanied by RAF planes dipping their wings in honour of the great man, it ran aground on a sandy bank. To say this was inconvenient is something of an understatement as at the docks, the mayor, dignitaries, crowds and a live BBC broadcast were waiting. By the time it was refloated, Campbell was on a tug boat and greeted mutedly by fewer people and had missed his BBC slot. To make amends, he was handed a telegram that informed him that the King had conferred a Knighthood on him. It was a surreal end to an odd day.

Campbell's name was now linked to virtually every product that needed an endorsement, and with the title 'Sir' ahead of his name, he was worth his weight in gold. His popularity was such that he was even pressed on political stories and somehow, albeit unwittingly, he managed to get his views aired publicly by a newspaper who had decided to publish a speech he'd made about the 'ills' of his country. The *Daily Express* was the paper, and although they later backed down on the reasons for publishing, it only served to make the Campbell name even more resonant than ever before.

A year later, in 1932, Campbell again returned to Florida with *Blue Bird*, and among what could only now be called a circus (there were boxing tents alongside the beach course where 'Negroes' were forced to box until only one continued to stand, or huts where the local 'hooch' was dispensed from bathtubs to beat prohibition), he took his car to the amazing speed of 253.97 mph, finally breaking the 'barrier' that he'd dreamt of. It wasn't enough, though, and he wanted the 260 mph mark almost immediately, but with the weather closing in and the mayor a little concerned at losing what was his biggest annual tourist attraction, permission was taken away and the beach closed to traffic. Within twelve months he was back, and again raised the record to 272.46 mph but, with the car showing its age and the beach bumpier than ever, this was no easy record. He described it as the 'worst ride I have ever had', but he again promised to return until he reached the next barrier, 300 mph.

These constant record attempts could only prove to be detrimental to his family life as long absences were necessary, but an indication of how difficult any relationship can be when one is striving for perfection can be seen in a much-discussed piece of Pathé newsreel shown in cinemas on his return to Southampton that year. An excited Donald, his young son, is seen rushing up the gangplank as Malcolm emerges from the crowd to be greeted by the press and supporters. Donald holds out his hand in the of-its-time way to shake his father's hand, yet Malcolm either doesn't see it or completely ignores it and poor Donald is stood alone not knowing what to do. It's an almost heartbreaking scene and goes some way to explaining Donald's later life, especially as he reports that his father once said to him, 'You'll never be like me, we're built different.'

At this time in his life, Campbell could quite easily have given up and let younger and more agile contenders take over. He was forty-eight years of age and had failing eyesight, yet his desire to be the first man to reach 300 mph on land drove him forward. In 1934, he handed over a bunch of post-dated cheques to Leo Villa and Reid Railton, and told them to rebuild *Blue Bird* and make it fast and sleek enough to shatter the dreamed-for barrier. He then went off to South Africa to search for diamonds in an arid desert after hearing about them from a friend. They of course were never found, but on his return he was mightily impressed with the new car that was presented to him. It had been redesigned around a Rolls-Royce engine that produced 2,350 hp and was described by an American journalist as a 'thunderwagon', but by Campbell as a 'really efficient streamlined car'. It was ready to smash through the 300 mph barrier. Initially it failed.

On 7 March 1935, back on Daytona Beach, Campbell broke his own record by a mere 4 mph to 276.816 mph, well short of what he wanted and expected. The sand was even more bumpy and unforgiving than before, the car was beset by tedious delays with tyres refusing to behave the way they had been designed, and the gales were so pronounced that as he approached the pier, he nearly ran straight into the wooden girders. Even the crowds were smaller than before, as the seemingly annual attempt was beginning to lose its allure and attraction. It was clear to Campbell that the beach was not the place to be anymore and, convinced that the car really could satisfy his ambitions, he went searching for another venue. He found it in Utah.

The Bonneville salt flats are now best known for regular speed record attempts, but were for years a place that offered no comfort or reason to visit. Lying in the state of Utah, they stretch some 300 miles by 150 miles and are so vast that the curvature of the earth is clearly defined. They lie some 120 miles west of Salt Lake City and were once a huge lake that has dried up down the millennium, leaving behind a landscape that is a desert of glaring white salt. During the summer months, the temperatures are achingly hot and the white salt painful to the touch, but in the winter when the rains come, it becomes completely flooded as there is nowhere for the rain to drain away, and so the water just evaporates, although that takes time. It is over 4,000 feet above sea level and, due to its remoteness, a place that hardly attracts the casual visitor unless you are there to break a speed record.

Three years previously, a local driver, Ab Jenkins, had laid out a circular course and broken a number of class records on the flats. He was a Mormon who didn't drink or smoke and his lifestyle meant he could indulge his almost near-obsession with driving cars fast. He effectively created the course that would in the future be used for speed record-breaking in the future. In 1935, John Cobb had tried out the place in his monster Napier car and decided it was ideal for breaking records. This of course alerted Campbell, and in August he and the *Blue Bird* were packed up and transported to the unwelcoming landscape. The temperatures reached 110°F during the day and the salt glare was so bright that heavy sunglasses had to be worn at all times, although Campbell still found this uncomfortable to his eyes. The car took an age to arrive by train and was severely damaged when it did, due to the jolting from the railway carriages, and the team (including fourteen-year-old son Donald) went mad with boredom. Instead of the thousands of spectators that mostly delighted in his Daytona achievements, this bid was played out to virtually no one, as virtually no one had the means or the desire to get to the place. It was a bizarre and solitary business, but the expanse of flat ground meant that the car would be capable of going as fast as it was able without having to avoid any solid objects in its way.

On the 3 September 1935, early in the day when it was cool, *Blue Bird* did what it had been designed to do. It broke through the 300 mph barrier. This, of course, wasn't without its dramas – record-breaking can never be easy – and the two runs needed to break the record were as dramatic as could be expected. On the first run, a front tyre burst at nearly 300 mph, meaning Campbell had to wrestle with the steering wheel, all the time coping with noxious fumes leaking into the cockpit making him feel sick. At the end of the run, all six tyres had to be changed, but one was so hot that it couldn't be touched until it had cooled down and time was running out. Campbell sat in the baking cockpit becoming more and more agitated until, with 5 minutes to go, he was given the all clear to start his second run. That went faultlessly, but to his immense disappointment the timekeepers informed him that he'd broken his own record again but missed the 300 mph mark by 0.13 mph. It was a huge blow and he was determined to go out the next day to make amends, only to be told that they'd made a mistake and in fact his mean average was 301.129 mph! He *had* broken the 5 miles a minute barrier, but such was his anger at the timekeepers that all accomplishment was lost. Of course, due to the time difference between the US and the UK, the newspaper coverage was confusing to say the least. On his initial 'failure', reports were immediately telegraphed back to London and the papers went to press with the story. By the time the 'new' speed was confirmed, it was too late to alter the story, so the British public woke up to newspaper and radio reports of a new land speed record, but a failure to reach the targeted 300 mph. Twenty-four hours later, the papers had the story of the 'new' speed, but the anti-climax was all-pervading. As the *Daily Express* reported a day or so later, 'Rumour of 301 mph was officially denied, confirmed, unofficially denied, officially denied again and then unofficially confirmed. The speed of 299 mph was confirmed unofficially, denied officially (twice), reconfirmed, re-denied (both officially and unofficially) and finally both denied and confirmed (officially and unofficially). What torture! What suspense! What tedious rot!'

No matter, Sir Malcolm Campbell had just broken the land speed record for the ninth time and in those achievements had raised the speed from 146 mph to 301 mph. At the age of fifty, he had achieved his lifetime's dreams. Now it was time to give up?

He'd promised his wife, Dorothy, that once he'd reached that record he would walk away, and that's exactly what he did, losing immediate interest in *Blue Bird*, which proceeded to earn its keep with numerous public displays around the country. Campbell actually turned to politics to keep his public profile alive, fighting in an election as a Unionist candidate in the constituency of Deptford. Sadly, it wasn't one of his greatest moments as he managed to turn a 4,000 majority over Labour into a near 7,000 loss to the same party. Public speaking didn't come naturally and a lack of warmth meant he alienated most of the voters. He then spent some time rebuilding his huge home with his wife and family, adding a golf course to the surrounding grounds and co-writing numerous books on motoring and speed, but he was bored. It was then that he decided to emulate Henry Segrave and try to pair his land speed record with the water speed record.

15

FROM LAND TO WATER

In 1936, Campbell approached *Miss England II* designer Fred Cooper and commissioned him to build a boat that would be capable of beating Gar Wood's record of 124 mph on water. He'd earlier told Leo Villa of his plans, and had sworn him to secrecy. A few months later, *Blue Bird K3* was unveiled. It was a conventional hydroplane hull, some 24 feet in length, a 'V' below the waterline and powered by the Rolls-Royce engine that had been so successful with the car in Utah. The 'K' denoted the British insurance symbol and the '3' to indicate that this was the third boat to be built since the system had been instigated.

The boat was taken to Loch Lomond for trials, but they proved to be unsuccessful. A twig actually fell into the supercharger air intake, meaning the whole system had to be dismantled to retrieve it. Then the water was so choppy that only a speed of 80 mph was attained. Add to this, Campbell's eyesight now being so poor that the team hung enormous linen sheets on the rocks in sight of line to steer his boat, and it seemed to be a doomed process. He was not to be beaten, though, and his determination saw him take the boat to expanse of Lake Maggiore on the border of Italy and Switzerland. There he was again feted by the local populace and thousands turned up to see his attempt. The boat was even blessed and christened *Uccello Azzurro* by a local Roman Catholic priest, but the trials and tribulations of record-breaking returned. The boat overheated so that design changes were made, the water very rarely behaved itself and at one stage a large fishing net entangled itself around the hull, but on 1 September 1937, he became the second man to hold the world land speed and water speed records at the same time.

In ideal conditions he completed the two runs with no problems and broke Gar Wood's record, increasing it to 126.32 mph, an increase of just under 2 mph. Of course, he wasn't satisfied: 'She's a proper sow to hold – yawing all over the ruddy place. I know I can do better and all being well, I'll take another crack tomorrow.' He did just that and increased the speed again to 129.5 mph. One of the first to congratulate him was indeed Wood, who sent a telegram and also asked if he could buy his Rolls-Royce engine for £15,000. Campbell said thank you and politely declined, but agreed to a challenge for the Harmsworth Trophy. Within a month, however, his land speed record had gone, taken by George Eyston in his *Thunderbolt* on the Bonneville Salt Flats. He had raised the record to 312 mph, but by this time Campbell had lost interest in attempting to regain it and was single-minded in his pursuit of new speed on water.

There was a challenger to his water record in a research engineer from Bradford called Edwin Spurr. He was a close friend of T. E. Lawrence, and the two of them shared a passion with speed. Lawrence had long been involved in motorcycle racing and then turned his attention to water, so the two of them decided to build a boat that could take the water speed record. Unfortunately, in 1935, Lawrence of Arabia was killed in a motorcyle accident, but Spurr continued with their obsession and eventually designed and built a 16-foot vessel at a cost of £8,000 called *Empire Day*. It had a 1½-litre engine, designed to trial the boat at speeds of up to 70 mph, before being replaced by a 960 Napier-Lion aero engine that would challenge Campbell's record. Sadly, he was not remotely successful as on one of his trial runs on Lake Windermere, the boat caught fire after badly overheating at around 73 mph. The craft was badly damaged and Spurr spent some time repairing and rebuilding it. When it reappeared in 1939, now named *Empire Day II* and boasting a new engine and propellers, it failed to even take to the water. After spending some time in a Maidstone car showroom as a prelude to an attempt on the record, it then disappeared from view as important transmission parts were not available and Spurr called it a day. The onset of the Second World War also played a part in his decision, but it was a disappointing end to what could have been a glorious head-to-head between two British pilots.

As it was, Campbell had already broken the record for a third time when he took *K3* to a record of 130.91 mph on Lake Hallwilersee in Switzerland. The successful attempt took place on 17 September 1938, but it was originally due to have been at Lac Luman, where he'd won a Coupe des Nations meeting at 120 mph. Unfortunately, the underwater springs had caused problems with the stability of the boat, so a new venue had been found. By this time, Fred Cooper had been replaced by Peter du Cane as marine architect, and to prove his worth, he took *Blue Bird* out on the lake and actually achieved 120 mph himself. The record was broken once more, though, and with Europe in the midst of international tension and uncertainty, Campbell announced he would build a new boat for one last attempt at the record, hoping to push the speed so far out of reach of any other contender that it would stand for quite some time.

That fourth record proved to be the easiest of them all. A new *Blue Bird K4* was constructed, along the lines of a revolutionary design from the United States. The Apel brothers from Atlantic City had come up with a radical new idea for the hull of speedboats. It was basically still a hydroplane, but was halved longitudinally and a flat bottom inserted between the two halves. There were then two sponsons either side of the cockpit and a planing shoe ahead of the propeller at the rear, meaning that at speed the boat would only be touching the water at three points. It helped to reduce aerodynamic drag and rapidly increase top speed. Campbell had become aware of this and commissioned Peter du Cane to build the new boat to these specifications and to be ready for another attempt in 1939.

While it was being built (at some considerable personal financial cost), he went searching for a suitable venue for a boat that was expected to be considerably faster than anything seen before on the water. Another consideration was the possible onset of war and the restrictions being placed on travel around Europe, so Coniston Water was chosen in the Lake District in northern England. Coniston is seemingly a stone's throw from Windermere on the map and was chosen mainly due to the ghosts that still haunted Windermere following the tragedy involving Henry Segrave nine years previously. The town of Coniston was, and still is, a sleepy little hamlet on the west of the lake and had never seen this type of disturbance before. Its main claim to fame had been through the poet John Ruskin from many years past, and a conservationist group calling themselves the Friends of Brantwood (after the house where Ruskin lived) attempted to stop any speed records taking place on the lake. Another group, the Friends of Campbell (some 485 in number) opposed them and won the day. Campbell was welcomed with open arms and the local populace looked forward to the excitement of the record attempt and the ensuing publicity it would surely bring. They may have ultimately been disappointed as the attempt hardly lasted for more than a week.

After *Blue Bird K4* arrived on Monday 14 August, it was immediately christened by son Donald ('May God bless the craft and her pilot') then had a couple of trial runs where it seemed unstable at around 80 mph (forcing du Cane and Leo Villa to pilot it themselves to see where the problem was). After an all-night session of changes to the aerodynamics, Campbell went out on the 19th and shattered his own record. The two runs on a glass-like lake saw *K4* achieve an average of 141.74 mph, some 11 mph faster than his last record eleven months previously. It was a perfect attempt and by far and away the least problematical of all of his thirteen combined records on land and water, but it was also his last. Within a few days, Great Britain declared war on Germany.

The hostilities understandably put an end to any thought of record-breaking, and Campbell returned to the services, where he worked at Combined Operations testing new weapons. He'd actually warned of war many times in the years leading up to the conflict, and also wrote many books on the subject, so it wasn't the shock to him that it had been to a large part of the population. Unfortunately, the war saw the end of his marriage to Dorothy, who'd had a nervous breakdown due to the tensions in the family home. The two were divorced in 1940, yet remained firm friends until Malcolm's death. In fact, Campbell remarried in 1945 to Betty Humphrey, but they divorced three years later, although she'd disappeared to France after just three months of the marriage and never returned.

Once the war ended, Campbell, whose financial situation was not quite what he'd hoped, decided to have yet another crack at his own record. This was despite no one seemingly showing any interest in challenging him and the fact that he'd been advised time and again that it really wouldn't be the money-spinner or publicity-grabber that his previous records had been. He was of no mind to listen and immediately contacted Rolls-Royce to find suitable engines to power the now mothballed *K4*. They were in no position to help as the company was still recovering from the conflict, so he took the brave decision to radically overhaul *Blue Bird* and fit a de Havilland Goblin turbo-jet engine that created 5,000 lbs of thrust and had recently propelled a Vampire plane to speeds of 600 mph. It was a gamble, especially as the boat had to be redesigned to accommodate a thrust engine instead of the usual propellers, but Campbell was desperate to increase his record.

It's worth noting that at this time Malcolm Campbell's health was becoming a serious issue. He suffered from painful kidney stones, and his eyesight was failing fast. He'd been diagnosed with glaucoma, yet at the age of sixty-two he took the new and vastly powerful *Blue Bird K4* on to Coniston Water, struggling to see the marker buoys on the water and refusing to wear the half-moon glasses prescribed to him.

Bravery, stubbornness, desire and sheer guts are the words that can best describe him, yet ultimately the whole venture failed miserably. The boat was totally unstable, despite constant tests with models in a vast water tank in Hampshire. She purpoised badly and veered off course, so much so that she was a danger on the water. At one stage, the sheer power of her engine slew the boat out of control, where it nearly crashed into the support boats that accompanied her on the trail runs, and it was clear that the whole design was flawed. A boat that had been built to handle traditional propellers and had achieved a speed of over 140 mph was now expected to perform with a 5,000 lb thrust turbo engine that could conceivably travel at 250 mph. It was never going to happen, and despite more changes and trials on Poole Harbour, *Blue Bird K4*, in its new guise, was a failure.

Sadly, Sir Malcolm was never to see the project through to its fruition as his health deteriorated badly. His eyesight failed even more and then he suffered two massive strokes that left him paralysed down his left side. He'd already had major surgery on his eyes, where holes had been drilled to drain the fluid that was congregating, and with the strain of the operation and accompanying kidney problems, he blacked out twice.

His son Donald, who was abroad when his father fell ill, immediately returned to the family home and they were able to spend a Christmas together with the rest of the family – although Malcolm was bedridden throughout – but on New Year's Eve 1948, at the age of sixty-three, Sir Malcolm Campbell died.

In his life, he had achieved more than most. He'd broken the world land speed record an astonishing nine times, a feat never to be repeated, and the water speed record four times. He'd served in two world wars, written numerous books, become a treasure hunter and even stood for Parliament. In his life, he had cheated death many times while at the wheel of *Blue Bird,* yet he died from natural causes. He left behind a huge legacy and one that was inherited by son Donald in years to come.

16

THE RACE FOR 200 MPH AND ANOTHER CAMPBELL

By now, Sir Malcolm Campbell's record had stood for nearly ten years and it would only be a matter of time before someone attempted to break it. That someone was Canadian band leader Guy Lombardo, who, with the automobile industrialist Henry Kaiser, had already made an attempt on the 'American' record of Gar Wood of 124 mph the previous year, albeit unsuccessfully. Kaiser was a sixty-seven-year-old billionaire from Oakland, who, as well as being a highly successful car maker, was also an industrial shipbuilder, and in 1948 had invested in the region of $60,000 for the Ventnor Boat Corporation to build a boat that could challenge all of the water records, especially the world water speed record held by Malcolm Campbell. They then produced a 32-foot, 8,500 lb beast that was powered by a 3,000 hp Allison aero-engine. It was designed by Arno Apel, the man who had rejected Campbell's advances when asked about building a new *Blue Bird*, and was another boat that embraced the three-point principle, with only those parts in contact with the water. Once built, it was christened *Aluminium First*. Sadly for Lombardo and Kaiser, the boat was a failure. Numerous runs on the Pontomac River had shown that the craft was unstable and not a record-breaker, but the publicity that Kaiser had garnered leading up to the trial runs had galvanised a certain Donald Campbell into action. Malcolm's son, hearing of Kaiser's attempt at wresting the record from his deceased father, had decided that the record had to be in a Campbell's hands and had to belong to Great Britain. This was the moment that brought Donald Campbell into the record-breaking arena on both water and land.

Donald Campbell was born on 23 March 1921 at Kingston Hill to Dorothy and Malcolm. He had been named after a friend of his father,

Donald Hay, a fighter pilot in the First World War who had been close to Malcolm, but had crashed and been killed when the two of them were indulging in aerobatics. Hay's plane hit the ground when the wings had failed and Malcolm then honoured him in later years by calling his son by the same name. At that stage, Malcolm had yet to break any of his subsequent world speed records on land and water, but he was an MBE and had enormous success in motor racing. Donald, with his sister Jean, lived a privileged life with the best education, large houses and acres of grounds to indulge themselves in.

What Donald didn't have, though, was a doting father. Malcolm was too consumed by his own career and record-breaking to be a generous and loving parent, and there have been many stories told – mostly by Donald himself – of Malcolm's lack of warmth and affection to his only son. Jean has down the years defended her dad and made a point of saying that at no stage did she ever see her father mistreat Donald, but it's fair to say that Malcolm was a man that Donald admired and feared in equal measure. The newsreel of Donald standing with his arm outstretched waiting for his father to acknowledge him is a painful thing to watch, and some of the quotes attributed to the successful dad when discussing his son's future are hardly encouraging, but everything that Donald was to do in later years was in some part an attempt to live up to his father's reputation.

Malcolm Campbell was away more often than he was at home. If he wasn't attempting to break a speed record, then he was off looking for treasure in a far flung part of the world, or simply taking himself on a cruise while the family moved into a new home. It meant that Donald's vision of his father was almost mythical, with the added lustre of a true 'boy's own' hero. He was taken along to a few of his father's record attempts, notably to South Africa and Cape Town and later to the Bonneville Flats, so the lure of speed was ingrained very early. Unfortunately, in his early years he had a few medical problems related to rheumatic fever, and a serious motorcycle accident that brought about headaches that bothered him for the rest of his life. The rheumatic fever was such that when the Second World War was declared, Donald rushed off to enlist in the hope of becoming a fighter pilot like his father, but Malcolm had sent him on his way with the condescending words: 'Nonsense ... the doctors will never pass you.' Sadly, he was to be proved right.

Donald had gone to the RAF Receiving Centre in Bedford and had gone through all of the rigorous tests in his quest to join the war as a fighter pilot. He'd even somehow managed to convince the board that he was healthy and well, but hiding rheumatic fever is not something that can be done easily and he was subsequently turned down. The disappointment was huge and Donald immediately left the service to return to 'civvy street'. His days in the war were advantageous, though, as he worked as a special constable, then later as an inspection engineer for a device that was installed as part of air field defences. His job was to take this device all over the country, which at least gave him the feeling that he was contributing to the war effort. Before the conflict, his first full-time employment had been in an insurance company. After the armistice, he turned down the chance to return and instead invested a small amount of his capital into Kline Engineering, a company that made carpentry tools. The interest in engineering had come about after he'd spent some time working for the Briggs Motor Body firm, run by his father and Leo Villa, and then later as a maintenance engineer at a factory that produced around 50,000 jerrycans for the Army and RAF. Kline Engineering was to keep him busy right up until his father's death on New Year's Eve 1948, when his life changed forever.

Shortly afterwards, Donald was sat in his father's old shed at Little Gatton. The estate and the house were up for auction, a difficult time for him as everything that he knew was about to disappear, and while he sat in the favourite chair of his father and finished off a bottle of whisky from the sideboard, he spoke at length with Malcolm's long-standing friend Goldie Gardner. It was at this point that Gardner mentioned the attempt on Malcolm Campbell's water record by Kaiser, and that suddenly prompted Donald into action. He would try to break it and keep it in the family name. He and Leo Villa would take the *K4* out of mothballs and try to increase the record so that it was out of bounds to anyone else.

Leo Villa agreed to work on the new attempt, but he surely must have had his concerns and doubts. Unlike Malcolm, Donald hadn't raced any type of vehicle, either on land or water, and was not encouraged by his father to follow in his footsteps at any time. There was always the suggestion that Malcolm felt there was no room for another record-breaker in the family while he was alive, but Leo agreed to work alongside Donald 'to the bitter end', knowing that the son shared the same attributes of the father in his single-minded pursuit of success. He kept his promise.

The first problem that Donald encountered was that he didn't actually own either the *Blue Bird* car or boat. Neither had been left to him in the will and he was forced to buy them both back from the trustees. This must have been galling to Donald, but once the deal was done, he drove down to Porchester, where the boat was stored, and spoke to Peter du Cane at Vospers to discuss how they could upgrade it to challenge for another water speed record. The jet engine was clearly not an option due to its failure with Malcolm, and the concerns over a rookie pilot meant that the whole project was effectively scaled back, but the three Rolls-Royce engines that had been used separately to power numerous record bids were brought back into play, with the R37 (the engine that had broken the land speed record at Bonneville) modified to take a more powerful fuel and giving approximately 200 hp more. Donald also renamed the boat *Bluebird* – in the future, all of his record-breaking cars and boats would be called *Bluebird*, as opposed to his father's *Blue Bird*.

Unfortunately, his father's wheelings and dealings before he died were to cause yet more problems for Donald. All of the mechanical gear needed for the *K4* had been sold many years before, and so Donald had to track down the owner, car dealer John Simpson, and was forced to exchange the 1935 *Blue Bird* car, plus a further £750, to buy back the old *K3* and its mechanical parts. It was becoming a costly business.

Later that summer, a very nervous Donald Campbell took the new *Bluebird K4* out on to Coniston Water in the hope of breaking his father's now ten-year-old record. It must have been strange for the many team members, among them mechanics Harry Leech and Sid Randall, plus of course Leo Villa, to see a new Campbell sit in the familiar cockpit of the boat, but despite his nervousness and anxiety, Donald performed admirably. Sadly, the Lake District weather didn't and the inevitable delays hindered any progress. Every morning the team would gather on the slipway used so many times in the past and hope that the lake would be calm. It hardly ever was as the wind whipped up the waves and Coniston chose to misbehave like a spoilt child.

Eventually, the elements calmed down and on 9 August 1949, Donald Campbell was able to take *Bluebird K4* out on to Coniston Water for its first run in anger with a new pilot in the cockpit. It was steady and a speed of around 80 mph was attained without too many mishaps on the water or behind the wheel. Campbell was so pleased with himself that he declared that he would go for a record speed the next day, only to be told in no uncertain terms by the experienced Villa that it was far too early to even think about such a thing. However, Donald was stubborn. For the first time, they had a huge argument over who was in charge of the whole attempt, and he made it clear that it would be he who would make any decisions as to when they would attempt a record. One day later, after the boat had badly snaked at 120 mph with 'hot plugs' giving the engine effectively more power, and following a near accident with a submerged log at around 100 mph, Campbell returned to the shore suitably chastened.

In a moment of light relief, he exclaimed to Villa, 'This job's bloody dangerous!' at which both smiled and the disagreement was never mentioned or repeated again.

The date 19 August 1949 was the ten-year anniversary of his father's last water speed record, and so it made sense to Donald to break it on that day. Of course, sentiment plays no part in such things, and the lake refused to cooperate. It was wild and windy and, despite the presence of hundreds of spectators on the shoreline, *Bluebird* wasn't able to take to the water. A frustrating moment, yet four days later the conditions were perfect and Donald had his first serious attempt at breaking the world water speed record. It has to be said that this was nothing short of remarkable. In his younger years, he had watched with awe as his father had travelled around the world breaking records on land and water, plus of course winning numerous races and time trials. In all that time Donald, had been actively deterred from continuing along the same path and had not so much as turned a racing car wheel in anger or surfed a wave in aggression, yet here he was about to succeed his father, in full view of a sceptical world, with little or no experience.

It was initially a fairy story. Donald fought the boat, which pitched and yawed violently, ignored the scalding oil that accompanied the white smoke that bellowed into the cockpit, and just kept his foot down when every instinct told him to stop. On his first run he exceeded 150 mph, then on the return, he hit his own wake from the previous passing and very nearly ran into a press photographers' boat, causing one of them to hastily jump overboard in a comedy moment. The speed of 135 mph was reached, although seemingly not during the measured mile. The boat came to a halt in the middle of the lake after Donald frankly scared himself witless (something he cheerfully admitted in his later autobiography) and was towed back to the slipway. Had the record been broken?

In an uncanny moment reminiscent of Salt Lake in 1935, Donald was initially told that he had in fact broken his father's record, albeit by the smallest of margins. This was greeted by delight by the whole team, and even the BBC then broadcasted it at 8 a.m. on their news bulletin on the radio, but of course there had been a mistake again. His mean average speed was in fact 135 mph, some 6 mph short, and the news had to be broadcast again. It was a shattering blow and a humiliation too, but Donald in particular took it all in good grace, mainly because he'd seen it all before with his father!

The team packed up and decided to head back down south to make modifications and to find out why the oil had leaked into the cockpit and why the boat had lost some of its power on the second run, leaving it unstable. *Bluebird K4* was in no state to make another run, especially as water had also seeped into the engine, plus the money was rapidly running out. Campbell felt inclined to return to his position at Kline Engineering, if for no other reason but to earn his salary, and the boat needed to be given a complete overhaul. As he left Coniston, the story is that he stopped his car, looked across the vast expanse of the now calm lake, called it 'a bitch' and promised that he would be back.

17

SLO-MO-SHUN

Campbell actually did return to Coniston a year later where he persevered with *K4* and managed to get it to reach a speed of 150 mph, but overheating problems and a lack of stability brought them to the conclusion that the old *Bluebird* had effectively reached the end of its usefulness as a record-breaker. That was also confirmed by some quite staggering news from America, where it had been announced that an unknown driver in an unknown boat had smashed the water speed record and taken it to over 160 mph.

Stan Sayres is revered in nautical circles in the United States, where his achievements, although not as numerous, are considered as great as those recorded by Gar Wood. He was born in 1897, and his early years had seen him obsessed with all things to do with speed. He had a desire to drive in the famous Indianapolis 500 motor race and had spent a large part of his youth in pursuit of speed. At the age of twenty-nine, now a car salesman in Oregon, he bought a hydroplane after the owner flipped it on Lake McKay, nearly killing himself in the process. Along with powerboats, he filled his spare time by flying aerobatic planes, much to the increasing concern of wife Madeline. In 1937, and now the president of the Chrysler car dealership in Seattle, he bought a small class boat called *Tops III*, which Madeline jokingly suggested he rename *Slo-Mo-Shun* due to his languid and relaxed demeanour. Sayres took this boat out numerous times and enjoyed a modicum of success, while at the same time continuing his rather eccentric aerobatics in the air. Eventually, his wife had her way and persuaded him to give up the flying, but the powerboating continued. *Slo-Mo-Shun I* didn't last long as it caught fire in a race at 80 mph and was destroyed, so the second version was commissioned and built by the Ventnor Boat Works. This again brought some success, although its top speed was around 90 mph. A third version was built soon after and it seemed as if Sayres' interest in boats was just a pleasant diversion, but what took place next was to rock the world of powerboating.

In 1947, Sayres contacted a Boeing aircraft engineer, Ted Jones, and suggested they could design and build a new hydroplane utilising aircraft principles. This meant that the 'three-pointer', where the stern of the boat is raised out of the water, is complemented by a strong propeller that becomes part of the suspension. The prop then does not become submerged, meaning the resistance is less and the blades provide the thrust of the boat. With its stunning aerodynamics, the boat could shatter any preconceived design idea of note. Sayres was happy with the design and asked an old friend, Anchor Jensen (an apt name), to build the boat. He owned the Jensen Motorboat Company, and by the summer of 1949, they had produced a 28-foot-long mahogany and teak sleek machine that looked fast even before it was launched. It was powered by a 2,000 hp Allison aero-engine and had financial sponsorship and backing of twenty-four companies, including the Mobil giant. It was launched in August 1949, and later Sayres wrote, 'When the boat was constructed, I had no thought straightaway of the record, feeling that it was beyond reach. In spring 1950, during our initial trial runs, we seemed to be running so fast so easily that I was urged to try for the record.'

The attempt on the water speed record was about as straightforward as it could possibly be. From 21–23 June, the boat, with Sayres at the wheel, had a few unsuccessful test runs, with bad weather and a broken propeller causing delays, but at 7.10 a.m. on 26 June 1950, *Slo-Mo-Shun IV* shattered the eleven-year record of Sir Malcolm Campbell by 19 mph. The first run on Lake Washington, watched by a handful of enthusiasts and workers from the company, was a frustration as the timer failed, but Sayres just turned his boat around at the south end and motored back north, passing the flying mile at a speed of over 163 mph. Seven minutes later, after refuelling, he reversed the course and recorded 157 mph to give an average speed of 160.323 mph. It was an astonishing performance, made even more shattering to all rivals when it was confirmed that Sayres hadn't even run to the maximum revs and that the boat was capable of going significantly faster. Stan Sayres, a shy and modest man, had just become the fifth man to break the 'official' world water speed record, yet no one outside of Seattle had heard of him. No one had been aware of the super-boat that had been built in secret and hardly anyone had witnessed its astonishing performance. One could only imagine the sheer desperation that Donald Campbell must have felt when he received the telegram informing him that his father's record had been completely destroyed, and that his very own *Bluebird* was not even close to matching this super-boat from across the ocean. It was the largest rise in speed since the records began.

The boat was a sensation. To prove its worth, Sayres then entered it for the Gold Cup and Harmsworth Trophy races, where it won comfortably. It also became the first boat ever to win a race at 100 mph, but none of these triumphs were with Sayres at the wheel. His wife Madeline had insisted that he would not be allowed to race due to the dangers involved, despite the fact he was the fastest man on water. Her reasoning was that if it was in a straight line (i.e. breaking a record), then that was fine, but racing against another boat was far too risky. So instead, Ted Jones piloted until he broke his wrist in a friendly arm-wrestling match, and then he was replaced by a wealthy businessman from Ohio by the name of Lou Fageol. He'd only had limited time in the cockpit, yet put his name on the record books with the 102 mph lap in the Harmsworth Trophy.

By the end of the year, Stan Sayres had become a household name in America, much to his discomfort. He was someone who had never really enjoyed the publicity surrounding his exploits, but he'd been voted Seattle's 'Man of the Year' and the UIM (Union of International Motorboating) had awarded him a medal of honour for 'the greatest boating achievement of 1950'. Sadly, this had also caused friction between himself and Jones, who felt aggrieved at the lack of recognition he'd received in actually helping to design the craft. An uneasy alliance continued between the two as the boat continued to impress on every outing.

At the same time, Donald Campbell was continuing with the now aged and uncompetitive *K4*. It was fast, and in fact in one of the trial runs on Coniston, it had just about reached a top speed of 170 mph, but this had caused massive overheating and damage to the engine. It still had stability issues at top speed, but was sufficiently balanced to win the Oltranza Cup on Lake Garda in Italy. Campbell had even looked into the possibility of attempting a record run at the same time, but the constant 'tramping' of the craft at speeds in excess of 80 mph was too problematic.

In his desperation, he actually contacted Stan Sayres in Seattle to ask for advice on how to improve *Bluebird* and make her more like *Slo-Mo-Shun,* and to show the true character of the man, the world's fastest man on water replied with all of the details of the build of the boat. It was a magnanimous gesture and spoke volumes for Sayres as a man.

The final demise of *K4* came after another difficult run on Coniston Water. Campbell had put Leo Villa in the second cockpit so that he could observe first-hand the problems the boat was experiencing at speed, and again the craft hit a very encouraging 170 mph before the usual overheating. Unfortunately, before the two had any chance to remedy the problem, a huge explosion took place beneath them and the boat stuttered to an undignified halt. Campbell later suggested the boat had hit a submerged railway sleeper, but others have maintained that the gearbox simply exploded. It was sufficiently loud to alert most of the villagers in Coniston, with some convinced that the two had been killed. As it was, *Bluebird K4* started to take on water and sunk as it floated to the shore, leaving Campbell and Villa to wade to the bank. Eventually it was rescued, but the damage was such that it was irretrievable and the battered and broken hull of the once beautiful boat was stripped of its engine and stored away in a warehouse belonging to a friend of Donald's. There it stayed for many years until it became such a rotting mess that the owner of the storage facility, Bill Coley, simply set fire to it. It was a sad and ignominious end to a boat that had held the record for eleven years. As ever, sentiment played no part.

It probably meant something to the patriot Donald Campbell that there was another British challenger for the water speed record at the time who was not him. John Rhodes Cobb was that man, a big, burly but shy individual, who was already a three-times holder of the world land speed record and the first man ever to take a car at a speeds of 350 mph and 400 mph.

Cobb was born on 2 December 1899 in Esher, Surrey, and at an early age had become fascinated by motor racing. The reason for that was quite simple – the only British motor racing circuit at the time, Brooklands, was on his doorstep. He grew up watching the exploits of drivers such as Kenelm Lee Guinness and Henry Segrave and dreamt of one day becoming a racing driver himself. That day came in 1925, when, already a successful businessman selling furs for brokers Anning, Chadwick & Kiver, he participated in his first race. He finished third, driving a FIAT, and a few weeks later recorded his first victory at the same track and in the same car. For the next decade, Cobb was a regular at the iconic racing circuit and, on 7 October 1935, he set a new record of 143.44 mph for the outer circuit lap record at Brooklands, driving the Napier Railton, eclipsing the existing record held by Tim Birkin. At one stage in his racing career, he held every speed record from 1 to 24 hours set at circuits such as Brooklands, Montlhery and Bonneville. Obviously the next step was a full-blown assault on the world land speed record, which at that time rested with Malcolm Campbell's *Blue Bird*.

He commissioned Reid Railton to build him a car, financed by his success in the fur trade, and while that was being designed, Cobb's close friend George Eyston had gone to Bonneville and increased the record to 312 mph in *Thunderbolt*. It was an amazing period for observers of record-breaking, as barely a year passed by without the speed being raised or another attempt being made. For the years between 1937 and 1939, the battle for supremacy between Cobb and Eyston was all-consuming, with each enjoying the challenge of raising the record while the other looked on.

Railton designed a stunning looking car for Cobb. It was a lightweight and streamlined 48-litre beauty that didn't just rely on pure grunt and power to reach its potential. It only weighed around 8,000 lbs and at 2,500 hp was more than capable of beating Campbell and matching Eyston's *Thunderbolt* in terms of looks and performance. It was also called *Railton,* after its builder, and that spoke volumes for a man who shunned any type of publicity, unlike his predecessor Malcolm Campbell, who breathed fame like it was oxygen.

In 1937, Eyston had taken the record and increased it to 312 mph, so the next obvious target was to try for the 350 mph barrier. He returned to the Bonneville Salt Flats in 1938, and on this occasion was joined by John Cobb – new to land speed record-breaking, but not to Bonneville, as he had set numerous class records there. *Thunderbolt* immediately broke its own record again on 27 August at an astonishing 345 mph (although this wasn't without the usual drama, as on a previous run the timing equipment had failed and so no speed had been recorded), but that just spurred Cobb on. Two weeks later, after numerous trial runs where he'd come agonisingly close to the record, Cobb took *Railton* out onto the glaring white salt once more and set his own mark by increasing the record to 350.20 mph, becoming the first man to exceed 350 on land. Unfortunately, he was only to have the record for 24 hours.

The following morning, after readjusting the cooling mechanism on the engine, Eyston took his *Thunderbolt* out and smashed the record again, this time reaching 357.70 mph, but in his heart he knew that it was probably the limit for the car and the next barrier of 400 mph was a step too far. Both Eyston and Cobb returned home to prepare for another assault the following year.

The year 1939, of course, when the world moved inevitably towards war, but for Cobb there was still one last chance to regain the record. George Eyston was having problems with *Thunderbolt,* which had been modified, but there were no such dramas for Cobb and *Railton*. On a perfect day, 23 August, with a small crosswind and nothing else to bother him, Cobb blasted the car over the two runs at an average of 369.74 mph, shattering the record by 12 mph. It was to stand for eight years, as soon afterwards the world went to war.

During the Second World War, Cobb served as a pilot in the Royal Air Force and then later in the Air Transport Auxiliary, and even appeared in a propaganda film, although he was uncredited. Inevitably though, once peace came, his mind returned to record-breaking and the possibility of breaking the 400 mph barrier. For this he brought the *Railton* out of retirement (now renamed the *Railton-Mobil Special* in deference to his new financial backers) and took it back to Bonneville. Sadly, the course was in a mess as it had effectively been abandoned for eight years, but after some heavy rolling work to rid it of uncomfortable and dangerous bumps, a smooth measured mile was achieved and the car was ready for its attempt.

As well as a record-breaking attempt, Cobb had one other duty in 1947, and that was to marry Elizabeth Mitchell-Smith. This in itself was surprising as he was well known to be shy around women and was very much a 'mother's boy' – he adored his mother and would listen to her opinions over anyone else's. Sadly, the marriage didn't last as Elizabeth died some fourteen months later of kidney disease.

As for the record, it was pretty plain sailing. *Railton-Mobil Special* was good enough for 400 mph and managed to achieve this speed on 16 September, although the mean average was 394.196 mph, an increase of 24 mph on his previous record. It should have been over 400 mph, but the bumps on the course had contrived to make the car unstable as it approached the measured mile, and unfortunately there was no opportunity to rectify it as the very next day the rains came and the flats were flooded.

Cobb sailed back to Southampton and received absolutely no plaudits at all. There was no ticker-tape welcome as was afforded Malcolm Campbell before the war. There was no knighthood bestowed on him and there seemed to be very little recognition of what he had just achieved. It probably had more to do with the prevailing mood in the country following the appalling conflict as opposed to anything perceived against Cobb, but this didn't matter to him. He had never chased fame or indeed fortune, and he was quite happy to slip back into the country unnoticed. He stayed unnoticed for the next three years, although in that time he remarried. The lady in question was Vera Victoria Henderson, and she was credited in later years for reigniting the spark in his life after the death of Elizabeth.

By 1950, his thoughts had turned to the possibility of holding the water speed record as well as the land speed record, so he turned to Reid Railton once more and asked him to build a boat that could accommodate a jet engine and challenge the record that had just been set by Stan Sayres. Railton agreed and set about designing and crafting a boat called *Crusader*.

18

SAYRES, COBB AND VERGA: A TRAGIC TIME

Slo-Mo-Shun hadn't disappeared. The boat (of which a replica was made and inevitably called *V*) was destroying all competition, but the news that Cobb and Campbell were looking to take the record back to Great Britain gave Sayres the impetus to attack his own record once more. He installed a new Allison engine into the craft, giving it a further 450 hp, and a group calling themselves the Greater Seattle Incorporated set up a fund to pay for the attempt. This helped Sayres, but also antagonised him. As he said at the time, 'There are penalties to being the Number One target. What started out as a hobby, is beginning to turn me into a slave.'

No matter how frustrated he may have felt at the demands placed on him, at just before 8 a.m. on 7 July 1952, *Slo-Mo-Shun IV* went out onto the East Channel of Lake Washington and smashed its own record once more. In front of 2,000 spectators, the 'Grand Old Lady', as she was affectionately known, recorded a mean average of 178.497 mph, some 18 mph faster than her previous speed. The cheering from the fans on the shoreline as they watched her race past, rooster tails of water following her, was enthusiastic and celebratory. The water speed record was placed out of sight it seemed, as there surely wasn't another boat that could get close.

After the record was won once more, Stan Sayres retired from competitive powerboat racing, mainly on the insistence of his wife again, but the two *Slo-Mo-Shun* boats *IV* and *V* continued to compete with Lou Fageol and Joe Taggart as drivers. The boats dominated wherever they raced, notably in numerous Gold Cup events, but the unlucky Fageol and Taggert both suffered horrendous accidents that sadly brought the *Slo-Mo-Shun* dynasty to an end. In August 1954, *V* flipped backwards while qualifying for the following year's Gold Cup race. There seemed to be no explanation, except that maybe the boat had hit a wave too hard, but Fageol suffered a punctured lung and several broken ribs. He recovered eventually, but the replica boat was completely destroyed and what was left of it was sold by Sayres to a Seattle group called Roostertails Inc. for $15,000. They then rebuilt the craft and called it *Miss Seattle*.

Two years later, the same thing happened to Taggart as he was reaching 140 mph on the Detroit River in *IV*. He hit the wake of a patrol boat, and the destabilisation caused the boat to rock back and forth before somersaulting and crashing back into the water. Taggart was rescued from the water unconscious, having suffered multiple fractures all over his body. *Slo-Mo-Shun IV,* the most ingenious design in boatbuilding history, and the craft that had absolutely destroyed the world water speed record, was a mangled wreck. Stan Sayres left the shoreline quickly on hearing the news, refusing to see the battered boat that had always been his favourite. It was towed back to the pits and then later exhibited in Seattle in its final state. Thousands came to pay their last respects to a boat that had put Seattle on the map. At the same time, hundreds of dollars were donated by those same people, in the hope that she could be rebuilt. Sadly, that was never to happen, as one month after the crash, Stan Sayres died of a heart attack while asleep. He was sixty years of age. His name is revered in Seattle, and the hydroplane pits at Seward Park bear his name. In later years, the *Seattle Times* nominated him as the seventh most distinguished sportsman the city had seen in the last 100 years, quite an achievement in an area known for its love of all sports. His success with *Slo-Mo-Shun IV* saw millions of dollars earned for the city, with the hosting of the Gold Cup races, following his annual victories with the boat. Stan Sayres may not be a world-renowned name in sporting circles, but his legacy is as great as anything that Gar Wood had left.

Meanwhile, John Cobb's challenger *Crusader* was ready. At a personal cost of around £15,000, the craft, a 31-foot three-pointer, made from birch plywood and an engine capable of 5,000 lbs of thrust that had also been fitted to the Comet jet liner, was taken to Loch Ness in Scotland. This lake was chosen simply because it was 23 miles long and over 1,000 feet deep, and seemed a perfect place to challenge for a water speed record.

It's worth noting that, up until this point, Cobb had never actually raced a powerboat of any description, yet here he was about to take this untried craft on the waters at speeds approaching 200 mph. It was an astonishing effort, but if he needed any support, then his old land speed 'nemesis', George Eyston, was there to supply it. He'd been asked, and accepted, to be the competitions manager for the whole team, and his technical knowledge, as well as his similar experience was expected to prove invaluable.

The attempt was being played out in front of a small media gathering, although it didn't match anything that Malcolm Campbell or Henry Segrave had commanded. In fact, the most interested in the curious, looking boat that seemed to keep the locals awake at night, and in the early morning with its booming engine noise, were the schoolchildren of the area. They flocked to the small steamboat terminal where the team had set up camp on a daily basis, so much so that Cobb had to plead with the teachers to allow his team to continue in peace. In fact, he didn't appear to want anyone to get too close, as the publicity surrounding any visit seemed to make him deeply uncomfortable. There is a grainy black-and-white Pathé film of a visit from the Queen Mother just before the official attempt. Cobb is seen in his rather cumbersome and heavy overcoat, standing awkwardly alongside the smiling Queen Mother as she looks over the boat. The spotlight certainly didn't come easily to him, even if the royal patronage was welcome. As an interesting aside, another visitor that day was a very young Richard Noble. His experience paved the way for his efforts with *Thrust*, and the eventual capture of the land speed record not once, but twice.

After the first run on relatively calm waters, where *Crusader* reached a comfortable 120 mph, Cobb likened the experience to 'driving a London omnibus without any tyres on'. The simplicity of the statement suggested that this was such a new venture for him that it may have been rather foolhardy to have continued until more experience was gained. That, however, would be an insult to the man who had faced every challenge in his usual stoic way, and nearly always succeeded, no matter what the danger.

September was probably not the best month to attempt a record in the heart of Scotland. The weather is always notoriously unpredictable, and it proved to be so in 1952. Numerous delays and cancellations followed as the Loch fell foul of the windy and wet weather, but, on the 12th, Cobb did a double run between Drumnadrochit and Invermoriston, where the boat went significantly faster than the 178 mph set by Stan Sayres two months previously. Four days later, the timekeepers arrived and set up in position, ready to record the next attempt, but again the weather refused to cooperate.

On the 23rd, *Crusader* averaged 173 mph over two runs, agonisingly short of the record; but Cobb was convinced there was a lot more to come. Unfortunately, time and money were running out and the feeling was that a record had to be set before the end of the month, especially as the rainy season was due (although any season in that part of Scotland could quite conceivably be described as rainy). There were also mutterings of impatience from the few media personnel present, as 'non records' didn't exactly make interesting copy. Six days later though, the pressmen had their story.

The morning of 29 September 1952 dawned like any other in that part of the world. It was wet, windy and misty, and not at all conducive to setting a water speed record on a choppy and agitated lake. The team, by now frustrated and fractious, retired to the Drumnadrochit hotel to discuss a way forward. Many of the members were of the opinion that no record would be possible that year, and they should return in the summer of 1953. In fact, constructor Peter du Cane was particularly concerned about how the planing shoe was distorting under pressure of high-speed runs, and had offered to take the boat back to Vospers for inspection, but Cobb was insistent that the run was possible once the weather had calmed down. This was odd to say the least, as he had told his mother and his wife of a premonition about having his last run in *Crusader*, but it seemed his main consideration was not to let people down who had been patiently, or in some cases impatiently, waiting. As luck (or not) would have it, by mid-morning the weather had abated and the loch was now serenely calm.

At noon exactly, *Crusader* was fired up and prepared to attempt to break the record for the world water speed. The timekeepers' boat – *Maureen* – was also in position, although Cobb was extremely annoyed to find that it had been gliding across the lake leaving a wake, instead of staying in the one position as had been instructed. Hindsight is always a convincing tool, but the turn of events could have been so different had the waves and the wake been allowed to subside.

Crusader sped off down the loch in a burst of speed and spray, and the few onlookers watched in wonder as it quickly reached a speed unseen before. Through the measured mile, the boat actually averaged 206 mph, peaking just afterwards at an unbelievable 240 mph, and at one stage it looked as if the craft was hardly touching the water at all. The record was within Cobb's grasp and it looked so stupefyingly easy – but then, disaster.

As the boat decelerated, it hit a wave, causing her to bounce aggressively twice. Somehow ,Cobb attempted to steer the boat to the calm waters, but then another wave hit and the boat buried its nose into the water. There was no explosion or bang to alert the spectators, but just an almost silent whoosh as *Crusader* disintegrated into the loch. In seconds, fragments of the machine were flying terrifyingly into the air, and then the whole craft disappeared under the water. It wasn't clear exactly what had happened, except to say that the wake had immediately destabilised the boat, and the already fragile front planing point just couldn't cope with the pressure. Where the wake had come from will always be a matter of conjecture, with the *Maureen* taking the blame from the immediately ill-informed. Some locals suggested that the famous monster that supposedly lives in the loch had been to blame, as it had been swimming immediately underneath. Whatever the reasons, John Cobb was killed instantly. His injuries were extensive, and it was believed that it was shock that had brought about his end. Ironically, the day before – a Sunday – had seen perfect conditions, but Cobb had respected the locals' traditions and refused to race on the Sabbath.

His wife had watched from the shoreline in horror, and after seeing his body transported back to the pier and then on to the Royal Northern Infirmary in Inverness, she was taken by car back to her home in London in a state of shock. The news was quickly broadcast around the world and, two days later, his body was taken in a hearse from Scotland back to Surrey, where hundreds lined the streets to pay their respects to an unlikely hero.

The timekeepers released their figures and it was confirmed that John Cobb and *Crusader* had reached a speed 206.89 mph on the first run, but of course as there was no second run, it could never be ratified as a record. At one stage, the boat had actually again reached the phenomenal speed of 240 mph, faster than anything seen before on water, but it didn't count.

Cobb was buried in Christ Church in Esher, and a plaque now stands proudly on the banks of the Loch near Glenurguhart near to the place of the accident. It was paid for by the locals. As if to prove the nature of record-breaking, and demonstrate how the elements have to be in tune with the attempt, just 1 hour after the tragic accident, Loch Ness returned to the serene and calm state it had been when Cobb had first looked at it as a place to take the record.

John Cobb was the second person to lose his life while attempting to break one of the most difficult barriers in sport and, shortly afterwards, Reid Railton – the designer of so many successful cars and boats in racing and records – retired at the age of fifty-seven. He had seen too many tragedies.

Within two years, the world of water sport was hit by another tragedy, as the quest to be the 'fastest on water' took yet another victim. Mario Verga was born in Milan in 1910, and had grown up alongside Lake Como. His fascination for speed started at an early age, and in fact was satisfied by racing motorcycles alongside the shore of the lake against numerous friends. Inevitably though, with the close proximity of the water, the attraction of speedboat racing took over. After the war, once he'd become the head of a small factory in Como that made silk screen printed textiles, and money seemed to be of no consideration, he bought himself a small motorboat that was powered by a 250 hp engine. He raced this with limited success on the lake, and soon he was looking for a more powerful and successful craft. That came with the purchase of *Lario I,* a Maserati-powered hydroplane, which he immediately entered for an international meeting on Lake Geneva. He wasn't successful, but he did meet up with a man by the name of Enrico Fracchia, who was to become his personal mechanic. The two then entered as many races as they could with little success, although the continued profits from his silk screen industry meant he could continue to finance his passion.

Like all red-blooded Italians (or so the story goes), he also kept a volatile mistress who seemed to have a big say in his life, and she appeared to gain as much excitement from his racing exploits as he did, although winning was something that eluded him. For many years, Verga had been described in the local press as 'The Eternal Second', which just about summed up his success rate. To try and shake off this unwanted tag, he commissioned a craft, later named *Balbianello,* which was powered by a 2800 cc engine and capable of three-figure speeds. In 1950, he took on fellow Italian Ezio Selva in races across the country in head-to-head battles, but again had to settle for second place. This was after one particular race where the boat flipped, and he was rescued from the water unconscious.

At the age of forty, Verga actually retired from speedboat racing and married Liliana Burlazzi, his second wife. They had a daughter whom they called Laura, and, two years later, when the racing bug hit him again and he came out of his self-imposed retirement, he immediately commissioned a new boat that he named *Laura I.* With this vessel, he finally had the success he'd dreamt of by becoming world champion in the 450 kg class. That was followed by *Laura II,* a larger boat that was powered by an Alfa Romeo 159 engine, the same one that had taken Guiseppe Farina and Juan-Manuel Fangio to the Formula One World Championships. It was an immediate success, and in it he took the 800 kg class at a speed of 140 mph, also winning the Campari Trophy in Milan – beating, among others, Donald Campbell in the *Bluebird* – and once again became world champion.

At that time, Verga had no inclination to chase after a water speed record, feeling quite content to walk away from the sport as a two class world champion, but the Italian Motonautical Federation, mindful of the success of their boats in recent competitions, offered a prize of 5 million lire (quite a lot of money in 1954), for the first Italian boat to break Stan Sayres' record using an Italian engine, Italian fuel and an Italian driver. Verga was immediately hooked, as were two other successful Latin pilots in his old rival Selva, and a pre-war champion called Achille Castoli.

Verga immediately commissioned *Laura III,* a smaller version of Sayres' *Slo-Mo-Shun,* powered by two of the Alfa Romeo engines. It was just less than 23 feet in length, and built of Lameira plywood with streamlined aluminium cowling and tailpiece. Painted scarlet red (at a time when the Ferrari F1 cars were still in their infancy), the boat was stunning. Of the other two, Selva also used a 159 engine for his boat *Moschettiere,* while Castoli fitted an 1800 hp aero engine into his *Mercedes.*

All three went to the United States to compete in the International Grand Prix at the Orange Bowl Regatta, and Verga then went on to become the first Italian to beat American and Canadian pilots at the prestigious Baker Palladium Trophy. That gave him the impetus to continue his quest for the water speed record, but seemed somehow to end the aspirations of the other two. Selva realised that his boat wasn't strong enough to hold the Alfa engine, and immediately withdrew, while Castoli had a huge accident at around 160 mph when the propshaft of *Mercedes* disintegrated. That persuaded the veteran that any further attempts would be too lethal, and so he too withdrew while he was still alive!

Verga continued though and set about testing his boat on the relatively calm Lake Iseo. This stretch of water was ideal, as a local wind called Tivano tended to whip up the surface into small wavelets that were ideal for prop riding the water. Verga was certainly confident, saying he 'had confidence in his ability ... and his boat'. He described her as 'like a stallion. It'll be a job to break her in.'

In the numerous tests that followed, *Laura III* managed to hit speeds of 190 mph, but there were the time-old problems of water cooling and stability. At one stage, neither he nor Fracchia could actually steer the boat in a straight line, and both spent some time examining the left sponson, which appeared to be dragging in the water and pulling the boat to port. There were problems with the front planning shoes that were causing severe turbulence when at high speed, and depending on the condition of the lake, these were altered on a regular basis, so much so that the team had almost become confused at to which setting was the best. All of this was being played out in front of an

American/Italian documentary crew, who were filming his every move, plus a Swiss photography crew, who were also present at every moment of failure. Patience and finances were running thin, and Verga seemed to be taking too many risks. With a cigar and double scotch for good measure in the morning, he would go out in the boat and try numerous settings, in an attempt to get the right stability for an attack on the record. There was no doubt the boat was not ready for an attempt and a delay should have been considered, but the effects of the pressure and the possible prize money was too pervading, and so Mario Verga continued when others may have realised caution.

On the morning of 9 October 1954, Mario kissed his wife and daughter goodbye, sped off at 80 mph on his motorcycle and arrived at the slipway determined to attempt to break the world water speed record. The Tivano wind was causing more than a few ripples on the surface and, despite warnings of the boat's stability problems, at midday, he strapped himself in and set off. The result was inevitable.

At a speed of 190 mph, in excess of Stan Sayres' record, *Laura III*, with its flame-red beauty flashing along the lake with a fountain of spray behind, suddenly lifted into the air, its stern down in the water. It stayed that way for a few agonising seconds before taking off to a height of around 10 feet, catapulting Verga from the cockpit before barrel-rolling numerous times back into the water. The boat destroyed itself on impact and Verga was killed instantly. Later, he and the craft were recovered from the bottom of the lake, and it was established that the volatile Italian had actually died from shock as opposed to any injuries he'd received. He was the third person to die attempting to break the world water speed record, and the second in just two years. The Italian Motonautical Federation never made the offer again, and Verga became another statistic, and sadly a rather unheralded footnote in one of the most dangerous activities in sport.

19

DONALD CAMPBELL DOMINATES

Two major tragedies in the space of two years might have put off many a man, but Donald Campbell was not one of them. He was made of sterner stuff. He was very much the son of his father, and for that reason he wanted to emulate everything his father did. That meant continuing unabated with an attempt at the water speed record attempt. By now, he had divorced his wife Daphne, and had married Dorothy McKegg, but it's fair to say that his domestic life was never one of bliss. Tales of womanising abounded, it took a strong woman to stand silently by while her husband entertained any young female that caught his eye. This was the Donald Campbell of the time.

The other Donald Campbell was one of single-minded pursuit, and once he'd set his mind on achieving something, there was little that could dissuade him. After the accidents that took the lives of Cobb and Verga, he and Leo Villa wanted to make sure they could build a new *Bluebird* that could reach 200 mph safely. For that reason they, and the Norris brothers, studied the film of *Crusader*'s accident frame-by-frame for hours, in an attempt to understand the reasons why she suddenly disintegrated at high speed. It was eventually decided that the design of the new boat needed jet propulsion – something that his father had failed so spectacularly in his last attempt – as that was the only power plant that could propel the boat forward at the required 14,000 rpm. For this reason, Saunders-Roe, who had helped and backed the team for so long, withdrew from the whole project, believing it to be too dangerous. Again, Campbell proved his determination by sourcing an engine, a Metropolitan-Vickers unit called 'Beryl', and had it delivered to his premises. It came with an instruction manual as to how to start it up, and Donald and Leo spent quite some time following the directions to understand the complexities of this new and advanced power source.

The engine developed 4,000 lbs of thrust, and consumed 650 gallons of fuel an hour, plus 3 tonnes of air a minute. It was a fearsome beast, and it was this that was attached to the new *Bluebird K7*. This boat was radical in its design, with its fuselage looking like a jet fighter and two outrigged sponsons giving it an almost crab-like appearance. The cockpit was ahead of the 'Beryl', and if ever a boat looked like it was designed to go fast, then this was it. There were the inevitable financial concerns, and much of the money had come from Campbell's own dwindling pocket, after numerous companies (Castrol being the main one) withdrew their support due to concerns about the safety of a boat that carried such a powerful engine. The prefix K7 came about because 'K' stood for unlimited class, and the '7' was the next in line. Since *Bluebird K4*, there had been two other boats built at this level – *Crusader 6* and *Laura III 5* – as have already been mentioned.

The boat was christened by his wife Dorothy, with almost the same words that Donald had used sixteen years previously when conducting the same duties for his father's boat: 'I name this boat *Bluebird*. May God bless her, and her pilot, and all who work with her.' Lake Ullswater was the venue for the record attempt. Donald had preferred to return to Coniston, but Sir Wakefield, who was the MP for Kendal, had agreed to build a boathouse and slipway on the shore, so, due to political reasons, it meant that the lake would be used, despite its rather unpredictable currents.

This particular attempt had captured the imagination of the press, as Donald had made a huge deal out of the so-called 'water barrier'. This arrived at speeds of around 200 mph, where the centrifugal forces could literally shake boats apart. It was similar to the way the sound barrier was used to inflate the already impressive achievements on land in later years. Neither were likely to cause any more danger than speeds slightly lower, but they made for a great story. Of course, the 200 mph barrier hadn't been reached on water, so many of the journalists who attended in the spring and summer of 1955 were there in the unspoken hope of a bigger story than just a boat going faster than any before.

Sadly for them, any chance of seeing a dramatic speed on the water was unlikely at first, as the bow of the boat refused to lift at full throttle, effectively dampening the engines. They may have found Donald's comments on the whole affair a little more interesting though, as his expletive laden commentary was inadvertently broadcast on a loudspeaker system to all on the lake shore. It helped to keep up the entertainment, at a time when *Bluebird* refused to travel faster than 20 mph without sinking its engines.

Weeks passed with the boat being redesigned regularly: changing the weight distribution and repositioning the tanks. Wind tunnel tests were done, and no fewer than forty-seven changes were made. The stupefyingly bored pressmen filled in their time with games and the spectators disappeared rapidly. Oddly, at this time, the US Navy started to show an interest in the boat, with a view to using the new technology and design in the future, something which enormously impressed Campbell, as well as frustrating the patriot in him, as the Royal Navy weren't showing the same kind of attention.

While all of this was taking place, Donald was carrying on in his usual fashion. There were many on the team, who, even at this early stage, doubted his courage and his ability to lead. Inevitably, he was always compared to his father, and in many ways he came a poor second. Whereas Malcolm was quite aloof with the team members (there are stories of him demanding that all personnel of the team stood to attention when he entered the breakfast room and could only sit down once he had taken his seat), Donald was part of the whole enterprise, 'mucking-in' when needed. Unfortunately, this sometimes translated as someone who didn't know how to take control. Also, his lack of experience at driving anything remotely fast before taking up record-breaking meant that a few members held secret, and not-so-secret, doubts as to whether he could 'cut the mustard'. Craig Breedlove, a later holder of the land speed record, maintained that Donald always drove with 'fear', something confirmed by designer Ken Norris. Fear of course is healthy when attempting to go faster than anyone before, but it didn't always endear him to an already critical and sceptical team and press corps. In fact, in later years, Australian Ken Warby, who is the current holder of the record, also maintains that Donald was 'fearful' when getting into the boat, but knew when to put his 'foot on the throttle'.

The interest from the US Navy had been publicised to such an effect that Campbell had decided to break the record on Ullswater, and then take *Bluebird* to America shortly afterwards to break through the infamous 200 mph barrier there. He felt that there would be more commercial opportunities in the States that would then pay for future attempts. So, the 23 July 1955 was a double-edged sword as far as he was concerned. *Bluebird* was ready even if he wasn't. His bad back – which afflicted him all of his life and was caused by a bad motorcycle crash – was particularly bothersome on this particular day, but he strapped himself in the boat and sped off along the now calm lake. In front of few onlookers (record-breaking, either on water or land, was losing its allure in the now space age), *Bluebird* completed the two runs in an easy fashion at 202.32 mph, smashing the existing record by 24 mph, and of course becoming the first boat to take the record at over 200 mph. He was pleased, but also frustrated, as a lack of radio signal meant that he had no idea what his speed was, and so his plans for taking the 200 mark in America were over there and then. Also, his back was agony and, as he waited for the timekeeper's confirmation, Campbell actually dangled himself from a crane to help ease the stress on his spine! When he did receive the 'good news', his first comments to Leo Villa were, 'The Old Man would have been proud wouldn't he?' His father was always there.

The 'Old Man' surely would have been proud. Some sixteen years after Malcolm last broke the record, Donald – without any real previous experience – had taken it at a speed some 60 mph faster, and in a brand-new *Bluebird*. The Campbell legacy, now in the hands of Donald, lived on, and to prove that he had escaped from the shadow of his father, he bought Leo Villa a Triumph TR2 and the Norris Brothers brand-new Austin cars as an appreciation of their hard work in achieving the record. That was the kind of gesture unlikely to have been seen from Malcolm.

The record had crippled Campbell financially, so an invitation from the Las Vegas Chamber of Commerce to visit Lake Mead in Nevada, 'with a view to attempting the new world record under ideal water and weather conditions', was one that couldn't be ignored. It also helped that NBC had arranged to have the record televised live in their *Wide, Wide World* programme on 16 October, although Donald and the team knew that trying to arrange an attempt on a set day was almost impossible, due to the many variants surrounding such a venture. No matter, the boat was airfreighted on a DC10 (after being almost completely dismantled so that it could fit into the carrier), and Donald and the team soon followed.

October in Las Vegas is like any other month in the glitzy town. Even in the 1950s, it was a venue of gambling casinos, nightclubs and all-night entertainment, and the arrival of the 'fastest boat in the world' just added to the attraction, although many of the visitors and residents were blissfully unaware of the boat and what it had achieved. The team set up in the Sahara Hotel and took *Bluebird* to the man-made Lake Mead, but any thoughts of 'ideal water conditions' were soon erased, as the lake was full of pleasure craft and local swimmers. NBC had arranged for Campbell to make a 'record run' at precisely 1.04 p.m., so that they could broadcast it live to nearly 50 million viewers. Although such a run was impossible, *Bluebird* lined up and waited for the signal to start.

Frustratingly, the lake was full of cruisers, rowing boats and spectator craft, and despite the best efforts of the local rangers, these were allowed to get far too close to *Bluebird*, leaving the inevitable wash for the boat to traverse. Somehow, Campbell pushed the craft to around 160 mph despite it bucking and bouncing all over the water, causing injuries to his shoulders from the safety harness that kept him strapped into the cockpit. He then refuelled and saw to his dismay even more boats edging closer, completely unaware of the problems they were causing to the water and the wash they were leaving. Again, *Bluebird* careered down towards the cameras at the finishing line at around 160 mph, well short of its own record, but impressive bearing in mind the conditions it was travelling on. Of course luck was not on his side, and as Campbell slowed right down, about a mile from the slipway, he ran out of fuel. This would not normally have caused a problem, but as yet more boats sailed closer for a better look, one large pleasure cruiser in particular caused a huge wave, flooding *Bluebird*'s engine, and soon the boat was taking in water. Seeing the craft start to sink, Donald quickly jumped out with mechanic Don Woolley, who almost drowned as he tried in desperation to cover the engine to seal it. The two were rescued and taken to the shore, only to watch in horror as *Bluebird* sank to the bottom of the lake, all of it live on television and in front of 50 million viewers. It was great television for a nation that had started to embrace the medium, but a disaster for Campbell and the team.

It took some 11 hours for the divers to attach cables to the boat and inch it gradually back to the shore, and, at around 1.30 in the morning, the sad sight of *Bluebird*, blackened by the high mineral content of the water, was lit by headlamps of the cars on the shoreline. The boat was badly damaged, but thankfully the 'Beryl' engine was reasonably intact. Almost immediately, a certain Gen. James Roberts, who had watched the proceedings at the lake, offered the full assistance of the Nellis Air Base some 10 miles from Nevada to help with the rebuild. It was there that the mechanics, ably helped by local engineers from the USAF Fighter School, spent long hours completely stripping and rebuilding *K7*.

By 9 November, *Bluebird* was back at the lake ready to run, but then the weather broke and the strong winds caused the boat to be beached for a week. The team filled in their time with the 'attractions' of Las Vegas, Donald in particular who enjoyed the female company of the town. On 16 November though, a record run was possible. The boat lined itself up at the start of the kilometre (the UIM had now decreed that a 1 kilometre run was required as opposed to the old 1 mile), but there were yet more delays. Firstly the timing wire, laid under the water, had been severed and stolen, and it took the local police a little time to locate it and have it relaid; then it was found that one of the timekeepers simply hadn't turned up! He too was located, in a bar and very drunk, and was driven down to the shoreline to take up his position, although not in the state of alertness that was demanded for the job in hand.

The two runs were reasonably uneventful. Crowd control was not a problem this time, as the patrol boats had been very strict about access to the lake. The water was calm enough for *Bluebird* to actually reach around 250 mph as it left the flying kilometre on its first run. That caused a mild panic when it looked like there wouldn't be enough room to slow the boat down, but Campbell zig-zagged as it approached the bank and disaster was averted. The second run was appreciably slower, after it hit a ground swell that was attributed to the severe winds of the previous day, and *K7* found itself airborne for a few dramatic seconds. The mean average was 216.20 mph – a second world water speed record for pilot and boat in four months.

The Americans, who had taken Donald to their heart, celebrated wildly, and that night a large party again enjoyed all the trappings of success. *Bluebird* was put on display by the swimming pool at the Sahara Hotel, and NBC conducted numerous interviews with the quintessential Briton. There was also a communiqué from the Foreign Office in London, congratulating Donald Campbell on the run and praising him and the team for boosting relations between America and Britain, particularly in an area where the United Kingdom was not seen in a particularly positive light. It delighted the patriot in him, as all along he'd said that his endeavours were not just for him, but for country too.

Not long afterwards, his wife, Dorothy, who hadn't made the trip to Nevada, was presenting her own live television show in the United Kingdom called *Quite Contrary*. She'd already received a telegram telling her of Donald's success, but the producer of the show decided he wanted to use the news in a more dramatic way, so engineered a moment at the start of the opening where Dottie was handed the telegram for the first time. The cameras then captured her reaction as she then read out, apparently without prompting, 'My husband Donald Campbell has broken the world water speed record at Lake Mead, and the speed is…' It was a sham, as the marriage was now in severe difficulties and they would be divorced within a year.

During the riotous evening of the record, a guest spoke to Donald and innocently suggested that he should go for the land speed record too, as he could then hold both the records that his father had all those years ago. That simple throwaway remark led to another chapter in Donald Campbell's life.

20

CAMPBELL AND BUTLIN: ALL ABOUT THE MONEY

Money was always a consideration with Donald Campbell. Whereas his father was wealthy and could always rely on the publicity surrounding his record achievements to finance the next step, Donald lived in an era where breaking speed records was hardly noticed at all by investors or the public. In an age where space travel was becoming the next 'big thing', and boys' comics were full of tales of spacecraft and flying saucers, travelling a boat at 220 mph on water hardly captured anyone's imagination. So it was fortuitous that Campbell became very good friends with William 'Billy' Butlin.

Butlin was a self-made millionaire, a man who had sold his campsites to the military during the war, and then bought them back at a fraction of the price and cashed in on the post-war family holiday boom, offering people cheap and cheerful vacations in his holiday parks around the country. He and Donald had formed a friendship, and somehow he'd been persuaded to put up a £5,000 prize for anyone who could break the water speed record in a British boat. As there was only one person who was interested in doing such a thing, it's safe to assume that this idea came from Campbell. He made the most of his opportunity over the next few years.

In 1956, he'd already made up his mind that he would continue to emulate his father and try for the land speed record. He had commissioned a *Bluebird* car to be built and designed by the Norris Brothers, but that wouldn't be ready for few years, so to keep up the momentum of his own profile, he undertook to break the water record again, back at his old and favourite haunt, Coniston. The idea was to eventually break the 250 mph record, but Campbell had formulated a plan that would see him receive the prize money more than just once.

He'd just been awarded the first of his four Segrave trophies, the trophy that was given to the British subject who'd achieved the most in the sphere of transportation on land, water or in the air. He also knew that *K7* had a limit to its top speed, and wanted to manage it effectively so that there was always another 'goal' to reach, in what was soon to become an ageing vessel. He'd been the unwilling recipient of a *This Is Your Life* television presentation (and anyone who has seen the programme will testify that he really didn't want to be a part of it), and in an age where British motor sport superiority was just a moment away, he was by far and away the most recognisable and famous of the lot. He needed to keep that profile if he was to finance an attack on the land speed record.

Sponsorship had started to arrive for a new record attempt – the biggest from Mobil who had agreed to put him under contract for a year, providing he broke the water speed record again, with the promise of more money should he reach 250 mph. He'd also stated a new relationship with a young girl called Dory Swann, and it was with this comfortable and serene outlook that he returned to the lake that he'd called 'a bitch' all those year ago.

Bluebird had received a few modifications since Lake Mead, not least the inclusion of a breathing mask and air bottle should the worst take place, but also a few small aerodynamic changes that would ensure a more stable ride. On 19 September 1956, he took *K7* out on its first run in the late afternoon on a calm and slightly misty day, and ran at a shattering 286 mph! It was nearly 30 mph faster than he'd ever gone before in the boat, which shocked everyone, not least Leo Villa, who was watching from the support boat nearby. He then radioed Leo and told him that he intended to go just as quick on the second run so that the 250 mark would be obliterated. On his return, he managed a far more sedate 164 mph, meaning the average was 225.63 mph, a new record and his third, but far short of what had been promised and certainly expected after the first run.

There were suggestions then, and indeed now, that Donald shocked himself with the speed on that first run, and with his speedo showing that he'd been travelling at 240 mph (it had been affected by water reaching the pitot head and so registered a slower speed), he'd then decided not to run as fast in the second run so that the extra that could be eked out, and *Bluebird* could be saved for another attempt and another prize of £5,000. Campbell said that the boat had behaved so alarmingly on the second run that he was convinced that a stabilising fin had been torn off, but subsequent searches underwater saw no evidence of it. He also had suffered from the fumes that had leaked into the cockpit: '[they] were so bad on the return trip that I nearly passed out and was just doing things automatically. I never had such a ride in my life.'

Whatever the truth, *Bluebird* never had such a poor second run again, and didn't run as fast until the fateful 1967 attempt. Campbell received the Gold Trophy, which was awarded by Billy Butlin, pocketed the first £5,000 prize money and revelled in yet another world record.

At the end of 1956, Donald Campbell was made a CBE, something that clearly delighted him. He was then invited by Canandaigua Lake Promotions to break the record on one of the many lakes in New York State – Lake Canandaigua. With more sponsorship rolling in, an increased deal with Mobil and numerous other small donations, the team shipped the boat out to America in June and set up camp lakeside. The entrepreneurs (CLP), who had invited the *Bluebird* team over, had also invested quite a lot of money in making the area a tourist attraction for the record attempt. New shops, restaurants and spruced-up hotels were prepared, and the profits that were made from the thousands of visitors would then help to finance the rebuilding of the area. They also built a huge Campbell 'theme park', where visitors could watch the team work and the boat run, plus look over his father's old Sunbeam car. There were displays and movies of previous record attempts and the opportunity of meeting Donald in person. Unfortunately though, hardly anyone came. Donald Campbell and *Bluebird* weren't the attraction expected, and the organisers lost a huge amount of money. The lake wasn't really suitable to high-speed running either, and the boat behaved in an erratic way, at one stage taking off at 200 mph after hitting a swell from a pleasure craft, causing Campbell to tell reporters he was 'lucky to come through alive'. The fastest he could get the boat to go on the unpredictable water was around 210 mph, not even close to a record.

The hosts were anxious to recoup some of the money they'd paid, especially as only around 30,000 people had turned up over the weeks, well short of what was expected. They sent the team to the Canadian National Exposition in Toronto where a few exhibition runs took place, and then finally they travelled to Onandago Lake in Syracuse in a last-ditch attempt to challenge for their own record. The place was eerie and unpleasant, with sewage in the water turning it to a dark grey. The team didn't stay long and, as time was running out for another £5,000 prize from Billy Butlin, Donald Campbell made the snap decision to head home and back to the familiar and comfortable surroundings of Coniston Water. Before he left, he did get the chance to witness Art Astbury break the water speed record for propelled-driven boats in *Miss Supertest II* at 184.49 mph, easily beating the previous record of Stan Sayres. Campbell actually had a ride in the boat afterwards, but it seems Astbury deferred when offered a similar opportunity in *Bluebird*.

On 7 November 1957, Donald Campbell increased his record by another 14 mph to 239.07 mph, after the early morning run had seen the boat hit 260. Again, the second was run well under that, but this time it because Leo Villa had witnessed the boat lift at the front with the planing points hardly touching the water. It was his fourth record, and each time it seemed that the increase was by just enough, never quite close to the 250 mark, but certainly enough to break the previous record. Another £5,000 was gladly received, and to prove his patriotism, Campbell then made a long speech to reporters who questioned why he carried on breaking records when there didn't seem to be anyone else even remotely interested in challenging him:

> Let us not forget that despite the activities of Sputnik we are the tops. We hold the world air, land and water records and we intend to see that we keep the lead. It seems to be the fashion of some people to run down the British and Royalty. It makes me sick and nauseated to hear them.

In the same press conference, he also hinted at the building of an incredible amphibian vehicle that would reach 300 mph on water and 500 mph on land. Nothing came of it, but his designs on the land speed record were still a reality.

Before that though, there was yet another record-breaking moment. One year and three days after his fourth water record, Campbell and *Bluebird* set another one. The boat had a few alterations, not least the addition of a tail fin that was supposed to house the slowing-down parachute, but it never worked. As Ken Norris said, 'All it did was get wet and fail to open properly.' There were changes under the boat too, with a water fin added to the transom in an attempt to stop the boat from lifting. The biggest change came from the professionalism of the team, who had now been taken under their wing by BP. They had added a huge sponsorship deal as part of the *Bluebird CN7* car that was nearly ready to attempt the land speed record, and so a purpose-built boathouse and slipway were built. Visitors weren't in any doubt as to who had supplied it, with BP emblazoned everywhere you looked.

Again, the runs weren't without their dramas. Campbell actually made three within the hour, as the first was problematic when the engine drowned once more. It wouldn't reignite, and then the support boat that was due to assist also refused to start, but eventually *Bluebird* hit her speed again and once more it was increased to 248.62 mph, tantalisingly short of the now attainable 250 mark, but that could wait for another day. Another £5,000 prize was gratefully accepted later in London at the Savoy Hotel at a Variety Club lunch where the guests included the new Formula One World Champion Mike Hawthorn, boxer Henry Cooper and actor James Stewart. Campbell's acceptance speech was again aimed at any of the snipers and doubters he perceived weren't taking him seriously:

> A world record perhaps has one meaning above all others. If you today achieve a new record then yesterday's unknown becomes today's known, and above all what you are trying to do is shed light on darkness and to further human knowledge. We are going – God willing – to press on.

Sharing the latest record of course was his partner of two years Dory Swann, and there is a Pathé film of Donald climbing out of *Bluebird* and kissing her gently on the forehead while making a teasing comment. They both looked happy and content, yet within three weeks Donald had married a completely different woman! On the night of the record, he and one of the team, Peter Barker, drove down to London and went to the Embassy Club for a celebratory evening. There they saw a lady called Tonia Bern, a Belgian-born nightclub singer, although the story from Donald is that he saw her that evening as a high-class stripper! Whatever the truth was of their initial meeting, and there are numerous different stories, he met her again the next day. Within two weeks, he had become so smitten that he married her. The newspapers certainly loved the story, as the whirlwind that was Donald Campbell had suddenly fallen for a whirlwind romance. Whatever poor Dory must have thought at the time is not known, but she later moved to the United States and lived in Manhattan for many years in a long-standing relationship with an American man. Donald Campbell and Tonia Bern spent the rest of his life together, although not in the most faithful of relationships on either side.

This level of dominance was not particularly healthy for the outside interests involved in the water speed record. Campbell reigned supreme, and his dream of holding both the water and the land records was uppermost in his mind as the *Bluebird CN7* was taking shape, Astonishingly, while that was being built, he again returned to Coniston to increase the mark once more. It was said that he had become obsessed about reaching a speed of 275 mph, but also adding to his anxieties was the news that at long last there was someone else who seemed keen on taking his record – an American called Les Staudacher.

In 1959, Campbell and the *Bluebird* team returned to their favourite haunt Coniston, with new wife Tonia Bern in tow. It was a relaxed attempt this time, with few problems to encounter. On 14 May, *K7* hit a smooth and relenting Coniston Water at 275 mph on the first run, and then a much slower second run after hitting disturbed water, to record yet another new world water speed record at 260.35 mph. It was his sixth, and this time raised his own mark by 12 mph, and with it another £5,000 prize money. Tonia was delighted and gloried in the success, while Donald only seemed to have one thing on his mind when he got out of his boat. As he said to Leo Villa: 'Unc, now that we seem to have got the old Bird behaving herself, given the right conditions, I'd like to have a crack at 300. I wonder what the Old Man would think of it if he could see me now? D'you think he'd be proud?' As always with Donald, it was father Malcolm he still wanted approval from. The team left Coniston and proceeded to concentrate on the land speed record attempt, leaving the American challengers to do their best on water.

That challenge came in the shape of Les Staudacher. He was a manufacturer who specialised in building hydroplanes, but also had the skill to branch out into a handy sideline in church pews! With pilot Ted Jones, who had unsuccessfully attempted to beat Campbell's old 202 mph record in 1955, they supplied and raced boats in all classes with huge success. It was inevitable that at some time they would attempt to take the water speed record back to the United States and, on 13 May 1959 – one day before Campbell's latest record success – the Aluminium Company of America (ALCOA), along with Staudacher and pilot Guy Lombardo, held a press conference where they displayed a model of *Tempo Alcoa*. This eventually had a 31-foot hull, was 11 feet from sponson to sponson, and was powered by a Korean-war surplus Allison turbojet. It took just over two months to build and, on 27 August 1959, the craft was launched into Saginaw Bay. It nearly ended in total disaster.

Driven by Ted Jones, a very accomplished and able pilot, the boat almost immediately hit 180 mph in a straight line, giving the team the optimism that they could easily attempt the record. One month later, they made their way to Pyramid Lake near Reno in Nevada, and with the press and the timing officials all standing by, *Tempo Alcoa* hit 275 mph easily on at least three occasions before making an official attempt at the record. As the craft slowed for the return run, Jones suddenly cut off the engine, aware that there was a problem, but the vessel refused to slow down. Instead, it veered out of control and hit a spit of land called Pelican Point, immediately became airborne and promptly disappeared over some rocks. Jones and the boat survived, but repairs to both man and machine were necessary before any further attempt.

The following spring, on Saginaw Bay, the boat was testing at high speed when one of the sponsons sheered off and it turned sharply right. The engine was ripped from the hull due to the dramatic force of the action and the vessel quickly sunk to the bottom of the bay. Again Jones escaped unhurt, but Lombardo had come to the end of his patience and decided to walk away from record-breaking attempts. Staudacher was made of sterner stuff though, and the following year he teamed up with Bob Evans, the president of the Nash Motor Co., and the two of them decided to build another boat that could challenge *Bluebird*. This prop-driven hydrofoil was called *Miss Stars and Stripes* I. This gave them the grounding to improve on it and build a fully aluminium engineered follow-up called *Miss Stars and Stripes* II.

That boat was taken to Lake Hubbard in 1961 and was driven by Staudacher – Ted Jones now deciding that water speed record-breaking was no longer for him. Reaching speeds of 200 mph, the boat seemed stable and powerful enough to go faster than any on water before. At 280 mph, the rudder suddenly came loose and the boat then veered sharply to the right, heading for the shoreline and the woods beyond. The fifty-year-old Staudacher fought the wheel and then attempted to climb out of the cockpit, but the wind pressure pushed him back. The boat was totally out of control and smashed onto the shore, ploughing through the dense undergrowth and shearing in half a small tree. Thankfully, Staudacher had somehow managed to jump from the cockpit, but the fall knocked him unconscious. He was rescued around 100 feet from the shore, but had broken virtually every bone in his body. He was a cripple for the rest of his life, and of course the challenge for the water speed record faded fast. Again, it proved the inherent dangers that water speed record-breaking brought, and for some time seemed to deter any who wanted to try to break the now seemingly insurmountable barrier that Campbell and *Bluebird* had set. He, of course, now had more pressing matters to attend to.

23 October 1978: Ken Warby and his jet hydroplane, *Spirit of Australia*, in which he broke the world speed record at an average speed of 510 km/h. He was the first man to break both the 300 mph and 500 km/h barrier. (*Getty Images*)

Donald Campbell in *Bluebird* at speed on Coniston Water. (*Getty Images*)

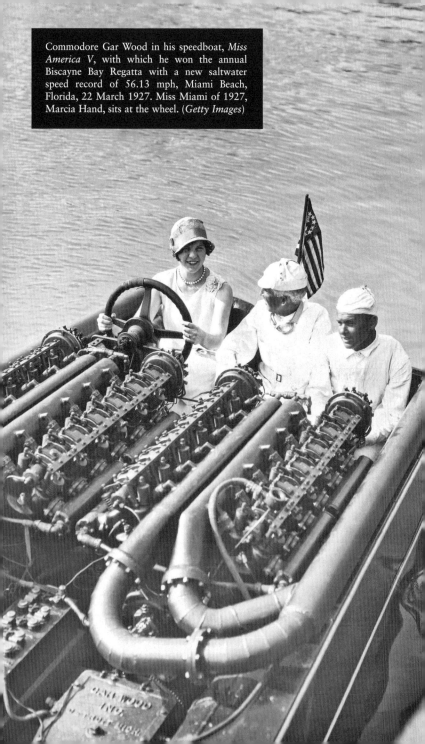

Commodore Gar Wood in his speedboat, *Miss America V*, with which he won the annual Biscayne Bay Regatta with a new saltwater speed record of 56.13 mph, Miami Beach, Florida, 22 March 1927. Miss Miami of 1927, Marcia Hand, sits at the wheel. (*Getty Images*)

Above: Donald Campbell's speedboat *Bluebird K7* crashes at Coniston Water in the Lake District during an attempt on the world water speed record, 4 January 1967. Campbell was killed in the accident, which happened at more than 300 mph on the return run of his record attempt. (*Getty Images*)

Below: Sir Henry Segrave puts on a steel lifebelt to protect himself during a world water speed attempt on Lake Windermere on 13 July 1930. The £25,000 speed boat, *Miss England II* broke the record traveling at 98.76 mph. It later capsized, killing mechanic Victor Halliwell and seriously injuring Michael Willcocks. Sir Henry Segrave died in hospital. (*Press Association*)

The jet-engined *Bluebird*, piloted by Donald Campbell, streaks along Coniston Water, Westmorland, England on 19 September 1956 to set a world water speed record of 225.36 mph. During the run the *Bluebird* touched 286 mph. (*Press Association*)

4 January 1967: British racing driver Donald Campbell's fatal crash while attempting to break 300 mph on water. He was killed when his *Bluebird* turbo-jet hydroplane crashed on Coniston Water, Cumbria, England. (*Getty Images*)

Above: Rescue attempts at the wreckage of *Miss England II* after Sir Henry Segrave crashed after breaking the world water speed record on Lake Windermere, England, on 13 June 1930. (*Press Association*)

Below: Gar Wood, veteran Detroit speed pilot, congratulating Kaye Don, his English rival, on the Detroit River on 6 September 1931, after the latter had beaten Wood's *Miss America* in the first heat of the Harmsworth Trophy races. (*Press Association*)

Right: Sir Malcolm Campbell, piloting his speedboat *Blue Bird II*, set a new world water speed record of 141.74 mph on Coniston Water in the Lake District. He is shown with his mechanics after the record-breaking run at Coniston Water on 19 August 1939. (*Press Association*)

Below: Kaye Don breaking the world water speed record on the Paraná River, Buenos Aires, Argentina, on 14 April 1931 with a speed of 103.49 mph, in Lord Wakefield's *Miss England*. (*Press Association*)

Above: Kaye Don following Gar Wood around the first turn in the course during the first lap of the second heat of the race for the Harmsworth Trophy, at Detroit, Michigan, on 14 September 1931. *Miss England II* leapt into the air when it reached the spot where Wood's boat is in the picture and overturned. (*Press Association*)

Below: Donald Campbell and Leo Villa in the 'side car' after the 140 mph run over Coniston Water, in the racing boat *Bluebird II*. (*Press Association*)

Lee Taylor receives a happy embrace from Rich Hallett, builder of the jet boat *Hustler*, on Guntersville Lake, Alabama, on 1 July 1967. Lee and his craft broke the world water speed record with speeds up to 285.21 mph. (*Press Association*)

Above: Bluebird after being salvaged from the botton of Coniston, thirty-four years after it crashed. (*Getty Images*)

Below: Water speed record holder Ken Warby displays his new boat *Aussie Spirit* in which he hopes to break his own record on Blowering Dam, NSW. Ken set the record in 1978 on Blowering Dam with a speed of 317.6 mph (511.11 km/h). (*Press Association*)

21

LAND AND WATER IN THE SAME YEAR, BUT ONLY JUST!

Despite breaking the water speed record six times, it was the land speed record that Donald Campbell now desired. This was simply because his father Malcolm had been defined by his breaking it, and Donald always required the approval of him in everything he did. During the years that he was busy pushing the water record further and further out of anyone else's grasp, he had also been busy attracting sponsorship and financial backing for an attempt at the land speed record, which at that time was still held by John Cobb at 394 mph (set in 1947). With the help of Alfred Owen in particular, who was head of the Owen Organisation, and whose offshoot company had helped construct the car, along with significant financial input from BP, Dunlop and Lucas, the *Bluebird* team were ready to take on the land speed record in Utah in 1960. The car was a beautifully streamlined monster that had a 4,100 hp gas turbine power unit with four-wheel drive. It looked the part, and as Campbell and the team arrived in stately fashion at the now familiar salt flats in Bonneville, it was his dream to break 500 mph on land and 300 mph on water, and maybe in the same year.

The salt wastes had deteriorated badly since his father had been there in 1935, with the top layer mushy and gripless, but the track had been laid out and the challenge was there. Donald Campbell wasn't to have things his own way though. The Americans, rather tired of British teams coming to their country, wrapping up a speed record and going home, had produced four worthy challengers themselves. All five teams shared the same salt lake that summer of 1960.

Athol Graham, a Mormon preacher, after having a particularly vivid dream about breaking the record, built a rather crude looking device called *City of Salt Lake*, setting set a speed of 344 mph the previous December. He arrived the following year, saying he now needed to know nothing else about speeds below 400 mph, and was ready to smash the record once conditions prevailed.

There was Californian hot-rod star Mickey Thompson, who, with a very small team, had built a device that was named *Challenger I* and had gone even faster than Athol at 362 mph. With the added superchargers that he had bought, he was convinced that the LSR would be his before the year was out.

Then there was Art Arfons. He'd brought along his *Green Monster,* a car not too dissimilar to *Bluebird,* with its 3,800 hp engine, but the least attractive. There was also seemingly the most effective car, the *Flying Caduceus* with Dr Nathan Ostich at the wheel. This was a pure jet-engined machine that could produce 7,000 lbs of thrust, and although it looked decidedly weird, it certainly was fast enough to take a record – although, at first it wouldn't be recognised by the FIA (Federation Internationale l'Automobile), due to it not having driven wheels, but it was soon the norm when it came to land speed record attempts.

While Campbell and the *Bluebird* team made slow and testing runs up and down the salt flats in an attempt to get to know the car, Graham decided that he was ready to make an immediate attempt in the *City of Salt Lake*. He'd been cautioned about the crosswinds but had disregarded the advice and, watched by the other four pilots, plus his wife and son, he sped off down the black painted line. At a speed of around 300 mph, the car lost traction and went off course, hit by a severe wind. It then veered into a sideways tumble, ripping the tail fin off, somersaulted and eventually landed upside down after a series of barrel rolls. The car was destroyed and Athol Graham lay there with a broken spine. He died on his way to hospital.

The story of that car didn't end there though. After an insurance pay out, his wife Zeldine paid for son Anzjon, then seventeen years of age, to return two years later in the rebuilt machine to try again. It was another disaster with more horrifying accidents and sadly, shortly afterwards, Anzjon died of leukaemia. Astonishingly, a year later Zeldine financed another attempt with driver Harry Muhlbach at the wheel, but for the third time the car crashed badly and he was lucky to walk away. It was only the sponsor's (Firestone) refusal to back her anymore that persuaded the insistent Zeldine to give up on the dream by 1964.

This first avoidable tragedy that summer persuaded Arfons to withdraw *Green Monster*, as he felt the car wasn't yet ready, but in later years he was to return and break the land speed record three times. Ostich proceeded to have so many problems with his challenger that he effectively gave up after two terrifying runs at over 300 mph, where the *Flying Cadaceus* veered alarmingly off course and only the braking parachute saved it and Ostich from disaster. Thompson, who had become good friends with Campbell despite him being an all-American type compared to Donald's typically British stiff-upper-lip countenance, was the closest to success. His *Challenger I* actually reached a speed of 400 mph on one of his runs and nearly had the record in his grasp, until a drive shaft broke on the return to thwart him. After repairs to the car, the salt had then reached a new low in its compatibility, and he too gave up. So, again it was left to the British *Bluebird* team to take the record once more. As ever, it didn't go according to plan.

Donald Campbell was quite a superstitious man. He'd always carried a small teddy bear in his cockpit called Mr Whoppit and, as a religious man, he attached a St Christopher's medal to the steering wheel of his car and boat challengers. The latter, in particular, seemed to have been necessary on the run that very nearly killed him. Before he'd arrived in Bonneville, he'd spoken to a psychic who spoke of a premonition that he wouldn't return alive. The events of 16 September 1960 were to be a serious warning as to how dangerous the whole record-breaking business really was.

Bluebird, by now adept at speeds of 300 mph after numerous runs and tests, sped off down the black line with Campbell intent on attempting a record run. This was despite the strong advice from Leo Villa and other members of the team, who were erring on the side of caution as they didn't believe the car was quite ready. Campbell was insistent. It may have been because he genuinely felt he and the machine were ready, or rather more likely because the whole attempt was eating into the finances. With the Bonneville Salt Lake costing around $1,000 per day to rent (and this was back in 1960 remember), it would be advantageous to go for the record as soon as possible. Whatever the reason, it was a bad decision.

As CN7 reached about 350 mph, it veered off course in a way similar to *City of Salt Lake*. Soon it was spinning sideways, and there seemed to be no attempt by the pilot to correct its course. That was followed by a series of rolls, a jump into the air, then a few bounces on the ground, before resting on its side two wheels down after an enormous skid. Campbell was still strapped in the cockpit when the distraught team finally arrived, Tonia being told to stay clear for fear of what she may see. Donald suffered a cracked skull, a pierced eardrum and cuts and bruises all over his body, and was immediately taken to hospital. The car was completely wrecked. The land speed record stood and all five challengers had failed.

Donald Campbell later said that he felt his brain had been affected by the oxygen supply being pumped into his helmet, which had made him light-headed when he was driving. That may have explained his lack of reaction when the car veered off course, but it hadn't affected his sense of humour. He reportedly said to Tonia, in the ambulance on the way to the hospital, that she shouldn't worry too much as he'd checked and the 'crown jewels' were still in one piece! The press back in Britain reported that he'd survived the fastest accident in history, and Alfred Owen – so impressed with the bravery and courage of his pilot – promised that if Campbell wanted to try again, he would finance a complete rebuild of the car. This was an astonishing gesture, bearing in mind the whole failed project had cost in the region of £40,000 in 1960s terms.

Campbell recovered from his skull fracture, but the psychological problems emanating from such a serious crash would stay with him for many years. Despite that, after a year of recuperating, he was ready to start another project. He was now ready to go for the 'double', the water and the land speed records in the same year.

Donald suffered from many panic attacks following his accident, and was advised by doctors to give up on his land speed record aspirations, but he was never going to be someone who would listen to such things. These attacks came in all forms, such as driving down the highway at 20 mph while other cars beeped ther horns at him for going too slow. He had become scared of travelling among other traffic. He carried on regardless. The car was repaired, as opposed to rebuilt, as promised by the now Sir Alfred Owen, and was ready for another attempt in 1962. The relationship between Owen and Campbell had sadly suffered during the time Donald had been recuperating, with the industrialist insisting publicly that he was the owner of the team as he'd spent so much money on the project. Campbell countered that Owen was just a sponsor, although a big sponsor at that. With the tensions behind the scenes mounting, and the questions about Campbell's suitability as a driver being raised regularly, it was essential that a record bid take place as soon as possible.

Utah was rejected by Campbell, as he really had no desire to return to the place, and so Lake Eyre, 450 miles inland from Adelaide in Australia, was chosen, helped by financial and local employment inducements from the Australian government. The place was about as inhospitable as anywhere on the planet, although a sheep station some 37 miles away would be used as a base station for the team.

The vast, dried lake was to be converted into a track, for the car to take the record at 400 mph with the help of a local workforce. This team wouldn't include any of the Aboriginals, as they regarded the place as a plague and wouldn't go anywhere near it. It was a 4,200 square mile of dried mud, in a desert of 500,000 square miles and a place that could kill a man in a moment. There is a story told of an Australian family who, one day in 1963, set off to the lake to watch the *Bluebird* team in action, only for their car to break down in the empty surroundings. They were found some time later after dying of thirst and dehydration.

It hadn't rained on the lake since 1955, but of course the moment the new CN7 was put on display at an exhibition in Adelaide, the rains poured and poured relentlessly. The attempt was postponed for a year and the cost continued to rise.

The following year, the team set up camp and attempted to run the car at low speeds, but the weather had decided not to accommodate them, and for the second year it poured it down. At one stage, it rained so heavily that the team had to rescue *Bluebird* before she sunk, but this did little to negate the intense criticism that Campbell was attracting back in the UK. The few pressmen who had accompanied the team to Australia had been bored senseless by the lack of activity, and had openly questioned why he hadn't run the car at higher speeds before the predicted rains had arrived. This had been reported back in Great Britain, with many commentaries suggesting that he didn't have the courage to drive the car at any high speed following his crash in Utah. This wasn't helped when Stirling Moss, the country's greatest racing driver and a man revered in motoring circles around the world commented, 'I believe a racing driver would have a better chance than a professional record-breaker. Campbell carries the image of being a motor racing driver, and this is unfortunate for the motor racing industry ... I do not think he has ever driven a racing car in his life.' The most damning criticism came from Sir Alfred Owen, who suggested that too much time had been spent on publicity, and that he and the country were disappointed in Campbell. It made for a fractious time.

The team returned in 1964, but all the poorer for the withdrawal of BP as a sponsor. They'd wanted to replace Campbell as the manager of the team, but Campbell refused as it had been his team since day one. One by one, other sponsors also withdrew, and it was left to a smaller Australian oil company to come up with extra funds to keep the attempt on track. There were also huge tensions within the team, with more rain delays causing tempers to be frayed once more. For the umpteenth time, Campbell was being questioned openly about his ability to drive the car, especially as he'd reported severe vibrations at runs of around 300 mph, something the Dunlop tyre representative and substitute driver Andrew Mustard refused to believe. Leo Villa eventually found that the salt from the lake bed was affecting the wheel alignment, but Mustard and other members were dismissed after lengthy disagreements. Campbell also had problems with the official stewards, who had proposed that he be replaced as they felt he wasn't fit enough to drive a car at that speed, citing his panic attacks from the old accident and a nervous disposition. Donald dealt with them in the same way, by simply dismissing them.

Back in the United Kingdom, *Bluebird* was becoming an embarrassment, and the subject of constant ridicule in the newspapers. Cartoon drawings regularly lampooned him, claiming Campbell was no nearer to becoming the hero his father was than if he'd never set foot in a record-breaking machine. Somehow, through all of the adversity (including more rain delays), a lack of finance, a lack of support on a personal level from people who he trusted and some simple bad luck, he finally succeeded.

On 17 July 1964, Donald Campbell finally achieved his dream of emulating his father, and broke the land speed record. The two runs, of which the second saw the tyres sheer rubber at a frightening rate, created a mean average of 403.10 mph (actually both runs were exactly identical!), and so not only smash through the 400 barrier, but break the seventeen-year-old record by 9 mph. It was a moment to savour after all of the criticism, but he seemed to accept it with a trace of bitterness, believing that the car could have gone even faster had the conditions been better. As he told motoring correspondent and respected author Cyril Posthumus, 'I felt a wave of resentment that it all had to be so difficult, and relief that I'd got the bastard at last.'

One of the interesting stories to come out of the record success was one Donald told numerous times afterwards. He said that, as he sat alone in the cockpit, he saw his father in the reflection of the windshield, who looked at him and said, 'Now you know how I felt then (referring to his experience back in 1935 on the same salt flats), but it'll be alright boy.' Whether this happened or not, it was a great way of embellishing an already impressive story.

For the third time in history, following Henry Segrave and his father Malcolm Campbell, the land and water speed records belonged to the same man. Now it would be time to try for the record of holding them both in the same year. That was to be achieved, but by the time it took place, the land version had been blasted to 536 mph!

The success of the LSR was appreciated by what seemed like most of Australia, even if back in Great Britain it hardly registered a murmur. In fact, the well-respected *Motor Sport* magazine had more than a few disparaging things to say about the whole project, suggesting that the speed was a let-down when the finance it took was taken into consideration. The press coverage took on the tone of 'about time' rather than a celebratory one, while, in Australia, Campbell was feted wherever he went. *Bluebird* did a demonstration run on the streets of Adelaide, and thousands cheered him on, followed by numerous civic ceremonies and celebrations. The team effectively disbanded, and sadly tales of bonuses not being paid became the norm, leaving a bitter taste with the individuals who were left out of pocket. This was while Sir Alfred Owen gloried in the success and Donald Campbell enjoyed the trappings of fame. It's interesting to note that many years later, a certain Ken Warby (now the current 'fastest man on water') witnessed the aftermath of the Lake Eyre success, and the subsequent water record that followed. Despite his utmost admiration for Campbell, he was very critical of the way Donald played up to the notoriety and fame. Like his father, publicity became like oxygen to him, and in business dealings he had inherited his father's way with money. One of the criticisms aimed at Campbell by Warby, was that all of the expenses on his Australian jaunt were charged to *Bluebird*, but '*Bluebird* didn't have a bank account!'

After the celebrations died down a little, Donald Campbell and his much smaller *Bluebird* team then started to look for a suitable lake for *K7* to attempt a seventh water speed record. They were initially invited to a lake called Bonney. This was about 150 miles from Adelaide, and at first seemed ideal. The boat was transported there, and Campbell seemed to be more at home in the cockpit of the *K7* than he ever was in *CN7*. Unfortunately the rains, which had been blight on his time in Australia for so long, came once more and the lake found itself flooded. The snow on the mountains nearby was also beginning to melt, and so gallons of water were dispersing into the lake, meaning that *Bluebird* had no chance of reaching its maximum. As early December, a new lake was sourced.

Lake Dumbleyung near Perth was finally chosen, helped somewhat by generous offers from the local mayor (of a population of around 400), who, seeing an opportunity for some great publicity for his small town, promised to make any amenity available to the team while they were attempting the record. This entailed building a new slipway, a boathouse and offering 'accommodation' by the lake – consisting mainly of caravans. It wasn't ideal, but it was good enough. The lake was 6 miles long and 3 miles wide, which was just about enough. The only downside, apart from the isolation of the place, was that usually around 3 p.m. every day, it was visited by a wind called the Albany Doctor, named for no apparent reason apart from the fact that Albany was nearby. This would manifest itself on the water with large 4-foot waves, which would race across the surface at an impressive speed.

The team arrived during both the duck hunting and water skiing season, meaning that both were suspended for the duration of the team's stay by the mayor. This was actually not resented by the locals, as the excitement of a water speed record on their lake was recompense enough. Of course, the ducks soon got used to the idea of not being shot at and spent a lot of time on the lake getting in the way. They had to be scared off each time the boat took to the water by firing blanks in their direction. There were also numerous old gum trees sticking out of the water that needed clearing, something that caused a fair amount of discord. By the middle of December, everything was ready for yet another attempt at the water speed record.

Of course there were many delays with the weather once more refusing to co-operate. The timing equipment had to be flown from Perth, as did the timers who cost a lot of money. Christmas came and went, with *Bluebird* taking to the water just a handful of times and reaching respectable speeds. Each time, a new swell arrived, or high winds curtailed the run. Finally, on the last day of the year, and of course on the very last day that the 'double' could be completed, the weather relented. It was very nearly missed by Campbell, as in his desperation he'd set off in his small plane to look for another lake nearby, but a local waterskier had raced back to Leo Villa, after being out on the lake to say that the centre was as smooth as glass. This meant a panic-stricken drive to the airstrip to alert Donald, who took off anyway to inspect the water from mid-air. Very quickly, he was back at the shore, and without even changing into his overalls, he climbed into the cockpit wearing a t-shirt, shorts and fabric helmet with his radio device, and set off to break the record.

It went smoothly, apart from Campbell stalling the engine at the start. *Bluebird K7* set a new water speed record of 276.33 mph, with the Albany Doctor following at a similar rate. Tonia swam out to greet her husband as the boat cruised to a halt. Once on the shore, Donald asked the handful of spectators to bow their head in memory of his father, who had died sixteen years earlier on that date.

Donald Campbell had achieved his dream of breaking the land and speed records in the same year, although his land record had been broken four more times since July, and was now 133 mph faster under Art Arfons. He was at the top of his profession, yet his words in an interview in Australia show a certain weariness in the constant probing into why he continued:

> The question is always asked, what good do these attempts do? Well, if the human race no longer wants to better the four-minute mile, conquer Everest, the skies and the oceans, then it will stagnate.

22

1967: THE DEFINING YEAR

On his return to England, Donald Campbell seemed to become a quite sad and unhappy man. His relationship with Tonia started to fall apart, as had all of the previous ones in his life, and the recognition he'd craved just didn't materialise in his home country. The people of Great Britain just weren't interested in record-breaking anymore; the 'swinging sixties' had taken hold, British music had taken over the Western world and England had won the World Cup. With the excitement of the space race between the United States and the Soviet Union heating up, the fact that a car could travel at around 500 mph or a boat at nearly 300 was of little interest. The knighthood he'd so clearly craved never came, and so Campbell was lost. His water speed record was under threat by an American called Lee Taylor, and it was maybe this that persuaded Donald to bring the old *K7* out of its resting home for a crack at 300 mph. It may also have been a way of publicising his next dream, building a car that could travel at the speed of sound, plus an amphibian vehicle that could travel at unlimited speeds on land and water.

The *CN8* was the jet car that he'd asked the Norris Brothers to design, so that an attempt at the speed of sound could be undertaken by the early '70s at least. They had taken the project seriously, but when Donald had organised for a model to be displayed at his Roundwood house, with the press invited, the response was completely underwhelming. No one seemed interested at all. Add to that a huge bill for damage to *CN7* after it was crashed by a reserve driver in an exhibition run, Campbell was again short of funds. His answer to the problem was to take *K7* to a new water speed record of 300 mph on Coniston Water again. It would be his eighth water record, and a precursor to a bigger attempt that would eventually see him break the sound barrier on land.

Coniston – 1966/67

The events of the record attempt in the last months of 1966, and the first few days of 1967, have been documented so thoroughly and regularly ever since, that there is little if nothing that I can add to the story. So much has been said, theorised, guessed at and fantasised, that all I can do is attempt to relate the events leading up to one of the most shattering news stories in recent times in chronological order – a 'moment in history' that has defined all record-breaking attempts, whether on land, water, or indeed air. From the moment Donald Campbell had the discussion with Leo Villa about resurrecting the *Bluebird*, to the last moments on the surface of Coniston Water, the Campbell story had taken on a new dimension. Yet it was never meant to be that way.

The team arrived in the beautiful and haunting Lake District in early November 1966. It was a threadbare effort compared to previous visits, with the biggest absence being that of any real notable sponsorship. BP had steadfastly refused to supply any finance, or fuel the endeavour, despite an almost pleading and begging letter from Campbell. One of their internal mail letters suggested that he would 'carry on until he killed himself', and that wasn't something they wanted to be involved in.

The familiar boathouse was supplemented by a rudimentary blue tarpaulin sheet to keep out the rains, and a small caravan was used for shelter and, among other things, a telephone for the handful of press who had bothered to turn up. In fact, there seemed to be hardly any interest at all from the media, and the crowds were conspicuous by their absence. *Bluebird* looked as sleek and as purposeful as ever, even if now rather dated, but even before the team set up camp properly, there was a bad omen. The driver of the transporter that carried the boat attempted a short cut to the slipway to avoid a tree, and managed to get totally stuck in the cloying mud of the adjacent field. It took some time for it to be retrieved.

The boat was equipped with a run-in Orpheus engine, with a new tail fin added to the craft to give more stability. Add to that the new paint job, and in effect it was almost like a new challenger for the locals to delight in. The local population of Coniston had very much taken the Campbells to their hearts over the years, and each time a record was set on 'their' lake, they embraced the glory. It's fair to say that they were, and still are, very protective of the *Bluebird* years of both father and son. It's said that the initial resting place of the *K7* at the bottom of the lake was a closely guarded secret by the good people of the village, determined to allow things to be kept peaceful and undisturbed. The author encountered that same protectionism a few years ago, when innocently asking a shopkeeper where the cottage was that housed the slipway for the numerous record attempts. She quite cheerfully told me, and it was only later that I realised she'd sent me in totally the opposite direction! It was deliberate as she had been there for most of her life, and the cottage in question was no more than a mile from where we stood at that time.

The mood of the camp that November wasn't helped by the weather. The Lake District is truly one of the most spectacular and stunning places in the United Kingdom, with Coniston in particular a jewel in a glittering crown. It can also be numbingly cold. The wind can sweep across the lake and penetrate any outer protection, plus the rain unleashes its torrent on a regular basis. At that time of the year, you can watch as the snow caps of the hills and mountains that surround the lake creep lower and lower as the winter weather takes hold. Strong cups of coffee and industrial heaters were called for and it has to be said that never has record-breaking seemed less glamorous. Add to the fact that it was being played out to a virtually solitary environment, and there must have been times when it became simply soul-destroying, but Donald Campbell and his loyal, small team just carried on.

They were forced to carry on when the 709 Orpheus engine (which had a further 1,000 lbs thrust added) decided to suck out the rivets of the air intakes during a static test. It was effectively destroyed there and then, and with immediate haste a couple of men were despatched down to London at 10 p.m. to pick up a replacement 711 Orpheus, returning after an hour's rest so that it could be fitted the next day. That in itself was a remarkable achievement, bearing in mind how few motorways existed back in 1966.

For the next week or so, while checking the new engine and launching the boat for a few low-speed tests, gale-force winds caused all kinds of problems for the team in the freezing conditions of the boathouse. The plastic sheeting was being ripped from the scaffolding, and the whole exercise was becoming more and more miserable.

The team had set up their base camp at the Sun Hotel, run by Connie Robinson. This had become a real home for Donald and the rest, and in fact she'd behaved almost like a mother towards him. She had been part of the previous attempts when running the hotel, preparing sandwiches and coffee each and every day. It seemed to be a place where he felt comfortable and protected, and every night he would hold court with the members of the team and the few press people who had stayed on. Sadly, Tonia didn't stay long. She'd now decided she wanted to pick up her old show business career and had stopped enjoying the numerous record attempts. She left and returned to London, but it's fair to say that the marriage was unravelling at that time anyway.

The problems continued. The weather played a big part in the struggles and the stability of the boat came into question, especially when Donald kept on 'putting out the fire'. Every time he pressed the accelerator, *Bluebird* plunged downwards at the nose, allowing water to enter the engine and cutting it off – this was sorted when Leo decided to tie some heavy sandbags to the rear to see if the weight at the back would counteract the problem. It did and the team had to go about looking for heavy sheets of lead to add to the boat as ballast. At one stage, a seagull flew straight into the cockpit when the boat was at speed. This killed the poor bird and very nearly killed Donald. It made for good newspaper headlines, although it was difficult to tell whether there was a hint of sarcasm and ridicule in the way they reported the incident.

On one of the runs, the boat hit a submerged log and slightly damaged one of the sponsons, but soon, on successive outings, Donald got the old boat up to around 200 mph. It was difficult, and his moods, of which there had always been quite a few, were progressively becoming worse. There are pictures and film archive of Donald Campbell at that time clearly looking stressed and haggard. The glint in his eye had gone and the whole episode was something that had stopped being enjoyable. It was hardly surprising that the press coverage was for the most part quite negative, despite claims he was doing it for the old Queen and Country. One esteemed journalist who spoke to Campbell's biographer David Tremayne – Geoffrey Mather of the *Daily Express* – said he felt that Donald retained 'the jargon of war long after it ended'. As the boat progressed slowly to its ultimate goal, so Campbell seemed to regress to an inner state of unhappiness. Many observers have suggested that he drank too much, and there are numerous stories of empty brandy bottles. For a man who was putting his life on the line on a regular basis with seemingly no one caring about it, that might be understandable? Campbell said to Mather:

> You've got to believe what you're doing, no matter what that is. Money is sugar
> in the tea, but no amount of money can make a man do something he hasn't
> got within himself. You know the old story, before the curtain goes up or the

bell rings, the old stomach is turning over at a rate of knots, the adrenalin is pumping through the system. You know, well we've all got this fright process. There are days when you're at a low ebb, and days when you are high. I can get frightened during an attempt and before it. You need to be frightened. It is like a curve, if you could plot it. If you are not frightened, you are a dead duck, and if you are too frightened then you slip down the other side. The act of dying? That most certainly worries me. I enjoy this life far too much, but you can be just as frightened of failure.

They were interesting words, and saw deep into the soul of the man who was struggling with the reasons to carry on. Financially, the team were in trouble too. The whole attempt was costing around £10,000 in 1960s terms, and only a tenth of that had been sourced away from Campbell's wallet. It was clear that the whole escapade had to be successful for any remuneration to make it worthwhile. The delays continued when, on 20 December, heavy snow on the tarpaulin distorted the scaffolding poles around *Bluebird*, and trapped her until the whole thing could be dismantled. It was frustrating as the day had been clear and the lake calm. On another day, the official attempt had to be cancelled when word had got out that the boat was about to go for a record. This meant that hundreds of cars packed the small country lane that perimetered the lake, meaning the timekeepers couldn't get to their positions! The local police had the frustrating job of calling off the run.

On 21 December, Campbell fell out with officials, who had rightly said they wanted to go home for Christmas. One-by-one, the team all said their goodbyes and returned to the bosom of their families for the festive holidays. It meant that Campbell was virtually alone over the Christmas period, but on Christmas Day he took *Bluebird* out on the lake and managed around 250 mph in one run, certainly the fastest she'd gone since the return to Coniston. The next day (Boxing Day), Campbell went even faster and recorded an unofficial 285 mph. It didn't impress Leo Villa when he returned, as he rightly felt it was an unnecessary risk, especially if the boat had hit a problem and there was no support for either pilot or vessel. It proved a point to Campbell though, and he entered 1967 convinced that an eighth water speed record was within his grasp.

In between those runs and the fateful day in early January, Campbell had also fallen out with the radio technicians who supplied the equipment for communication between himself and the team on the support boats and on the shore. Thankfully, an Army corporal came to the rescue. In a way, this constant tension surrounding the dealings with people belied a harmonious and happy team who believed in what they were doing with a siege mentality. It didn't matter that the rest of the country had long since lost interest in what they were trying to achieve, they *knew* what it was they were attempting. It's testament to his popularity that Donald Campbell kept his small band of helpers and employees together, even in the worst extremities of adversity.

On New Year's Eve, Campbell threw a fancy dress party for everyone still at the Sun Hotel. It was a raucous and enjoyable evening, but at the stroke of midnight a sombre mood fell over it when Donald shook the hand of every man and woman in the room to thank them for their efforts. He reduced Connie to tears by describing her as a 'darling Mum to us all', and he goaded some of the journalist who had written constant negative articles about this latest attempt. It was two years since he'd last broken a record and eighteen years since his father had passed away. Everyone who was there that night said that Campbell was in a very reflective mood.

The night of 3 January saw Campbell in a pensive mood again. Hindsight is always a great tool to use when talking of the past, but the stories that have emanated from the Sun Hotel that evening suggest that there was almost a sense of foreboding about him. One of the main tales to have gathered momentum was when Donald played Russian patience and turned up the ace of spades followed by the queen. This was supposed to be the 'death' combination and prompted Campbell to say to David Bensonone, one of his journalist friends, 'That's it. Mary, Queen of Scots, drew the same combination the night before she was beheaded.' Benson told him not to be silly and concentrate on another game, but later Campbell was heard to remark, 'I have the most awful premonition that I'm going to get the chop this time. I've had the feeling for days.' Again his friend told him to cheer up and that it would soon be all over, but the reply was, 'Well, it's somebody in my family that's going to get the chop. I pray to God it's not me.'

Since these stories were reported, people closer to him, including daughter Gina, have denied he could ever have said such a thing, suggesting it would be completely out of character. It's also worth noting that the night Mary Stewart supposedly turned over her own cards, she was aware of her fate in the morning anyway, and so it wouldn't have affected her destiny no matter which combination of cards she'd played with. In a way, it's all a little trivial on its own, but it does give an insight into the state of Campbell's mind on the eve of another attempt at what was becoming the most dangerous of endeavours. His last telephone conversation with wife Tonia has been extensively reported, and for accuracy's sake, I repeat it here so that any reader can make up their own minds:

Tonia: Hello?

Donald: Hello Bobo, how did it go?

Tonia: Oh marvellous. I'm the toast of Bristol, didn't you know?' (a reference to her show she was appearing in in the city)

Donald: Now listen darling, I'm going for the record tomorrow?

Tonia: Tomorrow?

Donald: Yes, I've told all the press and television boys. It's all set. My time's up now.

Tonia: You promised them?

Donald: The Boat Show starts tomorrow, you understand.

There was a pause on the end of the line.

Donald: I've been outside. No wind, and the conditions are perfect. I've got it all worked out. We'll go to the Boat Show, celebrate, have a few laughs, then fly off to Courchevel, do some skiing. How about that? I've already cabled Gina, it's all laid on.

Again there was another pause.

Donald: Bobo are you there?' (Bobo was an affectionate name he called Tonia in their time together)

Tonia: Oh yes Donald. I'm sorry. Listen, I'm coming up there. I want to be with you.

Donald: Oh, you will be with me, don't worry. As soon as this is over we'll go away, we'll have a wonderful time. Just you and me.

Tonia: Darling I should be there. I'm your mascot.

Donald: Don't worry, Mr Whoppit will look after me. He's always here.

Tonia: Go get some sleep yes?

Donald: Yes I will. Don't worry about me.

Tonia: And you don't take any pills, you old hypochondriac.

Donald: 'No, I won't. *A bientot*.

Tonia: *Bientot*.

Another pause.

Donald: Bobo? Do take care of yourself, won't you? You're awfully important to me, you understand?

There was then silence.

Tonia: Donald?

Silence again.

This conversation was made public by Tonia in her book on Donald, although there have been numerous suggestions that it may have been slightly embellished. Nonetheless, it paints a rather sad and almost tragic picture, bearing in mind how the next day's events were to unfold.

On 4 January 1967, Donald Campbell walked down the slipway at around 8 a.m. towards the waiting *Bluebird*. The conditions seemed right for a run, with the lake calm, although Leo Villa later said that he'd advised Donald against making a run due to the water not being exact, but was told, 'Don't mess about Unc, let's get her out.' He'd effectively brushed past the handful of pressmen who were present, but, without attempting to make each and every act of those final moments significant beyond the norm, it seemed as if he was in a hurry to get the whole thing over with. This was a record attempt that was being played out to a totally disinterested country, with little or no financial backing, and for what seemed a personal crusade to constantly prove himself as good as his father. The omens weren't good, but then if the attempt had been successful, none of this would have mattered.

Ten minutes later, he was strapped into the cockpit, but there was a delay while Mr Whoppit was located. Once found, Campbell was ready to go, announcing he would make a few slow runs to test the water. By this time, a few spectators had arrived along the shore, and it finally appeared that a record was about to be witnessed and yet more history made. The 'slow runs' were not to be taken seriously, as Donald had made up his mind to go for the record there and then. To be fair, all the team knew that to be the case. The support boats were in place, the timekeepers in position and the television and film cameras at the ready. After all of the frustrations of the previous few months, this would be the successful result that should again capture the public's imagination and give Campbell that step up to the proposed 'speed of sound' barrier he'd talked openly about.

At 8.45 a.m., *Bluebird* raced off in a flurry of spray and noise, disappearing quickly into the distance. The first run down the south of Coniston Water was actually the best Campbell had ever made in the boat. It flew majestically without a blip of complaining murmur. As ever, Donald gave full commentary to his team as he was driving, and it's appropriate to reprint it here to give an idea as to how the whole attempt was shaping up:

> I've got a fair amount of water here and, er, without the mask on, just as soon as I'm heading down the lake, er ... don't know. Here we go, here we go, here we go.

Four and five coming up. A lot of water. Nose beginning to lift. Lot of water coming again … and the nose is up. Left and right sponsons are up. It's up and away. Vision clear. Tramping very hard at 150. Very hard indeed. Trying for full power, I still can't get over the top. Full house, full house, full house. Now that's three.

The words may not make a lot of sense to the uninitiated, but the three referred to the fact that the boat had reached 300 mph and already the latest record was within his grasp. All it needed was another run of similar dimensions, and he and the team could celebrate, pack up and go home. Sadly, what happened next has baffled and bemused many people since, and has only gone on to add to the myth and legend that has become Donald Campbell.

The normal scenario after a first run was for Donald to talk to Leo Villa extensively and wait for permission to start the second run in the opposite direction. The rules state that it had to be completed within an hour of the start of the first run, so there was a lot of time and no need to rush. Afterwards, Leo stated he was surprised that, among the many radio conversations that took place as the boat came to a stop, only one was directed to him. Immediately, there seemed to be a problem with the link as he couldn't reply. It seemed inconceivable that the only radio link to have failed at that crucial time would have been the one from Donald to himself. Writing in his book, *The World Water Speed Record*, he said, 'I could hardly believe my ears when I heard, "Stand by. Am making my return run." Helpess, I stared down the lake.'

It was barely 4 minutes since the first run and *Bluebird* hadn't refuelled, so was lighter than before. The lake was still agitated with the wake of the boat, especially as Donald had used the water brake on the transom to stop. Then, in an act of complete mystery, Campbell set off on a second run without any thought to these problems. This was not an amateur who had no understanding of the patience and respect that a record attempt needed, nor was he someone who didn't understand the vagaries of water conditions in moments like these. This was a man who had broken the land speed record and done the same on water *seven* times! That alone made the decision to set off again so quickly, without the guidance of Villa and his team, even more unfathomable. In the immediate aftermath, some people suggested Donald Campbell now had a death wish with the strain too much for him, and indeed these next actions could pay testament to the fact. Those who knew him – and truly knew him – would say that it would never have entered his mind. Whatever the truth, within seconds, *Bluebird* and Campbell were to come to an end in a most spectacular way.

The film of the accident has been viewed time and again, and can now be seen anywhere in this digital age we live in. It has become the defining moment in the story of the water speed record, with those who don't even have a passing interest in the sport aware of that fateful day. There are those who still ask the question, 'Where were you when Donald Campbell was killed?' Almost like people ask where they were when Kennedy was shot, or when Princess Diana died. It was that significant in the nation's consciousness of 1967.

The boat set off and almost immediately hit a wave. Campbell's commentary obviously describes it better than I, or anyone else, ever could, and so again I print it in full detail:

> The nose is up. Pitching a bit down here as I drive over my own wash. Stabilising, up blind track ... rather close to Peel Island, tramping like mad ... er ... full power, and er, tramping like hell here. Can't see very much, the water's dark and green. I can't get over the top. She's lost a bit of her bloody track. I can't see anything. Hello, the bow's up! I've gone! Oh.....

Bluebird had struggled in the rough water as it rocked from side to side on each sponson (called tramping). Then, with around 150 yards of the flying kilometre left, they lifted out of the water, the boat glided into the air, arced, somersaulted and returned to the lake on its back, nose first, and disintegrated. Parts of the boat just careered across the surface before sinking slowly, and debris exploded into the air, before hitting the water in a frightening splash. Within seconds, the boat and pilot had disappeared. The following radio exchange is as poignant as it is unemotionally accurate:

> Tango to Base. Tango to Base. Over.
> Base to Tango, over.
> Tango to Base, Tango to Base. A complete accident I'm afraid. Over.
> Roger. Details, over.
> Tango, no details as yet. Stand by.

Almost immediately, Leo Villa and the other support boats rushed to the scene of the accident, but Donald was nowhere to be seen. There was a brief moment of hope when his crash helmet bobbed to the surface, but of him there was no sight. Gradually, pieces of wreckage appeared, plus the air bottle, life jacket and amazingly the teddy bear Mr Whoppit, but it soon became clear that a full rescue operation would be needed. There was the belief in those first moments that Campbell was still strapped in the cockpit and needed to be located quickly, but later it was confirmed that the G-force would have killed him instantly. Onlookers on the shore prayed for him, and soon the news was being relayed to the press at the slipway. Within minutes, the story was being broadcast around the world, meaning that the record attempt that no one was interested in had suddenly become the biggest story for quite some time. Professional divers and search crews turned up in the hope of at least finding Donald's body, as it was clear after around 30 minutes that he could not possibly have survived, but they found nothing. *Bluebird* and Campbell had sunk to the bottom of the murky lake, where they were to stay for some time. The two sponsons floated to the surface and they were taken back to the boathouse, while members of the team continued to skim the lake in their boats and the freezing conditions in an almost hopeless quest to find some trace of him. It was too late. Donald Campbell had become the most high-profile of record-breakers to be killed in an attempt at breaking the water speed record.

Despite his grief, Leo Villa actually appeared on a television programme that evening to discuss the accident, while news footage was shown around the globe. Tonia and Gina were informed by telephone and that night the Sun Hotel – now closed to custom – had a quiet and reflective 'party' to honour the man they all knew and loved. Most of them shared the irony that Donald had got the new record in his grasp, and would surely have taken it beyond 300 mph, had he done what he'd done countless times before, waited and listened to the advice of Leo Villa. It could never be explained.

23

THE AFTERMATH

Donald Campbell was later posthumously awarded his fourth Segrave Trophy, and it was a bitter Tonia Bern who made the acceptance speech:

> Many people today say that Donald Campbell was a big hero. To say it today is one thing, but to have said it yesterday when he was here to hear it is a much more important thing. The Segrave Trophy was given to Donald three times while he was alive. I know how happy he was. This Segrave Trophy honour goes to the *Bluebird* team and their skipper. Thank you, in his name.

In fact, the people who had been vocal in their criticism when he was alive, suddenly had different views in his death. Stirling Moss, so uncharitable when discussing Campbell's land speed record problems, said of him,

> He was a great man who took tremendous risks for his country. He was a very great ambassador, and from the country's point of view, he did a very good job. People who do this sort of thing have to have a tremendous strength of will rather than courage. Of course Donald had courage, but he also had the quality of strength and determination over fear. He had a tremendous amount of that.

On 23 February, a memorial service was held at St Martin-in-the-Fields in London, and was predictably packed for the occasion. It was attended by all those who knew and loved him, including Dory Swann who was on holiday from her new home in America. To give some idea as to the grief and shock that his death had caused, this is an extract from the address delivered by Campbell's lawyer, Victory Mishcon, that day:

Speed is not the only thing that manages to break through barriers. Amongst nations, among various sections of the community within a nation, among all creeds and colours, outstanding courage and outstanding characters break through barriers too of boundaries, languages, cultures and classes. Donald Malcolm Campbell did not break the sound barrier on land or sea, but he broke those other more important barriers during his all-too-brief life, so that we who are gathered here today are but a few of those who loved and honoured him, and who now mourn him in their many thousands in these islands, in the United States of America, in Australia and throughout the length and breadth of the world, where the spirit of adventure and bravery still thrill the blood of man.

And thou shalt love the Lord thy God with all thy heart, with all thy soul and with all thy might. These are sacred words in this House of God, often heard, as they are in the place where I usually worship. If ever a man gave all his heart and soul and might, it was Donald Campbell. So did he love his God. So did he love his Queen and Country. So did he love his ever loyal team, with its Leo Villa and the lady whom they call Fred (Tonia). So did he love the cause of human progress for which in his own field he was prepared to devote and indeed sacrifice his life. So did he love and cherish the memory of his father. So did he love people.

It soon emerged as to how deep his financial crisis really was. There were large debts, and a fund to the tune of around £20,000 – set up for the trust of Gina – had been regularly used. Gina was left £500 in the will, and with that she bought herself a sports car. The financial problems only served to heighten the suicide conspiracy – theorists who regularly went public with their views.

One year later, on the anniversary of his death, a plaque was erected at Coniston in memory of him. Hundreds turned out to witness the unveiling. It was attended by Leo Villa and Donald's dignified mother, who had now lost her husband and son. He actually received an OBE in June 1967 for his services to the land and water speed record attempts, and was briefly involved with Ken Warby years later with his *Spirit of Australia* challenger. Sadly, in 1978, Leo's wife Joan died, and one year later he passed away too.

That should really have heralded the end of the *Bluebird* story from its earliest beginnings under Malcolm Campbell, but, like all good Campbells, Gina also wanted to get in on the act. She became a successful powerboat racer in her own right, and with boats predictably called *Bluebird* recorded two class world records in 1984 and 1990. In an eerily fateful moment, she survived a similar accident to her father's at Holme Pierrepont in 1984. Later, she was quite outraged when a team built a replica *K7*, which they housed at the same boathouse in Coniston without the intention of setting any kind or record in it. The team hadn't contacted her or any member of the Campbell family, and after initially refusing to talk to them, she relented and watched as the gleaming blue boat – in every sense a complete reproduction of the *Bluebird K7* with the same Orpheus engine – fired its motors and glided onto Coniston Water. It must have been a truly surreal and emotional experience, but you have to ask why on earth anyone would go to so much trouble when all they have done is offend the very people they were supposed to be honouring? As it was, on its first venture onto the lake it sunk, and on the second it refused to plane across the water. Nothing was heard from it or the team again.

The real *Bluebird K7* was at the bottom of Coniston, having been there since that fateful day in 1967. As far as the locals were concerned, that was where it would stay, having become very protective of the Campbell tradition. In 2001, a local diver from Newcastle called Bill Smith decided that he would raise the wreck of the boat. He had originally called Gina, who was less than enthusiastic, and Lady Campbell, who was of the mind that everything should be left in peace. Smith was determined; with the help of a BBC documentary crew, *K7* was located and eventually brought to the surface of the lake on the 8 March. His crew also managed to find most of the accompanying bits and bobs of the boat and gathered them up too. It was quite a remarkable effort. Then, on the 28 May, Donald Campbell's headless body was also recovered just a few yards east of where the boat had lain all those years. The body was preserved by the low temperatures of Coniston, and his St Christopher's medal, given to him by his father, was still intact. It was also said that there was five and fourpence in his pocket – from the pre-decimal days of course.

The body was officially identified through DNA tests, and Gina now decided that her dad needed 'somewhere warm'. A funeral was arranged and his body was to be buried in a local cemetery in Coniston. The funeral was held in St Andrew's church in the village on the 12 September – a day after the 9/11 atrocities in America. The cortège was witnessed by hundreds in torrential rain. He was buried with the familiar blue-and-yellow racing colours of the family. The yellow came about when Malcolm, all those years ago, in painting his *Blue Bird* blue after watching the play, had run out of paint and so a splash of yellow could still be seen. From thereon there would always be a small part of any car or boat that carried the name that would have a splash of yellow.

Unfortunately, a legal battle followed between Gina and an enthusiast called Paul Foulkes-Halbard over the ownership of the boat. It was an unedifying end to what was an emotional story, but thankfully, a judge ruled in the Campbell's favour and *Bluebird* is now being rebuilt in a painfully slow and meticulous way, in readiness for a brief return to water and an eventual final home at Ruskin Museum in Coniston. The rebuild has taken longer than anyone could have imagined and it's one's hope that it will eventually be a success.

There is a feeling that the story of the world water speed record should end there, but sentiment is never a predictable thing. The record that Campbell strove for so earnestly was very soon in someone else's grasp. In fact, since Campbell's death in 1967, the record has been broken by two other men, neither who have become either household or world names. Lee Taylor and Ken Warby were to take over the crazy obsession that breaking the world water speed record could create.

AMERICA GRABS THE RECORD BACK

No American, or indeed any other nationality, had held the water speed record since 1952 once Britain's Donald Campbell had taken a stranglehold of the title. There were numerous suggestions of new record-breakers, such as Art Arfons, the successful land speed record challenger. He came up with the ingenious suggestion of taking his *Green Monster* jet car of 1960 and converting it to a boat, renamed as *Green Monster Cyclops*. In February 1967, a month after Campbell's death, he displayed the craft to the waiting pressmen. It was a curious, looking device to say the least. He'd added two Styrofoam-filled stepped sponsons to the front of the car and placed two wheels underneath. Arfons, who had never driven a boat before in his life, looked upon the whole process in a disarmingly charming and easy way:

> At 80 to 90 mph I'll be up on the steps. At 200 we should be planing on just the tyres and the tip of the steel rudder. If we have trouble staying on the water, I may put a wing fan up front, but I think the tyres will work.

The boat didn't deliver.

Another of the country's great land speed drivers, Craig Breedlove, who was the first to reach 600 mph on land, in his jet car *Spirit of America Sonic I*, was also equally dismissive of what was required to break the water version. He had commissioned *Acquamerica*, a two J47 turbojet-powered vessel that would be mounted forward on the sponsons while he would sit in the tail section. 'Speed on water is a matter of engineering, hydrodynamics and luck.' That too didn't work.

It was then Lee Taylor who would step up as America's next challenger for the world water speed record. He was born on 20 June 1934 in

San Fernando, California, and was the least likely water speed breaker one could imagine. He was educated in a poor suburb of Los Angeles, where he took up sports and excelled at football (American football as opposed to soccer). He was so good that he won an athletic scholarship in Washington, but that ended rather abruptly when a public scandal over bribe taking was revealed. He then settled down, married and became a factory worker for a cutlery business in Downey, California.

Apart from a recurring dream where he apparently owned a 'great big beautiful shiny black boat', Taylor showed little interest in water vehicles. He did help to rebuild a 1931 Buick car, but it wasn't until he got to know a man by the name of Rich Hallett that his interest in mechanical boats became pronounced. Hallett was the 'Drag Boat King', a sport only really known in California, but enormously popular. He had his own workshops where he would build and design his vessels for paying customers. The two became good friends, and as Hallett was also keen on trying out the relatively new sport of ski races, he invited Taylor to work in the shop and also get some experience in the sport. It was a fortuitous invite, as Taylor took to the sport like the proverbial duck to water. In 1962, he created a new world record for waterskiing at an astonishing 92 mph!

This quest for speed then materialised in a drag boat that he bought off Hallett called *Hustler*, after the nickname he'd had while playing football. This was an 18-foot streamlined beauty that managed speeds of around 90 mph. Two years later, in 1964, he bought an 18-foot hydroplane, calling it the same name, and managed to win sixty trophies with this 115 mph boat, plus his waterskiing too. All of this was in Californian waters, and it was clear that Taylor now dreamt of bigger things, not least a new water speed record, which at that time had belonged to Donald Campbell for nine years.

The only way to beat *Bluebird* would be to build a brand new jet boat, and for that he purchased a J46 Westinghouse turbojet that would create around 6,200 lbs of thrust. This engine had actually powered one of the US Navy's fighter planes, and with an afterburner fitted, he had the power but now needed the boat. That came from Rich Hallett, who, after seeing designs, built an oak and birch plywood 30-foot hull that promised speeds of up to 300 mph. The North American Aviation Co. supplied engineers to fine tune the engine, and Westinghouse experts were called in to look at the steering while the boat was testing on the Thompson Bay on Lake Havasu. Unfortunately, this wasn't an ideal stretch of water, as only around 3 miles were available, but *Hustler* performed admirably. A potential American water speed challenger was already beginning to attract the attention of the country's media.

That attention became greater after the events of the 14 April 1964. The boat was travelling at a speed in excess of 250 mph when Taylor suddenly found he couldn't slow down due to the throttle spring bending and refusing to retract. There was no drogue chute to stop him (something that successive WSR designers have struggled to get to work properly), and so as he and the boat headed towards the shore, and the immediate mountain that flanked the lake, he jumped clear with a great presence of mind. The boat raced up onto the bank and disappeared behind a bushy hill, causing extensive damage to the surroundings. The damage to Taylor was even worse.

An army helicopter had tracked the boat's path, and as soon as they'd seen the incident, they'd hovered above Taylor's unconscious body while a US coastguard retrieved him from the water. There then followed a comedy of errors that caused Taylor even more injuries than the ones he had already suffered. The helicopter pilot, keen to get away after landing on an uneven piece of rock, hadn't ensured that the coastguard and stretchered body were secure, and tried to pull away. Unfortunately, the weight of the two dragged the machine down and it crashed into the lake in a blaze of flames. The crew swam to safety and the coastguard unstrapped Taylor and managed to get him to the shore. The poor *Hustler* pilot was then flown quickly to a nearby hospital where an emergency tracheotomy was undertaken, as he was struggling to breathe. Soon he was transferred to Sunrise Hospital in Las Vegas where he remained in a coma for eighteen days. He'd suffered a fractured skull, a smashed left ankle and numerous bone fractures, including one to the eye socket.

Taylor's father persuaded the surgeons not to amputate his son's ankle, so they set to work on repairing it instead. They did a fine job, although it meant he would forever walk with a limp, with one ankle larger than the other. Of far more serious concern was the orbit of his left eye, which surgeons spent many weeks rebuilding – he would always suffer from double vision and would have to wear glasses for the rest of his life. Also, when he was woken he was asked numerous times by the nurses as to what his name was, to which he finally replied 'California'.

Taylor's injuries were horrendous. He was taught how to walk and talk again over a period of twelve months, and somehow put his life back together again. Thankfully, he didn't have to worry about the cost of his recuperation, as the National Drag Boat Association paid all of the $30,000 hospital costs. Sadly, the cost to his personality was greater. After the accident, and once he was released from care, Taylor became the victim of terrible fears of anxiety (similar to Donald

Campbell's after his terrifying crash in Utah), and was also prone to horrible and physical rages. This caused more than a few problems with potential sponsors.

He still had the burning ambition to break the world water speed record, and after his experience with the previous *Hustler,* he felt confident in his own ability to pilot a boat at the necessary speeds. With that in mind, he and Hallett salvaged the craft and rebuilt it completely. It took a couple of months but, in August 1965, he and the boat were ready for another attempt, this time on Lake Mead in Nevada. It turned out to be a thoroughly embarrassing episode.

Watched by one of the representatives of the main sponsor – Harvey Aluminium – Taylor couldn't bring himself to take the boat at a fast speed. His anxieties and fears had taken hold, so the representative quietly asked if the substitute driver, Bob Stipp, could take over. Taylor had no choice but to agree, but then went into an almighty rage when Stipp damaged a sponson after riding a wake left by another boat. *Hustler* was sent back into the workshop for repairs and Taylor then had a 'clash of personalities' with the Harvey representative, who had quiet correctly suggested that Stipp should be the main driver for the bid. The result was that Taylor withdrew the boat from the process, and Harvey Aluminium immediately withdrew their sponsorship. To make matters worse for Lee Taylor, his wife, Gloria, who had come to the end of her patience after caring for her husband throughout his recovery, decided to file for divorce. She also took custody of their three daughters.

There is something single-minded about record-breakers, and these setbacks would affect any normal person, but Lee Taylor was of course no 'normal' or 'ordinary' person. He set his sights completely on breaking the record, and at the expense of anything else in his life. After securing sponsorship with MobilOil and, oddly, the Guntersville Junior Chamber of Commerce (they were looking to boost tourism in their town), he took *Hustler* to Lake Guntersville in August 1966 and somehow got it to around 180 mph. It wasn't anywhere near fast enough, and after numerous and disappointing runs in front of a sceptical crowd and worried sponsors, the Guntersville officials also pulled out, citing a lack of money. It may have been more to do with a lack of faith, as it was clear that Taylor had lost whatever nerve he'd possessed before his horrendous accident. He returned to Los Angeles and prepared to go through the whole tedious process of contacting possible sponsors as his dream faded by each day.

In January 1967, Taylor had watched the news footage of Donald Campbell's accident and had even sent a telegram to offer his condolences. The record was still stuck at 276 mph, and Taylor still had the belief in his own ability to better it. In March, he found a new sponsor, a tyre dealer from Compton called John W. Beaudoin. In fact, the $20,000 he put forward was not so much as sponsorship, but more taking control of the team, as each member had specific tasks to perform. It didn't seem to worry Lee, and he himself had actually persuaded the Revd Doyle Hart, who ran the local Compton Youth Centre, to send out 7,000 letters to potential backers of the attempt.

In June, Taylor was ready for another full on attempt at the record. The lake was the perfect length – they'd returned to Lake Guntersville with the help of financial assistance from Revd Hart – and speeds of around 200 mph were required by the American Powerboat Association (APBA) before they would sanction another attempt, bearing in mind the psychological problems Taylor had been experiencing since his crash. It took four days, but eventually *Hustler* recorded 211 mph, meaning the officials were satisfied with both boat and pilot.

Beaudoin was putting the pressure on. His investment needed a quick return, and his concern over Taylor's well-being increased, especially as he was witness to another of the now famous tirades. After five runs where the speeds hadn't gone appreciably faster than 250 mph, well short of the existing record, there were suggestions that he may pull out all of his money. That seemed to spur Taylor on and a run of 276 mph satisfied all.

The next couple of days were frustrating, as firstly the boat hit a submerged log and needed extensive repairs to the sponson that had a hole ripped through it (although these repairs were made by a shower door made from the same plywood as the boat). The next day, strong winds prevailed, meaning there couldn't be a run. The 30th was supposed to be an ideal day for a record run, but the team had started to have serious doubts about Taylor's ability to push the speed at a far more dangerous rate, so they came up with a cunning plan. With the help of Rex Morton of the Redstone Space and Missile Centre, they advanced the throttle quadrant, so when Taylor applied only 70 per cent acceleration, he would in fact be receiving 100 per cent of the engine power. At the same time, other crew members moved the marker balloons further back on the course so that Taylor would hit the throttle sooner and keep it on longer. None of these ideas were disclosed to the unsuspecting pilot, and amazingly they worked!

At 9 a.m. on the 30 June 1967, Lee Taylor took *Hustler* through a first run of 299 mph after reaching a peak of 315 at one point. Frustratingly, on the return run, a lady in her pleasure boat ran across the route of *Hustler* and he had to slow dramatically, meaning he only clocked 250 mph to record an average of 274. This was just short of the record, and 5 mph off what was required for a new one to be officially guaranteed. Predictably, Taylor went into a fearsome rage at everyone around him. He only calmed down when Beaudoin promised to pay for just one more run before midday, and no more. It worked and, at 11 a.m., Lee Taylor and *Hustler* broke the world water speed record at 285.22 mph, only the eighth person to achieve such a feat since its 'official' inception, and only the third man to have taken a boat over the magical 300 mph barrier. Whatever his fears and anxieties, he was a new American hero.

The success brought with it many problems, and the fractious relationship between Taylor and Beaudoin simmered and eventually bubbled over. The latter had maintained that his financial input had effectively given him ownership of *Hustler*, something which Taylor naturally disagreed with. A number of court cases and legal representations took place, and within a year John Beaudoin became the official holder of the 'fastest vessel on water'. It must have been a galling experience for the thirty-eight-year-old water speed record holder, but he gathered his forces and went about looking for new sponsors and financial backing in an attempt to take the record over 300 mph.

As for Beaudoin and *Hustler*? Well, despite never driving a boat at over 30 mph before, the new owner went on a programme to hopefully take the boat eventually to a new record of over 300 mph. He took the craft to Lake Isabelle and managed to make successive runs that reached 250 mph, but a combination of many factors, including mechanical and weather constraints, meant that the record run was never attempted; Beaudoin eventually gave up. *Hustler* was then transferred in its ownership to someone else, and has since been renovated and displayed. Out of all the boats that had taken the water speed record, this one had the most radical design, and its pointed nose and intent gave it the look of a sheer racer. It has largely been forgotten down the years (and some would say the same of its original pilot), but it played a huge part in the history of this special endeavour.

In June 1971, the 'Daddy' of them all, Garfield Wood, died at the age of ninety. The man who had started the true contest of the world water speed record, and who had taken the record from 74 mph to 124 mph in twelve years, won numerous Harmsworth and Gold Cup trophies, and had also left a lasting legacy to the boating community, was mourned in his home city of Detroit and beyond.

25

AUSTRALIA ENTER THE RACE

The men (and the women) who have competed for the title of the 'fastest' on water down the years are a disparate lot. They have come in all shapes and sizes, and with unusual and inconsistent backgrounds. Some have been born into money and some have been driven by a goal that has seen them almost bankrupt from their dream. However, none of them could be regarded as athletes. In the early part of the twentieth century, the attributes needed to drive any vehicle at a fast rate of knots (whether on land or water) were courage and strength. A quick look at the snapshots from that era will testify that these were not the lean and hungry sportsmen and women that we identify with today. Physical fitness didn't play a huge part in their daily routine and, in the fashion of the era, a cigarette dangling from the mouth while fuelling the machine they had stubbornly pushed to another victory was hardly seen as unusual. If there was any physical activity that was used in training for their arduous attempts, it would probably revolve around the upper body strength and pummelling of the arms and shoulders. Even as late as the 1960s, the great Donald Campbell didn't exactly embrace a fitness regime. Heavy drinking and poor physical mobility due to a painful back didn't exactly hinder him when pushing for records. Attempting a record today requires the height of physical and mental fitness; Andy Green for instance, the man who currently holds the land speed record at over 700 mph and is aiming for 1,000 mph in the near future, is an RAF fighter pilot. This just wasn't the case just a few decades ago.

That is where Australian Ken Warby steps in. In today's day and age, the idea of a bear of a man who had a 'weak heart', and who built his boat virtually in his back garden, would be regarded as fanciful. Yet, back in the 1970s, that's exactly what he did!

Ken Warby was born in 1940 in a place called New Lambton, a suburb of the Australian city of Newcastle. In those days, it was an area of poverty and the working class, yet today stands out as one of the more desirable areas of the city. He was one of five children, with four brothers and one sister, born to Evelyn and Neville. He had a reasonably normal childhood, except his mother was never a well woman and ran the household with an iron grip, leaving Neville to quietly go about his business. Evelyn suffered from constant blackouts and was bedridden for most of her days, meaning that one of the children had to be present to take care of her. Schooling was tempered by a rota that saw each child take turns to stay home and tend to their mother's needs.

Ken was the weak child of the five, suffering from a less-than-healthy heart. According to his father, when interviewed years later (and this was at a time when the two were estranged from each other), he 'wasn't interested in school and not interested in sport either. He was supposed to have had a tired heart and wasn't really energetic.' He rarely played sports at school and had the nicknames of 'Tum' and 'Doorknobs', which apparently referred to the fact that he liked tucker and never exercised. When friends played cricket, on the lawn in front of the Warby's house, Ken would sit on the porch and quietly play his guitar to the tunes of an Australian country singer called Slim Dusty – a passion he never lost, as Dusty's music seemed to accompany him wherever he went.

Warby did find an early interest in building models and, at one stage, actually completed a difficult mock-up of Sir Malcolm Campbell's *Bluebird*, which must have given some indication of his future interest. It was while he was attending a Boy Scout camp at Lake Macquarie, south of Newcastle, that his real passion was ignited. Buried in the shoreline sand, he saw a 13-foot speedboat, and decided there and then that he wanted one of his own. As he said in Bill Tuckey's biography, 'It looked so simple to me. I knew that I wanted a boat just like that. I sat down and designed what I thought a speedboat should be like.' That design produced a plywood and maple boat of around 10 feet in length, powered by a 1934 Ford four-cylinder engine. He borrowed money off his father, and trailed it on a wooden box with some springs to take it down to Croudace Bay, but when it hit the water it was a flop. Each time he pressed the throttle, the boat would almost somersault backwards with its concave bottom, but it was an encouraging start for the sixteen-year-old. At that stage in life, most teenagers haven't a clue as to what they will do with their lives, apart from partying and getting to know the opposite sex, but Ken Warby had already decided what he wanted to do. He wanted to break the world water speed record.

That first boat, which he called *Hellcat* by the way, was sold and a new one purchased. At the same time, Warby had started to make models of the boats that took Malcolm Campbell and Henry Segrave to their records, and would spend endless hours racing them across the pond near his home in New Lambton. He also started to spend a lot of time at the Newcastle Royal Motor Yacht Club, becoming what was referred to as a 'pit pest', meaning he was getting in everyone's way. Eventually, the money was found to buy a second boat, a 10 footer called *Rebel*, meaning that, by the age of eighteen, he'd already owned and piloted two boats. Sadly, the second one was as bad as the first, so with the help of friend, he designed and built his own again. This was 'a beaut little runabout' that would get up to 40 mph, courtesy of a six-cylinder Dodge engine. At last he could take to the water knowing that he wouldn't sink, drown or splutter his way across the lake.

This boat was such a success that he actually recorded the fastest time for its class at a Royal Motor Yacht Championship (RMYC) meeting, and although he'd signed on as an apprentice at the local Broken Hill Propriety factory as a mechanical engineer, the quest for speed was now all-consuming. A hydroplane called *Raider* was his next port of call, which he rebuilt for its owner and raced himself at speeds in excess of 100 mph, but it was another craft – later called *Monte Cristo* by Warby for no apparent reason – that really set him on the path towards record-breaking.

This was a 15-foot V8 crude device that just wouldn't run correctly for its owner, so Warby tidied up the mechanicals and took it to the water faster than it had ever been before. He was then asked to compete in the 1967 State Championships in Sydney, and ran away with the evocatively named Whiskey Cup. As his father later commented, 'Ken was only eighteen and Mum used to worry about him, but not too much. She used to come Sundays to watch him. It never occurred to me that he would go on – it was just that it was instead of cricket or football with his tired heart.' It was clear that father Neville hadn't seen what virtually everyone had seen at that time. Ken Warby's passion was boats, and would now become a lifelong interest as well as career.

The green-and-gold *Monte Cristo* went on to defend the Whiskey Cup successfully for two more years, also taking the New South Wales Championship title for its class, meaning that Ken Warby was beginning to get a reputation in nautical circles in Australia, not that it seemed to impress his family too much. His father was rather blasé about the whole thing, while his brothers were more interested in riding bikes and speedway, but Ken continued with his racing career, and very successfully too. He'd also built a reputation as someone who was stubborn and always knew best, plus having a fanaticism for doing things exactly right. Every nut and bolt had to be perfect and every inch of the boat had to be in its best state before taking to the water. It's said he got that particular trait from his mother, who although seemingly bedridden for most of her time in the house, insisted on an almost fastidious attitude to cleanliness.

Despite this obsession with powerboats, he did have time to date, eventually marrying a girl called Jan. They wed on 22 January 1963, and were to stay married for twenty years. It's fair to say it wasn't a relationship made in heaven. She was a strict Catholic and seemed to close her eyes to Ken's constant wanderings, not only with boats but with the females who tagged along at race meetings. She did follow him to many events, but always seemed to be the quiet one who sat in the background looking lost. Even Ken was forced to admit that he and 'The Führer', as he affectionately called her, were 'never on the same wavelength'. He'd actually fallen out with his mother for four years over the marriage, and it's reasonable to assume that Ken Warby was quite a selfish and self-obsessed man who couldn't give himself to any woman permanently. His new-found fame had taken over his life, and Jan could come for the ride if she wanted, and if not, well that would just be tough.

At the age of twenty-seven, Warby left BHP and set up his own sales company called JK Trading, which led him to Worthington Australia as a sales representative. He'd also attracted sponsorship for *Monte Cristo* from the oil giant STP, plus Dulux paint and, by 1972, he'd moved the family (now with three children of his own) to the suburbs of Gordon. It wasn't a happy move, as now Warby was completely absorbed in designing a boat for the world water speed record. It took up most of the money he was earning, and at times Jan was the only real supplier, but as always she stood by him. Again quoting from Bill Tuckey's book, Warby said this of the relationship and situation at the time: 'I was never one for sitting beside a river and having a little family picnic. I don't think the kids were treated like royalty, but then again they really didn't do without much.'

Warby's trail to the record attempt continued, and in his backyard he'd got three RAAF ex-Neptune Westinghouse J34 jet engines that he'd bought off the government. In a move that very nearly backfired on him, he agreed to be interviewed by the *Seacraft* magazine, where he stated that he would 'do 200 mph on water'. It made for a good story, especially as Warby hadn't even built the boat yet, but as the article had pictures of the *Bluebird* and *Hustler* boats, they obviously took him very seriously. He also sold *Monte Cristo*, mainly because he found the boat too boring as it won virtually every race it entered and gave him no satisfaction.

The boat wasn't designed by any high-tech computer or by a skilled draughtsman who measured every centimetre, it was done by Warby on his kitchen table with a pencil and a piece of paper. It was a conventional hydroplane with two sponsons at the front and one at the back. It would be made from plywood, over a frame of Oregon (cut by a retailer called Whittakers) and stiffened with fibreglass material. There were no stress calculations, but just a knowledge that if it looked good, it would be good. For the next year, he single-handedly built the boat in his backyard, while his long-suffering wife and children went about their day-to-day business without the input of a husband and father. He invited ABC to film a documentary on the whole project, but that wasn't taken at all seriously, especially when one of the crew arrived and saw the sheer chaos of his 'workshop'. The hull was virtually complete and had one of the engines attached, but it was such an odd-looking machine that the film-maker left, convinced that Warby would kill himself before getting even close to a record.

At this stage, Ken was attracting a lot of publicity, although most of it self-garnered. Numerous newspapers had run articles on the project, although quite a few misreported certain details. This didn't matter to Warby, as any publicity would be good in his relentless search for finance for the attempt. Soon he attracted the attentions of a couple of jet engine technicians, who fine-tuned the engine. To make the boat look a little more professional, he painted *Spirit of Australia* along both sides in black paint. The craft, half-finished, was then trailered on the back of an old Ford Falcon down to Griffith and the lake, and for the first time was set on water.

The boat should have been an absolute disaster. How can someone build a record-breaking machine in their own backyard without any input from technicians, computers and engineers? It wasn't. In fact, it was a remarkable success. After firing up the engine (it actually hadn't even had a static test before hitting the water), Warby set off and the *Spirit of Australia* immediately hit 160 mph before running out of lake. Then, in typical bravado he announced that he would try for the Australian water speed record, held by Tom Watts at 163 mph, something the press jumped on with glee.

Unfortunately, those same journalists ridiculed Warby and his self-made boat at every possible opportunity. On the next run, the boat hit a beer can and actually started to sink, before being rescued by a tractor, which the newspapers reported with hilarity. Even when he did take the record in September 1974, he was hardly given the credit he deserved, but it did alert the Maritime Services Board. They actually refused to let the boat run until it had engine cooling and the registration numbers were painted on the side. That was followed by a noise meter test, but Ken Warby answered each and every criticism, and in that typical bullish way of his, just carried on – embarrassment seemed to be missing from his psyche.

Despite the publicity and the success, raising money in Australia for a water speed record seemed almost impossible. That in itself was surprising, bearing in mind the affinity the country had with Donald Campbell and his *Bluebird* cars and boats, but the Australian business community just wasn't interested at all. Warby had always been a huge fan of Campbell, but had started to resent the success he'd had, as he felt that too much money had been spent (particularly in Australia) for too little recompense. His feeling was that the speeds on both land and water should have been far greater, bearing in mind the financial outlay. This was confirmed when he spoke with Leo Villa about his new boat and the Australians' refusal to commit, asking whether it was a direct result of those days. It in a way, it changed his perception of Campbell, who went from being an idol, to someone he started to lose respect for.

The problem of raising the money was then solved in a completely unique way, and surely could only have come from the radical mind of Ken Warby. He started painting for a living as a means of raising money. He'd seen a couple of friends at a shopping centre building the world's biggest jigsaw puzzle for money, and had been persuaded to paint a couple of miniatures to display alongside it. He'd never painted before, but soon realised he'd had a talent for it and embarked on a strange career. Starting in a Canberra shopping centre, he painted small maps of Australia in miniature. He sold these and larger versions at a profit, and soon thought of the idea of displaying the boat at the same time, so as to raise enough interest. It actually worked! The money came in and, bit by bit, he was able to pay for the craft to be finished.

With the help of Professor Tom Fink (who had worked successfully on Campbell's *Bluebird K7*), the boat received a tail fin after the UIM had ended their ban. Fink then naturally asked Warby where his wind tunnel model was to test the aerodynamics, so Warby went off and built one in his kitchen, returning a month later with a model that was as good as anything any technician in a laboratory could achieve. Between them, they polished the rough-looking creation into an aerodynamic machine that now looked capable of taking the record. The next problem, as well as finding the finance, was finding a suitable lake to run on.

In December 1974, a press conference was held to announce that an attempt would take place at Lake Dumbleyung (where Donald Campbell had been successful), even though the boat was far from finished, with alterations still to be made due to a lack of finance. It was in the press conference that he came out with the great quote that has been used so many times since: 'Obviously I don't want to have the fastest coffin on water!' The following January, the boat did a couple of demonstration runs, and he announced that the record would take place in December. At the same time, an ABC documentary was aired for the first time. This was fortuitous, as watching the film was a certain Graham Thompson. He was the president of the Tumut Progress Association, a group looking to further the appeal of the small town of Tumut. Nearby was a dammed lake called Blowering (this didn't exist when the *Bluebird* team were in Australia, as it came about through a huge civil engineering project that irrigated a large part of the south-east of the country), and he suggested that Warby and his team fly down to check the lake for its suitability. This they did, finding it almost perfect, simultaneously turning the officials and population of Tumut into immediate boating enthusiasts! In a way reminiscent of the Lake Canandaigua Promotions back in 1957, when the whole area was transformed to accommodate the tourist attraction of Campbell and *Bluebird* (which of course ultimately failed financially), Tumut predicted that around 15,000 spectators would turn up to watch *Spirit of Australia*, and free accommodation and emergency services were offered to Warby and the team.

The 6 December was actually named as a date for an attempt, which seemed rather foolish given the vagaries of record-breaking, especially on water. That was then altered to sometime in January 1976, as it was clear the boat wouldn't be remotely ready, as the tail fin was yet to be built. In January, the lake was cleared by divers who removed any possible implement that could derail the attempt, including logs and waste products. Tumut started to get ready, although not everyone within the small town were keen on the record bid taking place on their lake and interrupting the skiing season. Then there was another delay. A date of 13 March was set for a few test runs, before a proper attempt at the end of the year. By now, his main sponsor Shell was becoming anxious and keen to move things on; they arranged a meeting for the second week in March where numerous records for other classes would be attempted. They paid for the timing equipment and all of the infrastructure needed for such an event, and so it was disappointing that *Spirit of Australia* could only average 177 mph on the lake, despite Warby breaking his own Australian record. The critics were out in force and the newspapers were now full of his failures as opposed to the heroics of previous reports.

Money had been tight to say the least, but suddenly not just one but two fairy godfathers turned up. Firstly, a millionaire called Ken Berkeley offered to pay the $7,000 needed to build and fit the tail fin, and that was followed by $25,000 of sponsorship from a traditional clothing store called Fossey's. It meant that all of the money problems were solved and Ken Warby could now focus on breaking the record. He immediately took to the lake again, but despite beating his own Australian record once more, he remained some way off the world record. He then named 20 November as a date for an official run at the record.

Of course, record attempts are never easy; if they were then everyone would do it. The November weekend at Tumut was as frustrating as anyone could have imagined. There were problems with the ignition, meaning the boat just refused to fire, then the wind arrived and the boat could only run at around 170 mph in the rippling conditions. The tail fin then buckled at high speed, and the final act in the exasperating drama was seeing the plane carrying the timekeepers' crash into an asparagus field after engine problems. Thankfully they were unhurt, but Warby retired from the lake and said he would return in 1977.

When he returned in April 1977, he wasn't as welcome as the last time. Some of the locals had become seriously annoyed about having 'their' lake taken off them, as he said in Tuckey's book:

> There had always been antagonism from the Blowering Boat Club, who weren't very receptive to me using what they considered their water. It was only a few people – one in particular – and some of it was jealousy, some thought I was an idiot, some I was disturbing a quiet haven. I had arranged for the water skiers to use an area down towards the dam where they wouldn't disturb the actual run area but some were still unhappy. The locals and the ski boaties thought that every time we went down there we'd get a record and that would be the end of it. One said to the press 'Tell Warby to go somewhere else – he's not welcome here.'

That antagonism manifested itself in quite a few ways, not least when someone actually cut the master timing cable before one of the runs and made an official complaint when he'd passed his allotted time on the lake. Warby was forced to shut *Spirit* down and wait for another day. At the same time, there were mutterings of concern about the stability of the boat, one in particular from Leo Villa, who commented, 'He hasn't cracked 250 yet. That's when his troubles start.' He would be even more concerned when he learned that Warby had decided to fit an afterburner to the engine, giving him at least 50 per cent more power.

Although the boat was regarded as being rather crude, its starting procedure was anything but, as Warby explained in an interview at the time:

> You switch on the fuel (just like lighting a gas stove) and crack the throttle open, and within a few seconds you have a fire in the engine. You then get 35 per cent power, which is idle in a J34, and the boat is starting to move slowly in the water ... just a few knots. At 30 per cent you give the wave-off signal and they pull out the power plug and go like hell to get away out of there. If their motor stalled, the standard instruction was to dive overboard as deep as they could. The boat would be down in the water, just bellying along. I'd slide up in the seat a foot or so, so I could look around through 360 degrees to see everything and I'd stay there to the start point so I could see over the nose of the boat ... when I was confident I had the boat lined up, I'd settle back down and mash the throttle – but not full, because with the J34 that could over-fuel the engine. You could hear it growl behind you as if annoyed, but you'd give it a good footfull and if everything felt alright you'd go ... the faster you went the faster the acceleration was, like 100–200 was a lot slower than 200–300. The main thing was to keep the boat trimmed. The second marker was two spits of land – I didn't want buoys or anything out on the course.

Now Warby, would you believe, wanted to add even more power.

26

AUSTRALIA'S LOST SPIRIT

The afterburner was fitted, and Warby then immediately destroyed the engine in a static test. Somehow a screwdriver had fallen into the power unit and had been emitted as a set of marbles. Ever relaxed and calm, Warby just replaced the engine with another, but that refused to fire with the afterburner, so Ken simply decided not to bother with the extra power after all. He instead drove off to Blowering Dam, arrived at 2 a.m., caught a couple of hours sleep, and then took the boat out onto the water. Successive runs leading up to 245 mph (another Australian record) suggested he could now have a proper attempt at the record, so he made a date for three weeks later. After he got out of the boat, one of his team taped a note to the windscreen saying, 'Hit 300, then smile.'

On 18 November, they returned to the lake, along with Tom Fink, who had serious concerns about the use of an afterburner. It clearly refused to work, and so they came up with the idea that if they cut 2 inches off the rudder, they could save around 2,400 lbs of drag at 300 mph, in turn producing another 400 lbs of thrust. Warby immediately went to a Shell service station, picked up an oxy-acetylene torch and cut off 2½ inches, just for luck. He didn't have any safety goggles, so closed one eye in rotation to make sure no sparks entered! Two days later – the very last day that *Spirit of Australia* could use the lake as the agreement had run out – he took the boat onto the water and recorded a mean average of 276 mph, actually hitting 300 on the return run.

Frustrated as ever, he screamed at the timing officials as he believed they'd got the speed wrong, even though it was all being done by computer. There were two sets of concrete markers that held the timing wire under the water, and that was backed up by numerous stopwatches. All of the information was fed into a computer (although rather basic compared to today), and the times and speeds came out. This didn't satisfy Warby and he ran back to the boat, shouting to a film crew, 'Well, we've got Campbell, now let's go and get the other bastard!' That referred to Lee Taylor, who when he heard of it later was less than impressed.

As he climbed back into the cockpit, he was told that he'd actually done 286 mph and not 276! The timers had actually made a mistake, but that only spurred him on and he set off in the pouring rain to shatter the existing record. The first one was 'scrubbed off' because the rain was hitting the windscreen like 'pellets', but then he did an amazing 302 on the next run. All that was needed was for him to do a repeat run and the record was his, but just before he set off a powerboat screamed across *Spirit* and upset the water. Warby was incandescent, but the villain just replied 'it's our fucking lake'. He was one of the many who resented the record attempt disturbing the serenity and calm of their retreat, but his actions had left the water disturbed, with a wake like that wouldn't normally calm for at least an hour. This is where Warby's courage, and some would say stubbornness, came in. He set off and simply kept his foot hard on the throttle, buffeted by winds at 200 mph, his gloveless hands gripping the steering wheel as he guided the boat through the waves and bumps. On the shore, his mother stood there shaking, his father languid and unaffected as always, and of his wife and three children? They were nowhere to be seen.

It took the Australian Powerboating Association and the Union Internationale Motonautique 2 hours to check and recheck their findings, but eventually they confirmed that *Spirit of Australia* had beaten the speed of *Hustler*, and Ken Warby was now the holder of the world water speed record at 288.172 mph, just 3 mph faster, but he was the first man to design, build and race his own boat to the record. He was the ninth man to hold the 'official' record, and the immediate celebrations were wild and emotional, although they were tempered by many who were just relieved that he'd stepped out of his creation in one piece. The few spectators joined in the party, but the 'anti-Warby' brigade just breathed a sigh of relief that it was over and that they could have 'their' lake back again. Australia now had a world water speed record.

The country may have had a new record holder in its midst, but Australia celebrated with the sound of pin dropping. Yes, there was an ABC documentary aptly called *Hit 300 and Smile*, which aired shortly afterwards, but hardly anyone else noticed. Newspapers were more interested in the upcoming general election, giving the record a couple of paragraphs hidden in the sports pages. He did receive a presentation from the St George Motor Boat Club, where former Formula One world champion Sir Jack Brabham presented him with the official record certificate, and he was made ambassador for the city of Melbourne. The rest didn't even turn their backs on him, as they hadn't taken any notice to begin with. The interest was virtually nil.

To compound this feeling of unheralded achievement, even the APBA started to question the record, suggesting that for reasons only known to themselves, the speed was not what was stated and invalid. When the arguments died down, they printed a certificate that actually listed a slightly different speed of 288.60 mph, but didn't at any stage mention that it was a new water speed record. It took until the 2 December for the UIM to validate the record and send him a new certificate, but they charged him $70 for the privilege. Around the world, the record had hardly raised a ripple of awareness, as virtually not a single boating magazine reported it, and those that did took on a sneering tone about a crude machine that had 'lucked' itself to the record.

Lee Taylor had become aware, but was singularly unimpressed. He sent a letter in November 1978 that was about as ungracious as it was possible to be:

It is my pleasure to congratulate you for successfully setting a new world water speed record. Now with its fresh world-wide recognition, which it so rightly deserves, it will naturally create public anticipation for the future. My past record times have been enclosed. I would be very thankful if you would send to me copy (sic) of your times, runs and picture or pictures of your present record-holding craft.

The inference was clear. Taylor didn't believe that such a crude-looking machine such as *Spirit of Australia* could beat the machine he had driven ten years earlier. In that decade, he truly never thought anyone would take the record off him, never mind something as basic as Warby's boat. He then contacted the UIM and had protracted discussions with them over the validity of the new record.

Warby very quickly became bitter. He had made virtually no money from the attempt, and told a magazine in an interview the following April that he was going to achieve 300 mph. Warby exclaimed that the boat was now open to the highest bidder, even if that meant Idi Amin! ABC gave their 'Sportsman of the Year' title to someone else, and then he had an argument with the airline Qantas, who had used the trademarked *Spirit of Australia* for their aeroplanes. He demanded compensation and they paid him what he described as a 'pittance'. Invitations came from around the world for Warby to run and display the boat (now that the world had woken up to the record), but hardly anything came from Australia. Thankfully, an MBE came in June 1978 in the Queen's Birthday Honours List, and a chance meeting with Bill McRae of the famous Speedo Swimwear Co. resulted in a $60,000 sponsorship deal for the next attempt. That gave Warby the impetus to push the record beyond 300 and out of sight of Taylor, who was still questioning the original speed and was now pushing ahead with another challenger that was reportedly using hydrogen peroxide as power and producing 8,500 lbs of thrust!

In September, with the help of the Royal Australian Air Force, Warby had got the boat completely overhauled and trimmed. The RAAF engineers not only took the engine to pieces and put it back together again, they also did a complete inventory of the boat, finding numerous problems that needed correcting. The steering needed to be realigned, the gauges needed to be recalibrated and the craft needed a fine toothcomb inspection to make sure it could now repeat and beat the achievements of one year previous. In effect, the RAAF took complete control of the whole project, leaving Warby with little to do but sit on the sidelines and prepare to drive the thing.

While he was waiting for the boat to be ready, Ken Warby paid for the *Hit 300 and Smile* documentary to be edited to a shorter version, with the intention of selling it as a commercial enterprise. Many countries around the world bought it, but no one in Australia was interested. Channel 10, who were usually keen on such things, sent him away saying that the story wouldn't hold any kind of audience. Shell asked him to front a short series of films about safe boating, but when he was put on the public speaking circuit, there were hardly any bookings. Warby just wasn't marketable. Despite this, he was a record-breaker and, in October 1978, he did it again.

The weekend of the 7/8 October was scheduled for the attempt. The boat was ready, although the afterburners still weren't working correctly, and the lake had been cleared. The opposition from the residents of Tumut wasn't as great this time around and Blowering Dam looked ready for another record attempt. On the 7th, Warby got into *Spirit* and had the ride of his life, although not one that he particularly appreciated. As he recalled to Tuckey,

> I was fine until I hit the rough area in the timing zone. It was full of white tops
> and the boat buffered and shook and generally danced all over the place. I got

two or three feet in the air for a couple of hundred feet and I remember hitting down on one of the bounces and I slipped forward in the seat and my backside was under the wheel and my head was where my backside should have been and I was looking at the sky. My knees were jammed under the screen but luckily my foot slipped off the power. The boat took a long time to slow down.

The boat had actually hit a wave and flew in the air for some 200 metres at around 200 mph.

The next day, there was a delay while the timing equipment was made ready. It took nearly 2 hours to arrange it, so Ken simply lay down on the trailer of his boat, put his hat over his eyes and fell asleep! When all was ready, he simply got in the boat and raced across the dam with tail spray roostering behind and the boat bobbing and skimming the waves, almost seemingly afraid to touch the water. A speed of well over 300 mph was recorded. There was then a frustrating wait as the fuel system had to be bled, as a blockage meant that nothing was getting into the tank. With just minutes before the official limit, *Spirit of Australia* turned round and went even faster! One hour later, it had been confirmed that Ken Warby had smashed his own record by 29 mph – the highest-ever margin in the history of the event – and had averaged the incredible speed of 317.596 mph. The run was so fast that photographers on the shoreline couldn't change the focus in their cameras and the few spectators that witnessed it only saw a flash of spray enveloping the boat as it pierced the lake. The team and the RAAF celebrated wildly, and this time it DID make headline news all over his home country, with the evening television news programmes headlining the attempt. His mother, crying again, made him promise to give it all up, but he quietly reminded her that she'd said the same when he'd taken his first 25 mph boat out on the water. He told the press that 350 was his next goal and the boat would be capable of producing such a speed. It was so different this time round.

The next day, he took the 'fastest vessel on water' to Sydney, where it was displayed in Australia Square. Channel 7 then surprised him by making him the latest in the *This Is Your Life* series. In fact, he was feted wherever he went, and the accompanying sponsorship fees and appearance monies made him almost forget what had taken place twelve months ago. Warby had at last been recognised for his achievement, an achievement which today still stands.

In a way, this is where the history of the world water speed record could end, as the speed set by the *Spirit of Australia* has never been bettered. The 'world's fastest coffin' has been suggested as the ultimate in water record-breakers, with nothing likely to beat it in the future.

People talk of the mythical 'water barrier' as something that cannot be broken through, but that barrier has progressively been pushed over the years. In 1978, one man was still determined to push that barrier back even further. Lee Taylor, plus Ken Warby, Craig Arfons, and even Donald Campbell, have a story to tell in the history of the world water speed record.

27

'THREE WILL DIE BEFORE THE RECORD'S BROKEN'

In 1979, Ken Warby went on a promotional tour to the United Kingdom, Canada and the United States. While in Britain, he naturally made a pilgrimage to Coniston Water, to the place where his 'hero' Donald Campbell lost his life. By now his marriage was failing, and so he went with a London friend and the public relations officer of his main sponsor Speedo. The three of them took a small boat to the spot on the lake and threw a wreath into the water. It said words to the effect of 'take care of the skipper'. They then all booked into the Sun Hotel for the evening, the last place of Campbell and the team back in 1967.

Warby said he didn't realise it, but he and his friend were sharing the exact same room that Campbell had made his home during that last record attempt. One night, the Australian had a most remarkable experience. Again, I quote from Bill Tuckey's interview:

> I was laying in bed ... I heard a hell of a scream ... it must have been the ugly early hours of the morning. I sat up. The bedhead was against the wall, but somebody, something came behind me and put cold, wet hands over my eyes and pushed me back down on the bed. Then the voice said , 'It's Ok. Three will die before the record's broken once.'

Warby is a typical Australian, gruff and down-to-earth, in that outback way that has become almost stereotypical. He'd been told that Campbell had used a medium to try to contact his father, but Warby had described that as a 'load of hogwash', so it's unlikely this is the kind of story he would make up. He also didn't know at the time that he was sleeping in the exact same bed as Campbell had twelve years previously. Whether the story is true or not, and the author tends to believe it is, the omens for Lee Taylor in particular weren't good as he prepared his new challenger for the record.

Meanwhile, Taylor had finally, after eighteen months of wrangling, handed over the trophy to Warby for the world water speed record, not that Warby had any idea such a thing existed! It was only after speaking to Leo Villa immediately following his first record that he knew there was one. Taylor, who just simply refused to believe that his speed had been beaten, was finally forced via legal means to let it go, and that was only after *Spirit of Australia* had moved the record up to 317 mph. It was sent to Australia on a plane and handed to Warby in April 1979.

Later the two met again – their first meeting in 1978 had not gone well at all – and Taylor showed Warby his new boat challenger. The record holder was not impressed by the boat, or by Taylor:

> He proceeded to tell me what a heap of shit my boat was and what he was going to do, and that I should keep the packaging the trophy came in because it would be needed very soon. He invited me down to Lake Tahoe but I said I didn't want to go and see him killed. I told several of his people his boat was badly designed and would bounce in the wrong conditions. It was obvious it was flexing … it had a whole heap of problems. In his final test runs he couldn't get over 186 mph and the boat buckled in the middle. They riveted in aluminium panels to stiffen it and pumped pressure into the rocket like it had never seen before.

Lee Taylor attempted the world water speed record on 12 November 1980. The boat, *US Discovery II*, was a 40-foot pencil designed hull sitting on skis. It was designed by aerodynamist Art Williams, and with the huge thrust pressure of its liquid-fuelled turbojet engine, it was expected to be able to reach 400 mph. The cost was a staggering $2.25 million, with backing from forty companies. It was simply the most ambitious and stunning-looking boat ever to attempt the world water speed record. It was also highly unstable.

Lee Taylor took *US Discovery II* to Walter Lake in Nevada, but the sponsors, of which there were many, weren't impressed by the location and so demanded a more accessible venue. Lake Tahoe was then chosen. After a few test runs, during which the boat seemed to struggle with speed and stability, Taylor told the press who were present that the original attempt date of the 13 November would now be used as another testing day, as he felt the boat wasn't ready. The media and spectators had already turned up in some numbers, and so Lee decided to give the boat a decent run to see if she could at least make a speed of around 250 mph to put on a show and not disappoint everyone. With a considerable amount of hindsight, this was a decision that many people said was wrong – he shouldn't have attempted to entertain the crowd. Whatever the reasons, it was a decision that Lee Taylor paid for with his life on that calm and serene November morning.

On the 24 November 1980, the magazine *Sports Illustrated* ran the following article:

Last Thursday, the 13th, 46-year-old Lee Taylor, a cheerful, dedicated man devoid of superstition, climbed into his 40-foot rocket-powered boat *US Discovery II*, intent on reclaiming the world water speed record he had once held for 10 years. The site he selected, alpine Lake Tahoe, 6,200 feet up in the Sierras, was ideal for such an extravagant gamble. The thin air at that altitude would not only afford less resistance to Discovery II as it sped along on a limited fuel supply, but would also reduce the risk of the craft taking off into the air – a common failing of vehicles that attempt water or land speed records.

The weather was perfect, the water conditions nearly so. The sky was almost cloudless, the wind so soft it could barely be felt on the cheek. On the lake surface there were slick, silvery patches of untroubled water, but most of the course over which Taylor would travel was darkened by two inch ripples that would help his sponsooned craft break out of the water and onto a plane. There were random swells a few inches high, but none seemingly as bad as those he had encountered on test runs at record speed a few days earlier.

At 10.58am, with his craft aligned for the first of her two required runs through a one-kilometre timing trap, Taylor reported by radio, 'Hydraulics on. Safety valve open. Inner safety valve open. Regulator, 100 psi.' He then gave the rocket engine two quick bursts, and 20 seconds later, two more. At 11.01 he reported, 'Regulator 525 psi.' At 11.02 he was off. At first *Discovery II* seemed to be struggling to escape the fury of spray and fuming steam she created. As the boat leaped higher out of the water, moving even faster, the spray and steam thinned out behind her. On the previous day, in a preliminary run over rougher water, *Discovery II* had bounced so violently that the panelling on her 40-foot fuselage had buckled.

... this time the trim of the boat, laterally as well as fore and aft, was obviously better. As the craft streaked through the trap, Jack Arden, communications director in Taylor's recovery boat, shouted to the radio network strung along the 6 mile course, 'It's looking good. It's looking good.' A brief moment later, two seconds, perhaps three, *Discovery II* was swallowed in billowing spray. In the next sliver of time, fragments of the boat flew 50 feet high. 'Oh God Lee,' someone cried. 'Lee, can you read me? Lee, can you read me?' Arden shouted.

In five seconds a helicopter was over the destruction site. Nearly 200 feet of the course was strewn with chunks of floatation foam. There were five identifiable objects afloat. The largest was the forward 22 feet of the fuselage, the smallest, Taylor's red helmet.

This excellent article, which I attribute to the respected and superb magazine, written by Coles Phinizy, went on to describe how the boat was travelling at 269.83 mph when the accident occurred. It was suggested that Taylor had started his run too early and had 'peaked' at the wrong spot on the lake. When Ken Warby learnt of the accident, he commented that it must have been the most 'expensive coffin in history'. Film of the accident showed that its left sponson had lifted and made the boat highly unstable as the boat 'heeled'. The cockpit was sealed, with the idea that if the boat was submerged, it would not be a problem, as that part of the boat would naturally float back to the surface intact. It didn't work. Taylor was the fifth man to die in a quest for the water speed record. Sadly, number six wasn't too far away.

Earlier in the year, Ken Warby had taken *Spirit of Australia* out for a couple of demonstration runs in Sydney, one of them nearly killing him when a film crew in a pleasure cruiser decided to get closer and cut right across him while *Spirit* was travelling at 200 mph. The wake it created caused the boat to jump into the air violently and then bounce along the water, seriously injuring Warby's back. He wasn't impressed. There was also supposed to have been another crack at his own record at Blowering Dam again later that year, where the intention was to break 325 mph, but a long-standing drought meant the water level had dropped alarmingly, and so it was called off. By the end of the year, the 'fastest vessel on water' was retired and made its home at the National Maritime Museum at Darling Harbour in Sydney. Thousands came to visit, and, to this day, it is still a top attraction.

Warby moved to America shortly afterwards, tired of the apathy of his own country. There he actually became involved with drag racing, and was incredible successful. The idea was to make enough money in exhibition runs to help finance a new 400 mph boat, but the lure of success on the drag racing circuit in the States took over his life. His mother died of a heart attack in 1981, and his marriage to Jan finally came to an end, so he made his home in America. Soon he heard that the National Hot Rod Association had sanctioned 'funny cars', and that was what decided his future. He met Craig Arfons, nephew of Art and son of Walter, two land speed record holders down the years, purchasing two of the cars off him. Arfons had already been successful at a similar type of racing and was making a handy living making customer cars. That set him off on the road to incredible success as he, and a female Australian driver by the name of Sue Ransom, broke attendance records wherever they went, while winning races and picking up a lot of prize money. Warby did this until 1992, when, after witnessing a friend die in a horrific explosion at Cayuga in Canada in a race meeting, he gave up and started his own business, mixing and selling concrete. It was an unusual career change for the gruff Australian, but then little that he'd done in his life could be described as usual or normal.

During this time, Craig Arfons had also decided to have a go at the water speed record. Record-breaking was in the Arfons family, as Art had broken three land records. Walt had also attended Bonneville Flats with his *Wingfoot Express*, which also broke the record, but with another driver at the helm. Art had looked at the possibility of attempting the water record himself a few years previously, but that had come to nothing.

Arfons had a workshop in a place called Bradenton in Florida, which was owned by a man called David Loebennerg. The two got on famously, and it was the latter's money and support that helped the young Craig to attempt his dream of becoming the fastest man on water. Actually, that wasn't his dream at all – his real dream was to build a car that was capable of achieving the speed of sound on land, but he felt that the publicity of a successful water attempt would help to finance his ultimate goal.

As already mentioned, Arfons had been heavily involved in drag racing in America, and in 1981 had suffered a broken neck when his almost uncontrollable machine had failed to stop while travelling at 325 mph in the quarter-mile strip. It didn't deter him though, as two weeks later he was heavily strapped up – his vertebrae held together by wires – while he tested a replacement car. That gives some insight into the mentality and strength that he had inherited from his family.

When the water bug hit him, he decided to go for the most radical and certainly most powerful of craft ever seen in the history of the record attempts. Called *Rain-X Challenger*, in reference to his sponsors Rain-X (who were the main backers of motor racing legend Mario Andretti in the Indy Car CART series), the boat was made of the new technology of carbon fibre, at the time making a big progression with the McLaren Formula One Team. The craft was effectively moulded in two parts – top and bottom – and glued together with a special density foam material. It was 25 feet long and weighed an astonishing 2,500 lbs. This included the General Electric/Westinghouse J85/CJ610 turbine engine, which gave out 3,500 lbs of thrust, and could be increased with the addition of an afterburner.

Aerodynamically, it was unusual. At no stage was the boat ever taken to a wind tunnel, but the needle point design of the *Spirit of Australia* was deemed unworkable for this boat, so a crab-claw front took precedence, with two inwardly facing tail fins at the rear. 'I truly believe that a wind tunnel isn't necessary,' said Arfons when asked about it.

It will only show the shape needed to lift its own weight. Instead Jay MacCracken, a computer expert friend, has developed a system of 18 tapping points at strategic locations on the hull – 12 on the deck and six underneath – and they all plug into a computer on the shore. Our plan is to work up to 100 mph, then hook up to the shore computer to feed in the data we obtain. Then we'll do the same at 150, 175, 200 and 250, each time getting the information to the computer ... if the thing is going to fly, one of the points will warn us.

They were brave and confident words, but Arfons genuinely believed he had everyting in place to not only beat the existing record, but smash it out of sight. He confidentally spoke of 400 mph on water, and then later a run of 750 on land. That confidence came from, not just the Arfons bloodline, but the fact that he designed and built the boat himself, in a similar fashion to Ken Warby. It also helped that Loebenberg had put up $250,000 to finance the attempt after Arfons had shown him a film of *Spirit of Australia*. This friendship had been forged when the two of them had run an offshore catamaran in a 1987 Mississippi River Race, and the entrepreneur had been taken in by the brash and confident Arfons.

The boat was taken to Lake Manatee on Florida for initial tests, but that turned out to be a waste of time as the local authorities refused to allow *Challenger* to exceed 20 mph, so a transfer to Lake Maggiore in July 1988 followed. They hadn't seeked permission to run on the lake, so the team just put to the water at 6 a.m. and answered any questions afterwards. It worked, as the boat managed to get up to 160 mph without too many dramas, but the lake was too small so any higher speed wasn't possible.

In August, they relocated to Lake Jackson near Sebring and immediately hit 250 mph, despite a choppy water and a crosswind. Arfons was elated, but said that he had 'gained more respect for the water ... believe me, you feel every bump!' He decided he would fit the afterburner and test again in November, which again went quite successfully. The following July was earmarked as a date for an official attempt at the record, and again Lake Jackson was to be the place. The local community had embraced Craig, and the media had turned out in some force. With the battle for the water speed record now effectively an American/Australian affair, with Britain seemingly now uninterested or unwilling to resume, the newspapers and broadcast companies had hyped up the possibility of the record returning to its 'spiritual' home, where it had started from with Gar Wood all those years ago.

The day in question was calm, and the water seemed amenable when *Rain-X Challenger* set off on its run, but almost immediately those in the know could tell there was something badly wrong. The boat was porpoising heavily and then corkscrewed wildly out of control when it reached the flying kilometre at high speed. By instinct, the afterburner was shut off by Craig, but the parachute failed and the boat didn't slow down as planned. The engine now pushed the boat onto its right sponson and then the craft bounced into the air, before crashing back into the water at incredible G-force, tearing the hull apart. Somehow, the cockpit survived the impact, as it had been designed to do, but the safety harness failed and Arfons was thrown through the windscreen at terrible velocity. He was later found to have broken both legs, his pelvis and suffered massive internal injuries and bleeding. He died in the ambulance on the way to hospital after being put on life support. At the age of thirty-nine, Craig Arfons had joined Henry Segrave, John Cobb, Mario Verga, Donald Campbell and Lee Taylor, as men who had been killed in their quest for the world water speed record.

There was no real explanation as to why the boat failed in such a spectacular and tragic fashion, but the fact that aerodynamics seemed to be given lip-service by Arfons seemed to have something to do with it. Even Ken Warby had suggested to him that the boat should be checked out in the Lockheed Marietta Facility, but Craig refused to even consider a wind tunnel. If there was any consolation to the shocked and grieving team who witnessed the carnage on the lake, it was that it was estimated by the American Powerboat Association that *Challenger* was actually travelling at 375 mph when she broke up – the fastest any boat has ever gone on water.

28

THE AFTERMATH

Ken Warby has always said that if there was a party held for the water speed record-breakers or challengers, then it would be a quiet affair, as he is the only member still alive and belonged to a very unique 'clique' of one. Despite the fact that there seemed to be no one at all interested in challenging the record following the horrific death of Craig Arfons, Warby himself set to build another boat in his Ohio home to raise his own speed. It followed his record-breaking boat in every respect, including the design, pointed nose, the two sponsons running to the front. It was made of plywood and powered by another Westinghouse jet engine, which, with an afterburner fitted, could create 9,000 hp. He even christened it *Aussie Spirit,* but despite the backing of the Australian government, who made Central Victoria's Lake Eidon available, the project never really got off the ground, or into the water properly for that matter. The main problem was Warby's reluctance to allow anyone else get involved in what was again a homemade craft, along with the familiar lack of finance and sponsorship.

He'd actually arranged for his son, David, to drive the boat once it was ready, as he 'had the fire', but after a public debut at the Cincinatti Travel, Sports and Boat Show in 2000 ('I'm launching my new boat in the United States to ensure it draws more attention and exposure throughout North America, but internationally as well'), it then disappeared again. Then, on the 19 December 2004, it had a test run on the Manning River in Taree (Warby had decided that Lake Eidon was of no use, despite the local officials saying they would cater to his every need, and made the choice of going back to Blowering Dam), but the speeds were slow, mainly due to the fact that the lake was nowhere suitable for a fast run.

Not long afterwards, his father Neville died. With the news that both Blowering and Eidon had suffered from an extensive drought, Warby simply retired. On 30 November, a month after another pilgrimage to Coniston to check of the progress on the rebuilding of *Bluebird K7,* he decided enough was enough.

Ken Warby is one of the last great pioneers in any form of endeavour. His stubbornness and raw courage has elevated the water speed record to something that the land has failed to do in recent years – provide a true extrovert who relies solely on his 'eye' for a good boat, as opposed to the extensive engineering and computer technology that is now essential for any vehicle that is ready to break another speed record. The fact that his record has stood since 1978 speaks volumes for how difficult it is to break. In fact, Warby is pretty convinced that it won't be broken for a long, long time, as the technology just isn't advanced enough to break through the water barrier.

Record boats at this time have to be hydroplanes, meaning they plane as the speed rises, with only three points of the boat barely touching the surface of the water. It's also understood that every time the speed is doubled, the aerodynamic lift is quadrupled, so the need to constantly manage the effects between the two is a major headache when looking to design a new boat. The current record is 317 mph, and seems unlikely to be bettered in the near future. There are a few challengers preparing for another crack at the record, however. One of them, the *Quicksilver*, led by Briton Nigel MacKnight, has been mentioned at the beginning of this book, and that seems the most likely to at least get onto the water and maybe succeed. Someone has to, as, in all life's endeavours, progress has to be made or the human race just stands still.

So what is it that all the pilots, from George Wood (the first man to officially break the world water speed record in 1928) through to Henry Segrave, Stan Sayres, Malcolm and Donald Campbell and Ken Warby aim for? Well, it certainly isn't for fame and fortune. Gar Wood was already a rich man from his business activities, which he used to finance his racing exploits. Segrave, Kaye Don and Malcolm Campbell were household names before they took to the water, and were as well known as Stirling Moss was in the '50s, Nigel Mansell in the '90s, or Lewis Hamilton is today. Stan Sayres eschewed any kind of publicity and seemed to enjoy the challenge, while Donald Campbell appeared to use his record-breaking career to fight his inner demons over his father, who he idolised and feared in equal measure. Lee Taylor had become obsessed after his terrible accident and Ken Warby was one of the world's great fighters, who ploughed his own furrow and couldn't care less if it was on someone else's land. None of them became rich simply because they'd broken the world water speed record.

The ones who died? Segrave and John Cobb's accidents seemed totally unnecessary, Mario Verga was the victim of untried technology, Campbell is the mystery that will probably never be solved, while Taylor and Arfons just made mistakes at the crucial time. It's astonishing that since the official ratification of the world water speed record in 1928, nine men have held the title and six have died in attempting it, although Segrave did break in the moments before the crash that led to his death.

What did they receive for their efforts? Well, in this day and age, a virtual passport to obscurity. If you were to ask any member of the public the question, 'who is the current holder of the world water speed record?', few would know the answer, although a minority may make reference to Donald Campbell due to the defining accident in 1967. It's also probably true of the land speed record, as jet fighter pilot Andy Green has hardly caught the public's imagination, despite the fact he has travelled at the speed of sound on land. Maybe it's apathy in this health-and-safety conscious world we live in. After all, why do something dangerous when you can simulate it on a computer game instead? Why travel at that speed when it benefits no one, as ordinary mortals would never need to travel that quickly in their lives? When space travel is becoming available as a possible holiday destination in the near future, the appeal of a car travelling at 1,000 mph, or a boat at 400 mph is negligible to most. Thankfully, there are still those who strive for such goals, who still embrace the sense of adventure that so marked our ancestors, and who are still willing to risk life and limb just to push the barrier back a little further.

The title doesn't hold much money, and today there doesn't seem to be much in the way of fame, but surprisingly there is a trophy that the successful can have their name engraved on. It's little known. In fact, when the author attempted to contact the Union Internationale Motonautique about it, they didn't even reply. One week later, I found myself in Monaco, and so attempted to visit their offices to talk to someone face-to-face. The office was closed, which says a lot about the trophy that represents the endeavour. It is a trophy that Ken Warby didn't even know existed. It's a silver plaque of Boadicea on a black wooden base. At the bottom it has an inscription that reads, 'This trophy was presented in 1870 by HRH the Prince of Wales, afterwards King Edward VII, for open competition by schooners.' Not a word about the water speed record. You can't help but think it was a trophy that just happened to be there, and not one that was specifically designated for the title. In fact, in 1934, after years of being missing, it was discovered in a silversmith's shop in Kent and represented to the Royal Motor Yacht Club. It was only in 1937 that they, in turn, presented it to the UIM for the holders of the water speed record.

It's true that the water speed record will never resonate with everyone while boating is classed as a rich man's pastime, but the men, and women for that matter, deserve the recognition.

The final word goes, as ever, to Ken Warby:

> A lot of people have died for it [the trophy], but it's an inaminate object made out of silver. It's like a cemetery. All the men who have held the record have died trying to raise it [not strictly true but it's easy to understand the point]. I can hold an annual reunion of the world's most exclusive club wherever I am in the world, because I'm the only member.

Let's hope he's joined by someone else soon.

STATISTICS

Steam-Powered Boats

Date/Year	Boat	Pilot	Venue	Speed (mph)
14/04/1874	*Sir Arthur Cotton* (GB)	Frank Haig	River Thames	24.61
1885	*Stiletto* (USA)	Nathaniel Herresh	New York	26.6
1887	*Ariete* (GB)	Unknown	River Thames	30
23/08/1893	*Feiseen* (GB)	Unknown	Unknown	31.6
1895	*Boxer* (GB)	Unknown	Unknown	33.75
27/06/1897	*Turbinia* (GB)	Charles Parsons	Solent Channel	39.1
1900	*Viper* (GB)	Unknown	Unknown	42.73
1903	*Arrow* (USA)	Charles Flint	Hudson Bay	45.06

Engine-Powered Boats

Date/Year	Boat	Pilot	Venue	Speed (mph)
1902	*Mercedes* (GER)	Unknown	Nice	22.36
1903	*Napier* (GB)	Selwyn Edge	Queensland	24.9
1904	*Trefle-a-Quatre* (F)	M. Thiery	Monaco	25.1
1904	*Trefle-a-Quatre* (F)	M. Thiery	River Seine	26.65
1905	*Challenger* (USA)	Proctor Smith	Solent Channel	29.3
1905	*Napier II* (GB)	Selwyn Edge	River Thames	29.93
1905	*Dubonnet* (F)	Emile Dubonnet	Monaco	32.46
1905	*Dubonnet* (F)	Emile Dubonnet	Juvisy	33.8
1905	*Legru-Hotchkiss* (GB)	Unknown	River Seine	34.17
1907	*Dixie II* (USA)	Clinton Crane	Hudson River	36.6
04/1910	*Ursula* (GB)	Duke of Westminster	Monaco	43.6

09/09/1911	*Dixie IV* (USA)	Fred Burnham	Huntingdon Bay	45.21
1912	*Maple Leaf IV* (CAN)	Tom Sopwith	Solent Channel,	46.51
1912	*Tech Jr* (USA)	Coleman du Pont	Unknown	58.26
1914	*Santos-Despujols* (F)	Victor Despujols	Monaco	59.964
1915	*Miss Minneapolis* (USA)	Christopher Smith	Put-in-Bay	66.66
09/09/1919	*Hydrodome IV* (CAN)	Casey Baldwin	Beinn Breagh	70.86
15/09/1920	*Miss America* (USA)	Gar Wood	St Clair River	77.85
06/09/1921	*Miss America II* (USA)	George Wood	St Clair River	80.57
10/11/1924	*Farman Hydroglider* (USA)	Jules Fischer	River Seine	87.392

Officially Ratified Records by the UIM

04/09/1928	*Miss America II* (USA)	George Wood	Detroit River	92.838
23/03/1929	*Miss America VII* (USA)	Gar Wood	Indian Creek	93.123
13/06/1930	*Miss England II* (GB)	Henry Segrave	Lake Windermere	98.76
20/03/1931	*Miss America IX* (USA)	Gar Wood	Indian Creek	102.155
02/04/1931	*Miss England II* (GB)	Kaye Don	Parana River	103.49
09/07/1931	*Miss England II* (GB)	Kaye Don	Lake Garda	110.223
05/02/1932	*Miss America IX* (USA)	Gar Wood	Indian Creek	111.712
18/07/1932	*Miss England III* (GB)	Kaye Don	Loch Lomond	117.43
18/07/1932	*Miss England III* (GB)	Kaye Don	Loch Lomond	119.81
20/09/1932	*Miss America X* (USA)	Gar Wood	St Clair River	124.86
01/09/1937	*Blue Bird K3* (GB)	M. Campbell	Lake Maggiore	126.32
02/09/1937	*Blue Bird K3* (GB)	M. Campbell	Lake Maggiore	129.5

17/09/1938	*Blue Bird K3* (GB)	M. Campbell	Lake Hallwilersee	130.91
19/08/1939	*Blue Bird K3* (GB)	M. Campbell	Coniston Water	141.74
26/06/1950	*Slo-Mo-Shun IV* (USA)	Stan Sayres	Lake Washington	160.323
07/07/1952	*Slo-Mo-Shun IV* (USA)	Stan Sayres	Lake Washington	178.497
23/07/1955	*Bluebird K7* (GB)	D. Campbell	Lake Ullswater	202.32
16/11/1955	*Bluebird K7* (GB)	D. Campbell	Lake Mead	216.2
19/09/1956	*Bluebird K7* (GB)	D. Campbell	Coniston Water	225.63
07/11/1957	*Bluebird K7* (GB)	D. Campbell	Coniston Water	239.07
10/11/1958	*Bluebird K7* (GB)	D. Campbell	Coniston Water	248.62
14/05/1959	*Bluebird K7* (GB)	D. Campbell	Coniston Water	260.35
31/12/1964	*Bluebird K7* (GB)	D. Campbell	Lake Dumbleyung	276.33
30/06/1967	*Hustler* (USA)	Lee Taylor	Lake Guntersville	285.22
20/11/1977	*Spirit of Australia* (AUS)	Ken Warby	Blowering Dam	288.6
08/10/1978	*Spirit of Australia* (AUS)	Ken Warby	Blowering Dam	317.596

Those Who Perished While Attempting the Record

13/06/1930	*Miss England II* (GB)	Henry Segrave	Lake Windermere	98.760
29/09/1952	*Crusader* (GB)	John Cobb	Loch Lomond	206*
09/10/1954	*Laura III* (ITA)	Mario Verga	Lake Iseo	190*
04/01/1967	*Bluebird K7* (GB)	D. Campbell	Coniston Water	303*
13/11/1980	*US Discovery II* (USA)	Lee Taylor	Lake Tahoe	269*
18/06/1989	*Rain-X Challenger* (USA)	Craig Arfons	Lake Jackson	375*

*approximate speed

ACKNOWLEDGEMENTS

During the research for this project, I have spoken to many people, but I am particularly indebted to some excellent books that have been published down the years on the personalities involved in the world water speed record attempt. The original and best had to be Gar Wood, the man who held the 'official' record four times from 1929. The best book I read on this remarkable personality and his various entrepreneurial successes was *Gar Wood*, written by Anthony S. Mollica Jnr in 1999. It gave an invaluable insight into someone who is now hardly known outside of the country of his birth.

Henry Segrave was a real 'boys own' hero and Cyril Posthumus's excellent biography called *Sir Henry Segrave*, published in 1961, was a remarkable source of enjoyment, pleasure and research. If ever a man deserved more credit for his achievements down the years, then Segrave was that man. Sadly, there are few books and little background on Kaye Don, so I hope with my research I've given this incredible man the credit he deserves.

The same cannot be said for Sir Malcolm Campbell, as there are literally hundreds of articles, books and column inches on a man who truly did live the life of a latter-day explorer and adventurer. I cannot hope to have lived up to this man's deeds; I can only repeat in my book the facts and opinions on someone who is as well-known today as he was while he was alive. An internet search for the name Malcolm Campbell will produce pages and pages of material on this amazing personality, and I hope I've portrayed him in a realistic light, which at times is not always flattering.

For Stanley Sayres – well if there was ever a man who eschewed publicity and turned his back on celebrity, then he did it better than any. Sadly, there is so little information, compared to others in the field, on someone who simply smashed the world water speed record beyond recognition in 1950 and 1952. Details on his life are sketchy at best. I hope my few paragraphs on this event-defining man have done him justice.

Donald Campbell has been written about so many times that his life story is as well known as any down the years. The image of *Bluebird* flipping on Coniston Water in 1967, and killing him outright, is instantly familiar. It's fair to say if you were to ask anyone who had absolutely no knowledge of the world water speed record for one name attached to it, then Campbell and the *Bluebird* would almost instantly be the stock response. Down the years, I have visited just about every 'Campbell-connected' spot in my quest to get to know the man better, and I have lost count of the number of times I have stood at the edge of Coniston and stared out to the approximate point. I decided early on not to contact his daughter Gina, as I reasoned (hopefully correctly) that she has probably had just about enough of being asked the same questions over and over again about her beloved father. The fact that she has recently published her own autobiography suggested that I would be just one more annoying inconvenience. I am indebted to her book and also two excellent publications I used for research: David Tremayne's *Donald Campbell: The Man Behind The Mask,* and *The Fast Set* by Charles Jennings, both published in 2004.

Lee Taylor's story is one that deserves a book all on its own, and surely is a story ready to be written, while the current holder Ken Warby is the only man still left alive of all the record-breakers. There is only one publication that seems to tell his story completely, and that is *The World's Fastest Coffin on Water* by Ken Tuckey – a fascinating read. Of course, I can't end my acknowledgements without a mention of the great Leo Villa, who down the years engineered, built, supported and lovingly cherished Sir Malcolm Campbell and then Donald Campbell, plus the numerous *Blue Bird* and *Bluebird* cars and boats. His book on the water speed record, co-written with Kevin Desmond in 1976, was a wealth of information.

There are many other personalities involved with the record down the years, some of them who sadly died in their attempts, such as John Cobb and Mario Verga, and I hope I've done them all justice with my reflections on their lives and achievements.

Finally, this book is by no means a technical attempt at explaining the history of the world water speed record, as I am in no way qualified enough to attempt such a thing. I have stuck to delving behind the mask of the personalities involved. I hope it doesn't detract from the book, and instead makes it more interesting to those who are not immersed in nautical terms. For those who seek the technical aspects of each boat, I can do no more but steer you in the direction of the aforementioned history from Leo Villa and Kevin Desmond. I don't ever expect *The World Water Speed Record: Fast and the Forgotten* to be regarded as the definitive version of the history of the world water speed record, as that is a book for someone with far more knowledge and experience to write one day, but I hope you enjoy it all the same.

Roy Calley
June 2014

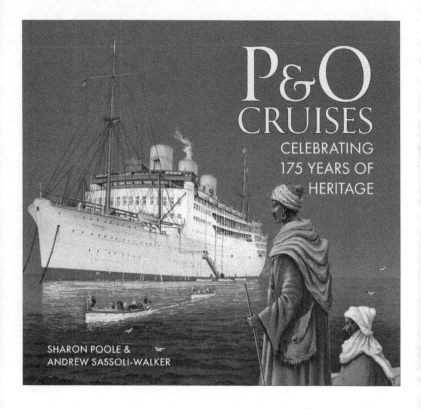

P&O Cruises
Celebrating 175 Years of Heritage
Sharon Poole & Andrew Sassoli-Walker

This book tells the story of how P&O Cruises reached this pinnacle
of achievement. It features, not just the innovative ships, but also the
stories of crew and passengers, past and present.

978 1 4456 0596 8
192 pages, illustrated throughout

Available from all good bookshops or order direct
from our website www.amberleybooks.com